ODYSSEY

THE LIVING MOMENT

Russell R. Hassler

ODYSSEY

THE LIVING MOMENT

Russell R. Hassler

21 Days to Living in the Moment

Train your brain to be wiser and braver in stress.

Increase energy, clarity and confidence.

Eliminate anxiety and depression.

Butterwort Books

Copyright © 2020 Butterwort Books

All rights reserved. No part of the contents of this book may be reproduced or transmitted in any form or by any means without the written permission of the copyright holder.

First edition, 2017, Odyssey Leadership
Second edition, 2020, Butterwort Books

Website: odysseythelivingmoment.com

Email: info@butterwortbooks.com

Edited by Helga Schier

Cover design by William Kent/The Kent Studios

If you would like to complete the Odyssey Program without writing in this book, copies of the forms that appear in this book may be downloaded from *odysseythelivingmoment.com*.

Note to the reader: This book is intended as an informational guide. The remedies, approaches, and techniques described herein are meant to supplement, and not to be a substitute for, professional medical care or treatment. They reflect the opinions of the late Russell R. Hassler, and should not be used to treat a serious ailment without prior consultation with a qualified health care professional.

978-1-7352979-3-4

FOR BARBARA ANN HASSLER

od·ys·sey (ŏd'ĭ-sē) *n.*
A journey of self-discovery.

Odyssey – The Living Moment **is a practical guide to living with increased energy, clarity, authenticity, strength and direction. The 21-day personal development program presents a framework that enables you to examine your unique challenges in a methodology of continuous improvement. The educational journey empowers you with the tools and skills you need to succeed in whatever you do, while the experiential aspect instills actionable habits that last beyond program end.**

Odyssey can assist you with becoming a better manager, parent, partner, and person. In three weeks, you can improve your managerial effectiveness and strengthen your leadership aptitude and spiritual resourcefulness. The journey of self-discovery is to live more mindful of the living moment. The quest is to gain a more enjoyable feeling of being alive.

The Odyssey Quest

Odyssey – The Living Moment is the introduction to *The Odyssey Quest*, a facilitated 12-week life leadership program which aims to strengthen personal authority and the capacity to live life authentically—in tune with your core values even under stress.

Clients of *The Odyssey Quest* report overwhelmingly positive results that include improved mental clarity and focus, increased energy, and better control in highly emotional states and situations. The proven approach places you at the center of your own hero's journey. You learn by doing.

The Odyssey Quest combines scientific perspectives with universal themes that empower the skills essential in combating stressful challenges in an increasingly complex world.

The Odyssey Mission

To engage the potential of clients through teaching a strategy for life leadership.

Contents

Forward 1
   The Living Moment 4
   Why Odyssey? 5
   The Quest Objectives 8
   Introduction 9

The 21-Day Odyssey

WEEK ONE - The Great Mystery: Life & Creative Power 13

Day One - The Great Mystery 15

Day Two - Dynamics of Feeling Alive 33

Day Three - Primal Intelligence 43

Day Four - The Human Condition - Part 1 57

Day Five - Becoming Consciously Attentive 69

Day Six - The Thought Inventory Exercise 81

Day Seven - Rest & Reflect 85

WEEK TWO - The Road of Life: Stress & Defensive Force 87

Day Eight - The Road of Life 89

Day Nine - eMotions: Energy for Motion 103

Day Ten - #1 Road Rule: SURVIVE! 117

Day Eleven - The Human Condition - Part 2 129

Day Twelve - Improving Intentional Focus 143

Day Thirteen - The eMemory Inventory 151

Day Fourteen - Rest & Reflect 159

WEEK THREE - The Living Motion: Dynamics of Life Leadership 163

Day Fifteen - The Living Moment 165

Day Sixteen - eStates: Energetic States of Consciousness 177

Day Seventeen - #2 Road Rule: THRIVE! 189

Day Eighteen - The Human Condition: A Summary 205

Day Nineteen - The Human Spirit 215

Day Twenty - The Odyssey Methodology 227

Day Twenty-One - The Never Ending Story 235

Postscript 254
   The Seven Universal Truths 255
   About Russell R. Hassler 256
   The Odyssey Quest 257

Forward

This life leadership program aims to empower my clients with the tools and skills they need to succeed in whatever they do. *Odyssey – The Living Moment* is the culmination of that ongoing personal journey.

In 1988, I was living in Knoxville, Tennessee, working as a statistical process control specialist in the quality control industry. Being new to the city, I spent an exorbitant amount of time reading and synthesizing self-development philosophies, psychologies and scientific discoveries that dealt with health and well-being.

The reason? I believed I was going crazy.

Young and keenly aware that the best years of my life lay ahead, I started to plan it all out, intent on embracing the wisdom of humanity and investing the emotional strength necessary to catapult my life to "success." Upon reflection, I was on a survival quest: to inject my anxious and often depressed existence with a more enjoyable feeling of being alive.

On the outside, I was as a very capable, intelligent and dedicated worker, technically and socially adept and quick to solve problems and please other people. On the inside, it was an altogether different story. I felt like an imposter. For years, I struggled with social anxiety: Was I good enough? Did I say the right thing? Would people find out what I really thought? I burned an amazing amount of energy analyzing my everyday interactions with people. In my waking moments, the constant chatter criticizing my every move consumed my conscious mind. Deep inside, I knew there had to be a more peaceful and powerful way of living.

On a typical day, I would swing on a pendulum between feeling angry or anxious. I found myself snapping at people, over-reacting to criticism, then feeling ashamed and exhausted from the confrontation. What is perhaps most ironic is that at the time, I was proud that nobody knew of my inner demons. I had mastered the art of living inauthentically—doing and saying things that were incongruent with my heart-felt intuitions, values and beliefs. I lived defensively, protecting myself from judgment and the painful complexities going on in my web of life.

In retrospect, my behavior wasn't surprising. My mother suffered social anxiety, which kept us kids isolated, and her locked in chronic depression. Our family relationships were naturally troubled and I grew up in survival mode, emotionally perplexed and anxious of the world around me. Through the chaos, I learned to be "good" yet fiercely competitive. When challenged, I pushed back strongly, then felt guilty and ashamed that I had been so assertive. My life was a constant roller coaster ride, and I wasn't having any fun.

All the while my cognitive chatter—the endless thoughts of self-doubt, self-blame, self-sabotage and self-regret—continued and grew worse. I went from one self-help seminar to another seeking wisdom that would fix me. I met with psychotherapists and discussed the same things over and over again. In many a session, I'd answer my own questions, leaving both my therapist and me frustrated. I distinctly remember one session: at one point I stopped and point-blankly asked my stunned psychotherapist, "Can you just teach me what's going on in my brain so I don't have to see you again?" Walking out, I set a goal: to figure out what was going on in my head so that I could watch a sunset with a clear, leadership mindset. I wanted to replace the feelings of inferiority and social ineptitude with an empowered feeling of being alive.

I began to invest significant time in learning how the human mind works. I read everything from psychology and theories of consciousness, to ancient mythologies, philosophy and human physiology. My quest provided two profound insights. First, I realized that the human body is not merely an incredibly sophisticated living machine, but a marvel of continuing evolutionary genius—an living mechanism that links the mind, the thought processes and feelings generated in our brain, to our corporeal reality, one affecting the other in subtle yet pervasive ways.

Second, I realized that, to an extent, we are in control of that evolutionary process in our minds and bodies. The human condition provides us with an extraordinary ability to use our cognitive powers to determine our emotional responses to external stimuli, and direct the energetic state of mind that we will apply to our daily challenges. Developing such heightened self-awareness gives us the power to either accept the life that is handed to us, or to intentionally create the life of our dreams. My quest was to achieve my dream of a clearer, more empowered state of mind.

Being in the quality control industry, I asked myself one day, "If my thoughts and emotions are part of my living biological process, what would happen if I began to apply the same continuous improvement method I used in optimizing manufacturing processes to control my turbulent state of mind?" Intrigued, I began collecting data on my pings—the moments in each day when external stimuli affected me in an emotionally negative manner—and looked for common patterns, applying the same quality improvement process that I used in my career. Instead of eliminating mechanical defects, my aim was now to reduce psychological defects—those annoying thoughts and negative emotions that disturb a powerful sense of self. Today, the eState improvement process is the basis for **THE ODYSSEY METHODOLOGY** you will learn in the next 21 days—the time it takes to instill a new habit of behavior.

In developing *The Odyssey Quest*, I realized that my thoughts and emotions were nothing but cognitive circuitry that had become hard-wired along my road of life. And as a living biological process, I simply needed some process re-engineering of the neural circuitry to regain what was lacking. Together with this understanding, I began to apply universal themes I found in my research, and endeavored to understand the scientific basis for universal truths found in many religious philosophies. By living the psychological intention of the 'truths', and applying **THE ODYSSEY METHODOLOGY**, I grew "wise and brave", and like the Lakota, became more present in everything I did. As I taught my brain how to deflect and negate the stress of people and things around me, I found myself better able to remain emotionally strong and resilient when stress did rear its ugly head. Soon, my anxieties diminished, my energy levels increased, and I went back to feeling enthused and motivated. I began living more effortlessly and powerfully, in a spirit of authenticity. My life journey became easier. And happier.

Today I have the privilege of sharing this methodology with smart, successful professionals, mentoring them to overcome a wide range of challenges. They learn to become wiser and braver by tackling the tough issues they may be facing head-on. Career pressures, managerial overload, marriage, divorce, unemployment, fatherhood, financial difficulty, the stress of an ongoing federal prosecution, childhood trauma, social phobia, spiritual crisis, chronic anxiety and anger are some of the life challenges successfully tackled in The Odyssey Quest. I've seen heroes emerge when real people step into stress and face their fears and anxieties.

As a leadership consultant, I aim to empower clients to succeed in whatever they do. My methodology has provided the tools and skills that enabled a top CEO win a multi-million dollar legal battle and become a better leader of his company. It also empowered a tennis professional with post-natal depression to have another baby and enjoy the experience. From enabling a top government lawyer to "feel again," overcoming a creative consultant's sabotaging behavior, helping executives kick drug habits to teaching hot-tempered supervisors to better manage their energy, the program has helped a variety of people overcome the stresses that had plagued their lives. They all found the means to change for the better the way their brain was interpreting the world around them. They discovered that the little things no longer mattered while the big things are calls to adventure.

For the next 21 days, set aside time to discover what you're really capable of achieving. Plan to spend 30 minutes each day for self-improvement. You will be presented with a set of readings, followed by a learning exercise. We'll explore recent scientific discoveries within a context of continuous improvement. The 21-day Odyssey will place you back in the captain's chair, at the helm of your consciousness. As life is a journey of continual growth and evolution, like me you'll soon experience what it means to feel alive, living empowered with a spirit of authenticity.

Russell R. Hassler
August 2016

*WOKSAPA MUKU YE HANTO YO,
WAKANYA HIBU YELO*

MAKE ME WISE AND BRAVE.
CLEAR THE WAY, IN A SACRED
MANNER I COME.

LAKOTA NATIVE AMERICAN SHIELD &
PRAYER

The Living Moment

For the Lakota Native Americans, this magic shield and prayer set their conscious focus as they rode thunder into battle. Regarded as one of the most courageous and persevering tribes of the American plains, the Lakota were driven by such emotional intensity that no one dared cross their path for they were feared by all. How did the Lakota use this image to develop such an undaunted warrior spirit?

Symbolically, the horizontal bar within the shield represents the road of life—the past, present and future; the fiery center, the life-energy of the here and now. Like most native cultures, the Lakota believe that we each have a powerful living force within us that is continually present, as if the moment itself were an intelligent living entity.

Today scientific research agrees: *What we think about and remember is, to our brain and body, no different than what is actually happening in real time. A thought that has not yet occurred or a memory you may dwell upon has the same physiological impact or emotional charge to the body. At every living moment, your brain is responding to real, remembered or imagined impulses in the same way, as if they were occurring right now.*

Every thought you have, every decision you make and every action you take affects the energy of your mind-body system. Anxiety, anger, addiction and depression are energetic disorders that can all be improved upon with an increased understanding of the subtle mechanisms we all live with. As thoughts intertwine with emotions, each living moment presents us with an opportunity to grow "wise and brave"—an Odyssey of self-improvement gleaned from every challenge encountered.

For the next 21 days, join me on a hero's journey that strengthens your warrior spirit.

The Odyssey Shield reminds us to live in the present moment.

Why Odyssey?

Stress will always play a part in our lives.

The question then, are you growing wiser and braver in stress? Or becoming lost in the chaos?

In one of humankind's oldest surviving tales, Homer recounts the story of Odysseus, who was tormented unmercifully by competitive gods bent on stopping his journey home. Under a supernatural assault that lasted ten years, Odysseus pressed forward through formidable challenges; his crew killed, he was fighting one-eyed giants and overcoming incredible tests to his stamina. For his wisdom and bravery, Odysseus is remembered two thousand years later as the iconic hero—someone who takes action amid adversity.

Such a leadership mindset is still required today. Living in the 21st century we are continually met with a never-ending borage of challenges, all of which distracts our attention and exhausts our energy. The modern world offers little rest for the weary. Tormented by the 24/7 gods of technology, economy and competition, in the endless assault even the best and brightest buckle and break. Today, mental and emotional disorders are at an all time high. Like Odysseus, survival means keeping your wits about you when the going *remains* tough.

What is Stress?

Stress wakes you up at night and exhausts you during the day. Stress is given to you by the people you meet and the situations you encounter. Even after those that irritate us are gone, their social stress remains encoded within our psyche. We fume in anger, quiver in fear or die in shame and depression. Even when sleep is desired, stress continues to ping our conscious minds with endless mental reminders of what's wrong and what needs doing.
Stress often hijacks our higher human intellect and auto-generates those annoying thoughts that prove difficult to turn off. Without mindful intervention, the cognitive chatter of self-doubt and judgment can grow louder to the point where self-sabotage and self-destruction are inevitable.

Stress erodes both the physical and metaphysical components of the body. Chronic stress typically manifests as a wide range of mental health concerns. Anxiety, panic attacks, manic-depressive behavior, anger control issues, ADHD, post-traumatic stress, suicidal thoughts—all warning signs that the complexities of the world have gotten the best of you. Without an in-tune consciousness, there's a real struggle to make clear, confident decisions in the moment. Without a trusted inner guidance system, life can become a self-created living hell.

If you are not in tune, it's time for a tune up.

Right now, your brain and body are continuously adapting to every stress-full encounter. Without conscious effort, your emotional system updates itself automatically with the people and events that are proving a threat to your survival. As a core competency, your subconscious remembers not the words, but the associated emotional energy. Without energy management (such as the yoga or mindfulness exercises included with this program), stress accumulates within the body as tension—spring-loading survival-based emotions that can wreak havoc on your health and relationships. Without intervention, stress can—and does—make you go primal.

Keeping your energy high requires energy management—an intentional improvement of the mental-emotional process. Like improving a manufacturing process, the living process of your mind and body can be updated and improved upon. I believe anyone with a conviction to improve can learn to control their thoughts and emotions. No matter what your current state of mind, your brain is always willing to learn and adapt. Even now, strength and trust in your core spirit can be restored by the lifting of emotional weight off your psyche. All that is required is that you put your mind to it.

Learning to deal with stress in the moment is key to improved health and happiness. Your Odyssey begins with a desire to grow "wise and brave", as a hero in your own life story. In the quest, you will discover what courage really means, and how taking action amid adversity is vital to navigating stress successfully. The aim is to become mentally sharper and emotionally stronger in the moment when it's needed most. The path to enlightenment is a hero's journey—a quest for self-improvement.

A 21-day Journey of Self-discovery

When the stress is on, how do you respond? When push comes to shove, what drives you forward? Keeps you down? What do you most value at an emotional core? In times of crisis, who are you authentically? Realistically?

For the next three weeks, join me in regaining focus and commitment to what really matters most. Invest 30 minutes a day to get to know yourself authentically, in the moment when the true you is required. I challenge you to Odyssey and connect with the warrior spirit alive within you right now.

Care for your spirit, and your spirit will take care of you.

Everyone is plagued with addictions, aggressions, and anxieties. When you are stressed, it is these primal behaviors that drive you to survive automatically. Without process re-engineering, you may find yourself locked in depression, angry at the world, afraid of strangers or addicted to ill sources of pleasure. As a habitual way of living, being in survival mode means that your potential is locked down by the very intelligence that is helping you survive. Taming the beast within requires reconnecting with your primal energy center and trusting it to move you effectively through the chaos of everyday life.

Over the next 21 days, discover the primal emotional energies that are running you right now. Learn to appreciate how they dictate the moment-to-moment thoughts and emotions that affect your energetic state of consciousness (eState). By strengthening your personal authority—living in tune to your core values under stress—you can quiet the cognitive chatter as those mental reminders are silenced by a confident state of mind. Without chatty rational analysis, decision-making becomes quick and intuitive. Self-doubt and criticism are replaced with a more optimistic outlook of your own abilities to succeed. This is the journey of self-discovery—feeling alive in the moment, appreciating the entire spectrum of emotion.

Are you ready to Odyssey?

THE QUEST OBJECTIVES

The purpose of *Odyssey – The Living Moment* is to hone your skills as a life leader. In order to deliver on this vision, this 21-day personal development program presents a shared context and methodology along with an open framework used to continually improve and strengthen your foundational character.

Over the next three weeks, you'll learn to live in the present moment. You'll begin to experience yourself as a hero, taking the steps to conquer stress in the moment using purposeful action. In terms of practical results, the entire program will build upon three key strengths:

CLARITY—Everyone is unique. Odyssey will uncover your own set of personal values that make you who you are. You'll understand your own internal decision making processes and gain a greater appreciation of the subtle yet pervasive biophysical mechanisms we all live with.

ENERGY—Life is energy. Odyssey will connect you to your living power center by developing personal strategies that naturally awaken higher energetic states. As a result, you feel more confident and enthusiastic in taking on the hard stuff. With improved life leadership, you'll TUNE IN and TURN ON energy automatically, doing more with less effort. Success builds on success.

CONTROL—Power commands force. A life leader responds positively rather than defensively to challenges. Living authentically means being in control of all aspects of your life, consistently making clear decisions and taking purposeful action based on instinct and intuition. Like a martial artist, you remain clean and clear in chaos, a true champion in stress, inspiring others with an enlightened spirit.

INTRODUCTION
#1 ROAD RULE: SURVIVE!

Life has provided you with a powerful impetus to survive. Science has discovered that the mind and body, acting as a single living system, adapt to daily challenges in a way that best ensures continued survival. Under stress, this living system can easily loose its integrity as life-energy becomes misdirected, creating an accentuated condition known by native cultures as the loss of spirit.

As a lost spirit, your survival instincts engage and dictate that negative thoughts (i.e. things that can go wrong) override positive thoughts (i.e. what can go right). That's why under stress, you tend to more easily think about and relive difficult people or situations. The survival brain is fear-oriented—meaning, in terms of survival, it is much more important for you to auto-remember the potentially harmful rather than the pleasurable. This fear conditioning is ancient in evolutionary design, yet continues to play a very active role in your well-being today. For optimum health and happiness, this subconscious survival programming must be consciously updated and maintained.

Neuroscience explains that our brains form habits, because neural pathways that are used repeatedly grow stronger. These subconscious pathways guide everything we do, from thinking to driving a car to solving complex problems. How we perceive, apply meaning and participate in the world around us is directly influenced by this dynamic world within our brain.

With over 100 billion neurons, the human brain suggests an awesome complexity. While still largely a great mystery, science, however, now knows that the living brain continually adapts to new challenges by creating new neural pathways. By exploring your road of life intentionally, an Odyssey begins. You begin learning from the stressful moments and rapidly gain a clearer, more empowered understanding of where you are now and where you want to be in the future.

"Odyssey saved my life."
52-year-old senior strategic executive to his HR Director

"I've been smiling for three days."
36-year-old sales executive when asked how his weekend had been.

"It's absolutely bloody magic. Long may it last!"
46-year-old advertising executive & creative consultant

"Wanted to call and say I'm still using your program."
ASX100 CEO, two years after his 12-week leadership quest.

"People and things just don't impact me negatively anymore."
43-year-old general manager—information services

"This is the first positive paradigm we've come across in our twenty year [heroin] recovery."
Entrepreneurial filmmakers

"Not only does he not get angry, but he hands my anger back to me!"
Wife of a 50-year-old senior consultant when asked how he was doing post-program.

"I've done years of self-development, and this is the first program that really gets to the heart of the matter and makes change happen."
47-year-old financial services officer

"Truly uplifting. I am able to willingly tap into an inner source of wisdom that gives me strength and inspiration."
38-year-old managing director

THE FIRST UNIVERSAL TRUTH

Live in the Present Moment

odyssey

WEEK ONE—THE GREAT MYSTERY

Life & Creative Power

Right now operating beneath your conscious awareness lies a domain that is inaccessible by thought or spoken language.

Yet, running beneath the surface of your conscious mind, a highly intelligent living process is occurring in your brain and body. It's driven by a spirit which strives to keep you alive—aware of and away from danger automatically.

For health and happiness, your Odyssey begins by learning to TUNE IN to this intelligent energy running beneath the surface. The quest is simple: to become wiser and braver every moment of every day.

odyssey

The Quest Objectives

At the end of Week One, you'll be able to…

1. Understand how your primal intelligence, driven by five core competencies, powers your every thought, action and emotion.

2. Experience how your primal intelligence affects your state of mind by using energy to move you.

3. Increasingly TUNE IN to the energy states operating within you on a daily basis.

NASA has made a startling discovery that points to the possibility that a primitive form of microscopic life may have existed on Mars more than three billion years ago.

Daniel S. Goldin, NASA Administrator, August 6, 1996

Day One—The Great Mystery

He was easy to spot. His body language gave him away. Unknowingly bouncing his knee up and down. Looking around, unfocused. Jittery. All subtle signs of anxiety. My soon to be client—I'll call him Doug—was sitting by himself in a Surry Hills cafe, two months after checking himself into a Sydney psychiatric hospital for severe panic attacks.

As I arrived, I glanced around and noticed many others in the cafe exhibiting the same anxious behavior. Smoking cigarettes. Talking excessively. Gesturing wildly. Their body language gave them away. Like an Australian Customs Agent trained to identify when someone is lying, I was aware how many were putting on a happy face yet running on empty. Once you learn to identify your own emotional states, it is an easy next step to identify the emotional energy in others. I brought my attention back from the surroundings, zeroed in on my new pupil.

From afar, he looked normal enough. Early-forties, dressed casually yet smart, looking physically healthy. On the inside was an altogether different story. His emotional health and mental wellbeing were in dire need of attention. I had been told that Doug was a nervous wreck. Unable to make confident decisions, a previous client had prepaid Doug's quest and sent him to me, assuring him that I would be able to help him identify what was happening inside him, and that the experiential Odyssey would give him the "warrior spirit." Doug happily agreed.

With a handshake, I introduced myself, sat down and ordered a coffee. Doug didn't waste any time. He immediately professed his anxious state of mind. With intensity, he told me that he had admitted himself to the hospital two months prior, and that he was on both antidepressants and anti-psychotics. He confessed that his anxiety spells were overwhelming that, at times, he thought he was having a heart attack. As we sat, Doug was becoming increasingly agitated and it was clear it was hard for him to sit still.

"Let's go for a walk," I suggested. We paid for the coffees and started toward the nearby park and up to a bench on top of Moore Park hill, where Sydney's beautiful skyline sprawled before us, with the crisp blue Australian sky as its backdrop and the sun shining bright, as it has been for billions of years. I reminded myself that I was once like Doug, and with a deep breath and sense of empathy, asked Doug to continue.

For the next hour, words spilled from Doug's mouth. He downloaded every woe and worry, from his impending financial disaster to a demanding girlfriend to his chronic insecurity at work. I listened willingly and patiently as he covered every tragic detail. Unfortunately, it was all too familiar: the feeling of insecurity and the lack of confidence permeating everything one does. It's an awful feeling. And it was obvious that Doug was really struggling. Doug was not on a path towards health and happiness. Doug was at a dead end. Was life meant to be such a painful struggle?

The great mystery lay in why Doug had fallen so far. How does anyone manage to stumble into such a discombobulated state? The diagnosis was common: A middle-aged professional male, with a good but high-pressured job, floating in a hefty amount of financial debt while supporting a high maintenance partner. In itself, this was neither unusual nor unmanageable, but Doug was overwhelmed and scared of it all. In his state, he had become unable to cope and resolve the challenges he was facing. Doug desperately needed to strengthen his spirit.

Behind the scene, Doug's anxious energy was negatively affecting those around him. At work, many were worried about him. His reputation was quickly shifting from that of a capable professional to that of a difficult colleague. Having just confessed his heart and soul to a complete stranger, it was obvious Doug was desperate, afraid of his own shadow. "Can you help me?" I remember him asking.

"Are you ready to help yourself?" was my gut response, and received but a blank stare. Doug had lost touch with his core spirit—the spirit that keeps us alive.

The road to health and happiness is not found out there—in medications, evangelists, illicit drugs, alcohol, promiscuous sex—but in here: somewhere between your soul and the cognitive conviction to improve. No one out there—no priest, no psychotherapist, no parent or partner— no one can help us except ourselves. Whilst wishing for a knight in shining armor, at the end of the day we each must muster the strength and courage to fight onward, for tomorrow brings more stress. In such a never-ending battle, where does one find strength?

With a can't-do attitude comes anxiety and alienation. Like Doug, many of us become our own worst enemy. We don't plan on it. We just wake up one day to find our lives aren't 100%. The life we are living is just not a good experience. Our professional lives may not be that awful, the circumstances we face not that dire. It's just that we've strayed off course and simply need to right the ship and put the wind back into our sails. In the end, we simply want to feel alive.

Nobody can feel for you. Being alive is a truly personal experience. No weekend seminar, no motivational speaker, no magical wand or book can snap you back on course and reconnect with spirit. Only you can reclaim the helm and begin to navigate your days more effectively. This is your one and only life. The time to take charge is now.

The upcoming 21 days are all about discovering what makes you tick. It won't be about me, or these readings. The journey will be about you taking the time to regain trust in your core operating system. You had a perfect connection to your core when you were a kid. As adults, however, we lose touch with ourselves, and begin to fear our own emotional depth. Follow this program with conviction and you'll find solid ground.

The first seconds of any stressful challenge, like a bad medical diagnosis, present each of us with a choice between a can-do warrior mentality or a can't-do victim mindset. Which do you choose when the heat is on? What is keeping you from being your best every moment of every day?

Enlightenment is Learnable. Really.

At the end of his Odyssey Quest, Doug was a new man. Within a few months, Doug was back to being a confident, productive professional. His financial debt was being managed successfully, and he had rectified the situation with his energy-draining girlfriend. He was happy, content, and was enjoying his rekindled desire to take the next steps that would excel his career.

Today, Doug is working on a notable global project, and recently told me that he remembers the insecure person he used to be. He can recall the anxious man who walked up the hill with me that day, sitting on the park bench purging his woes and worries, stuck in a situation reminiscent of post-traumatic stress disorder. To the new Doug, the old Doug was almost unimaginable. In his new empowered state of mind—developed during his journey of self-discovery—Doug *now knows how to never again* become so lost and out of balance. After three years, he continues to be wiser and braver with every passing day, inspiring others to do the same.[1]

Dedicate the next 21 days to getting back on course. Make time each day to rediscover being in command of the subtle mechanisms we all have to live with. You will learn to better utilize your

---

[1] The change in Doug's behavior had been so dramatic that others had taken notice. Wanting the same solid self-confidence for himself, Doug's boss soon became another Odyssey client, and, like Doug, is now inspiring others to lead their lives with more positive aspirations.

willpower to live authentically in the moment when you need it most. On the way, you will find yourself remaining cool and confident in the everyday madness of our lives. In the end, you will know what courage really means.

This program provides a simple continuous improvement methodology, which strengthens your ability to effectively deal with stress. You will learn to TUNE IN and TURN ON the person you know you can be. You will say what you mean and mean what you say. You will know yourself and love it. If life is supposed to be this amazing adventure, shouldn't the quest be to grow from every challenge you face? Life is short. Don't take it for granted. Treat life as a gifted opportunity to feel alive. Really alive. Because frankly, it's a cosmic miracle that we are among the living.

An Instinctive Directive

The great mystery isn't who you are or who you will become—it's that you're alive in the first place. It's the magic behind the spirit powering your existence at this very moment. To scientists, the miracle of life is the greatest of mysteries. Billions have been spent sending curious scientific rovers to Mars in search of the big answers. Are we alone? Is life unique? Are we a freak of nature ignited by a heavenly lightning bolt?

We have no clear answers as to where life comes from, and why we're here on this planet. How do you find yourself in such an unknowable paradigm? Religion? Retreats? Rest? In the end, it all boils down to making the best out of what life presents to us.

Consider this: Your enlivening spirit is the great mystery. The life-force within is a gift from the Universe. What you do with it is up to you. So, ask yourself: What are you doing with your spirit right now? Are you improving and strengthening it? Or have you completely forgotten that it is keeping you alive.

A few years ago, a friend spoke of the passing of his wife—I'll call her Jill—who died after a two-year battle with cancer. He was with her when she passed away, alone in their home, just the two of them. A truly rare occasion, I reckon, to be with someone the moment they move on. I was curious and asked to hear more about her death.

Fighting back tears, he told me what had happened the few weeks prior. After two long years of deteriorating health, Jill's weakened physical condition was taking its toll, slowing down everything to a near standstill. Eventually, her failing health completely immobilized her deteriorating body.

As each day passed, he knew the moment of death was getting closer. He recalled that on that particular morning, he felt her time was near. Within hours, she would be gone. He sat with her for the entire time, and as he held her hand, he could sense life leaving her body. He said that he could tell that the onset of death started in her feet, and slowly moved upward as her spirit grew silent and still. Then one last breath, and his wife was no more.

Jill was gone. Like a flame extinguished, her spirit was no longer enlivening her body.

He continued to hold her hand, as he sensed her spirit filling the room. He told me that he had a clear sense that her life-energy was occupying the space around him. In the stillness that followed, even that energy dissipated, and he knew she was in a different place.

Indeed, what is the difference between the moment before death and the moment after? What is there one moment that's not there an instant later?

The Spirit Within

The word spirit comes from an ancient Latin word spīritus meaning 'breath.' Even with our advanced scientific knowledge of the biomechanics of nature, the spirit of life—the intangible ghost in the machine—remains beyond the reach of rational understanding. The enlivening quality within us that makes us who we are remains a mysterious secret ingredient. Your spirit is without question a miracle. Never forget that it's alive within you—even right now.

Each breath and heartbeat provides the opportunity for us to feel alive. Sadness, depression, anxiety, guilt and anger all have a place in a well lived existence. However, if negative experiences outweigh the positive ones, your spirit weakens, and anger, anxiety and depression take over. At worst, suicidal thoughts encroach on our minds, and we become disappointed when we awaken in the morning. That's not a life well lived. That's a spirit lost.

A life leader knows how to live by embracing the entire emotional spectrum. Life leaders do not become stuck in any ill-fated state of mind. Rather, they flow with each circumstance in the river of life, calmly remaining above the chaos, knowing what to do when faced with the rapids.

Begin to think of your spirit as being on a sacred journey. Let's consider ourselves spirits enjoying a physical experience. Let's imagine that a mysterious life-force is enlivening our body and we are undergoing all the ups and downs, stresses and emotions for a reason: To experience a physical life. Our purpose may simply be to experience the rapture of being alive. As a spirit inhabiting a physical body, you are granted this privilege to feel everything from disabling pain to the exhilaration of pleasure, and all the joys, heartaches, and heartburns that come in between. Are you ready to embrace all that life has to offer?

> TUNE IN: Accept where you are right now—emotionally, mentally, and physically—so you can begin to get to where you want to go.

Physical death will catch up with us all, but until that eventful moment, our life quest should be to continually improve our experience of being alive: *to embrace both our strength and weaknesses, and to grow from knowing the difference; to surf the continuous wave of chaos with agility, style and courage; and to maintain our life leadership at all times, as helmsman in the forefront of our consciousness.*

For if in the afterlife we should discover that we were spirits blessed with a unique opportunity to be alive, what a great shame it would be to have not fully lived the entire spectrum of *feeling alive.*

The Ghost in the Machine

Life-energy, life-force, energy flow, Chi, Qi, prana, mana, vital energy—by whatever name it is known, it is the intuitive aspect of the human condition, a living energy that powers who we are. When this spirit is gone, so are we. No matter what religion, language or culture, the names describe an active energetic principle that exists in our mind and body and ultimately separates the living from the dead. This spirit is at the very foundation of our being alive. Without its animating life-force, we would cease to exist.

Because we are alive, our spirit seems perfectly natural to us. For the most part, we take our spirit for granted. We expect our lungs to breathe, our heart to beat, and our stomachs to digest food. We only wake up and notice when something's not right—a headache, heartburn, illness or emotional upset. Throughout it all, our spirit strives to maintain our health and well-being. What is it then about our spirit that engages the systems in our body to work together so beautifully, with such self-organizing elegance? How does our spirit command the countless cells and biological elements that keep us among the living?

Dr. Charles T. Krebs in his book, *A Revolutionary Way of Thinking* (1998), says that the self-organization of the organism suggests more than genetic programming. Krebs acknowledges that the "physical structure and repair of DNA is essential for the maintenance and health of an organism," but questions, "Is this all there is?" What else is there that may be powering our self-actuality?

Referencing *Vibrational Medicine* by Richard Gerber, M.D. (1988), Krebs proposes that there's a mysterious force at work. He states that if you were to gaze at the development of a human egg and sperm from the moment of fertilization, what you would see defies explanation. For the first ten days, the factors that organize development remain obscure. From day ten onward, scientists can recognize various chemical markers and gradients as biochemistry takes over. But before—from the moment of conception—the only process that can be detected is an electrical field generated with an axis that later becomes the spinal column—the very root of our human physiology.[2]

Dr. Krebs goes on to say, "In the East it is said that the etheric or energetic template of the body is what provides the directions for the organization of physical matter. And once that matter has been organized, the maintenance of its on-going structure is dependent upon a constant flow of subtle, nutritive energy coming from the energetic systems of the organisms." He conjectures that while decay and entropy reign in upon death, while we are alive, an active energy field commands a powerful opposite force: negative entropy—a tendency towards order.

All living creatures continually maintain themselves with this mysterious, self-organizing intelligence—a "tendency towards order" that is the prime directive of our spirit. And as you will find in the weeks to come, your own spirit is surprisingly smart at keeping you alive.

> You are fundamentally governed by a spirit that strives to keep you alive and healthy.

For the next 21 days, you will become more cognizant of your own health-inducing spirit operating within you. You will become familiar with how it powers your brain and moves your body without conscious thought. In a quest for improved health and happiness, let's venture forward to better understand how your spirit is driving your existence right now.

The Core Competencies

Billions of dollars have been spent sending sophisticated machines to Mars, to look for the telltale signs of life. These scientific instruments are seeking five key qualities or innate abilities that separate living organisms from non-living objects. Scientists have concluded that these core competencies are the foundational processes of life itself. Without these capabilities, living things wouldn't exist. Most important to our quest is that these instinctual drivers are at the heart of everyone's core intelligence even now.

These five skills or talents will become more evident in the days ahead. As you will learn, their primary directives play a powerful role in everyday life.

---

[2] Charles T. Krebs, Ph.D. *A Revolutionary Way of Thinking*, Hill of Content, Melbourne, 1998 pp. 326.

You are a unique life-form.
Independently operated, you are a self-contained entity, a living being unique in your own distinctive way. Your innate competency ensures that you maintain your own individuality at all times using an intelligent force that keeps you all together. The resulting boundary of skin maintains a vigilant physical separation between your inner and outer worlds.

Your spirit is one of a kind.

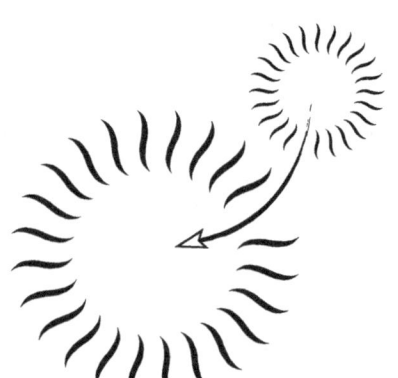

You are an energy being.
As a unique living creature, you need energy to survive. Each of our 100+ billion brain cells and the trillions of cells that compose our body are insatiably hungry, consuming an enormous amount of energy every day to sustain life in all cells, produce body heat, brain activity, heart and lung functions, voluntary movement and involuntary organ functions. Without food, water and air, our spirit would perish. This energy consumption includes the intake of emotional energy. Without connecting to the life-energy of others, you would die a lonely isolated death.

Your spirit requires energy.

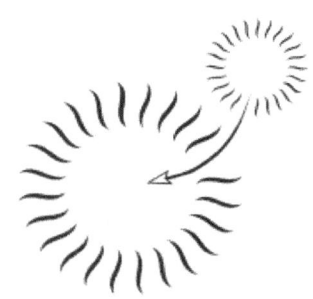

You are a self-organizing living process.
Every living system inside you is working together as one unique individual. Right now, a tremendous amount of internal living activity is organizing itself into the physical being you are. As a structurally complex organism, our primal intelligence is at the helm of our metabolism and ongoing well-being. Its impetus is to maintain our living systems, and orchestrate the trillions of cells, their tissues and organs into one dynamic life-form. Despite what you may do to yourself, your spirit works endlessly to ensure your ongoing health and well-being.

Your spirit is intelligent.

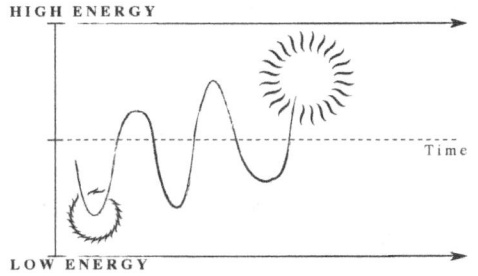

You are adaptable.
Given new stress or environment, your brain and body will adapt to the new challenge without conscious effort. You automatically grow smarter and stronger with every stressful experience you encounter. Your brain and body are geared for adaptation, learning instinctively from every experience of pain and pleasure. We normally think of learning as being a rational process, but as far as the brain and body are concerned, our emotional system is continually updated with new knowledge on a daily basis.

Your spirit learns by doing.

You are sexual.
Nature's most powerful force is our sexuality. Without it, we would not be here. It is the instinctual drive to build relationships and reproduce. It powers our social needs and cultural constructs. Our sex organs are displayed front and center, their prominent location on our bodies a testament to the importance of sex in our lives. Being sexual and social are two of humankind's most pleasurable experiences and as such, we must honor the life-force that directs the joy and happiness of being alive.

Your spirit connects you to others.

These five core competencies form your primal intelligence. They are the key instinctual drivers that strive to keep you alive and healthy. You did not learn them in school. Nature has provided them free of charge, deeply encoded within your DNA. These preprogrammed smarts play an important role in every thought, decision or action you make. Collectively, your core competencies form a powerful force that runs every living aspect of you. And as we will learn, these five instinctual drivers exist in our spirit, which is genuinely brilliant at keeping us alive.

One Very Smart Spirit

In terms of evolution, your core competencies are vastly ancient. As a survivor of a 100+ million year life journey, your ancestors adapted and learned to survive a multitude of obstacles. You are a survivor of the fittest. The knowledge and experience of your parents, grandparents, and their lineage dating back to prehistory is encoded deep within your DNA. There is no doubt about your innate brilliance. You may not feel bright. But the same intelligence that keeps you breathing, birds flying or kangaroos jumping is informing your instincts right now.

By tapping into this primal intelligence, you will learn to grow "wise and brave" from whatever stressful challenge is thrown your way. Therefore you can tackle any challenge with confidence: Every instruction to combat any challenge is already encoded in your instincts. Your quest is to strengthen trust in your own innate intelligence, and capitalize on the life-force that is already there. Connect with your spirit and your spirit will take care of you.

I've had the honor of sharing this program with Harvard CEOs and Oxford graduates. They were all very intelligent people with IQs far greater than my own. Still, I believe that no matter how smart a person is, they can become smarter by learning to listen to their primal intelligence. With a deeper connection to such pure ancient wisdom, the ill-fated disorders of self-doubt, self-blame, self-sabotage and self-regret all but fade away. As long as you're alive, your spirit will ensure that you navigate life effectively. Trust it and you will find true confidence.

By honing your thoughts and emotions with a strengthened spirit, you can become an Olympic athlete of life, a mountaineer of your peak potential. With the mastery of self comes the ability to rise above stress and conquer challenges in ways once considered too daunting. In the strengthening process, your mind becomes sharper and clearer, your body stronger and less anxious. By increasingly utilizing your own core intelligence—connecting to your spirit—you'll come to trust yourself when the stress is on. Self-confidence will ground your decision-making process. Self-reliance and resilience will become your authentic nature. All this by simply tapping into the smart spirit that is alive and working within you right now.

Day One Exercise

From a quality improvement perspective, every process can be improved upon. This is particularly true of the self-organizing living process going on within you right now. Adaptation is a core competency, which means you can learn to control attention deficits and improve how the brain and body are impacted by stressful challenges. Like building muscle requires going to a gym, becoming "wise and brave" requires the lifting of emotional weight.

Positive adaptation is the key to better health and happiness. The Odyssey to enlightenment calls us to better understand ourselves in the here and now. At this moment, emotional memories are charging the way in which you see others and react to the world. The goal is to become more conscious of those reactions and strengthen your state of mind to respond positively when you next meet with stress.

For example, most everyone resents being stuck in traffic. Bad drivers often ping us into bad states of mind. Our reaction to bad drivers is a subconscious habit. Unfortunately, reacting with negative emotions such as anger places the brain and body into stress, and our health suffers.

Better to respond positively in the moment, a leadership skill this program will endeavor to develop over the next three weeks.

We also tend to react negatively when we are subjected to a stressful environment. An unemployed client of mine accepted a job as the sales manager at a training company. Although he did not have previous experience making sales calls, he courageously took the job as a pathway to growth. Like many, he found he resented being rejected and soon became anxious. To make matters worse, his office space was in an open plan and everyone could hear every word he said—every negotiation, every rejection. In his new job, he was under pressure to be his best under stress.

After every sales call, he used process re-engineering and examined the pings of being rejected—the annoyed tones of voice, the short, terse conversations—and elevated the eState of what those triggering moments meant. Using greater self-awareness of his energy, he better managed his emotional state to persist tackling the hard stuff until his brain adapted in a positive, healthy way. Rather than becoming wired in fear and apathy, he stepped in with courage and responded with higher emotional responses. With every ping of rejection, he became "wise and brave."

eState	eMotion	
Experience	Feeling	Energy
Enlightenment	Nirvana	1000
Peace	Bliss	600
Joy	Serenity	540
Love	Reverence	500
Reason	Understanding	400
Acceptance	Forgiveness	350
Optimism	Willingness	310
Trust	Neutrality	250
Courage	Affirmation	200
Pride	Scorn	175
Anger	Resentment	150
Desire	Craving	125
Fear	Anxiety	100
Grief	Regret	75
Apathy	Despair	50
Guilt	Blame	30
Shame	Humiliation	20

Along the road of self-discovery you will find what is real and valuable. You will uncover the emotional programs that fuel your ongoing energy levels. If you examine your pings closely, you will gain wisdom into what really makes you tick.

What is a Ping?

A ping is a significant emotional experience. In physiological terms, a ping is a stress response. Pings can be positive, like a ping of joy at seeing a loved one, or the ping of optimism at what lies ahead. For this exercise, negative pings will be examined as benchmarks for self-improvement. You easily remember pings because they are charged with eMotion.

Pings can be about people, places or events. You can be pinged by your boss wanting a meeting or by your partner suggesting a different set of clothes. You can also ping yourself by mentally dwelling on a negative situation such as financial debt or the political system. Pings are associated with shifts of emotional states. You will get to know what "pings" you in the days to come.

Pings trigger eMotions (energy for motion) and are experienced as feelings. An eState is the energetic state of consciousness eMotions put you in. eMotions exist to move you to action. Consequently, eStates are the resulting energy states which power your thinking process. By focusing on the eState that you find yourself in, and seeking to raise that response to a higher level for future encounters with the same stressful experience, you can reduce the stress of a ping experience.

The chart of eStates and eMotions is adapted from the work of David R. Hawkins, M.D. Ph.D., in his book Power vs. Force: The Hidden Determinants of Human Behavior (2004), in which he used kinesiological studies to determine a hierarchy of power generated by the life-energy of different emotions. I've adapted his work for my own practice with clients, as it provides a useful and tested tool for measuring the nature of an emotional response.

For example, the client faced with having to make sales calls routinely experienced the eMotions of Anxiety and Despair, triggering an eState that put his mind in the corresponding emotional energy. By becoming aware of the events that pinged an eMotion, and becoming aware of the eState of his thinking process, he improved his state of mind by handling the stress until a more positive eState became habitual. As adaptation is a core competency, improving your eState permanently is accomplished with conscious continuous improvement.

The Odyssey Methodology

Step One: TUNE IN

The journey to self-improvement begins when you TUNE IN to your current eState. Since memories are charged by eMotion, close your eyes and **REMEMBER** the pings of the day. Using visualization, relive the day and choose three significant emotional experiences that affected you in a negative way. Clients routinely report pings of annoyance at their partner or peer, getting into an argument, feeling nervous about a daunting task, being snubbed by clerks, receiving criticism, trouble at work, financial worries, and other everyday stresses. These are all pings: people, places or events that disturbed your emotional energy.

PING—a significant emotional experience
[box 1]

Received an email from a client wondering when his problem would be resolved.

Duration: ___ hr. ___ min.

TUNE IN [box 2]
Fear (anxiety)

TURN ON [box 3]
Trust (all will be okay)

> What do you **REMEMBER** about your day? Were you pinged by any person, place or event?

Close your eyes and think about your day. Start in the morning, then remember going through your day, to this moment. What were the significant people or events that impacted you? Did something happen that shifted your mood? Was your energy pinged in a negative way? When you have three pings in mind, **RECORD** each in the PING boxes [box1] using a brief description. Include the person, place or event. Do this for each of the three pings. If the ping stressed you for a while, note the duration.

With eyes closed, think about the ping and **REFLECT** on the emotional energy brought on by the ping experience. Focus on the physical aspects of the eMotion—the tension of the muscles, the forceful movements and the feelings that dominated the ping experience.

Referring to the chart of eStates, intuitively choose the eState that best fits each ping. **RECORD** the eState you experienced during the TUNE IN process [box 2]. Before continuing, again pause and TUNE IN to the feelings associated with the eState. Become familiar with what each ping felt like in your body. Label that eState in your mind's eye. This will teach your rational brain how your emotional brain responds to stress triggers. This TUNE IN process builds trust in your intuition (in-tune-ition) a skill that will become self-evident in the days to come.

The next step in the continuous improvement effort is to TURN ON your higher brain functions. To strengthen your ability to deflect the impact of future pings, replace the negative memory with a more powerful one. Train the brain to TURN ON when pings next occur. Here's how it's done.

Bring the charged memory to mind by the **REPLAY** of your day. Close your eyes and place the palm of one of your hands on your forehead. This facilitates blood flow into the frontal cortex, the seat of your higher brain functions. This has a calming effect and facilitates learning. REPLAY the ping in your mind's eye. See the ping—the person, place or event—in its entirety. Visualize the face of the person, their tone of voice, what they were wearing, etc. Intentionally relax and allow the charge of the eMotion to dissipate with the calming palm on forehead.

Step Two: TURN ON

Once you have the ping in-tune, **RAISE** your eState. From the eState chart, choose an eState higher than the one experienced using quick intuition. RECORD this higher eState in the TURN ON section [box3].

Ideally, this eState will be one at or above the line of courage, and will seek to resolve the ping in a positive way. You can choose to TURN ON trust that all will be okay, or TURN ON optimism that things will work out. You can TURN ON acceptance of the situation or TURN ON the courage to seek greater understanding of the challenge. In these first days of the Odyssey, it may seem difficult to imagine how a stressful moment can be re-imagined as a moment of optimism or acceptance. But as we follow the Odyssey, and as you learn to understand the values that drive your own emotions, the task will become habitual.

Keeping your eyes closed, and with your palm on forehead, again REPLAY the ping, this time in the higher eState. Imagine living that high-energy eMotion in the moment the ping occurred. See yourself acting in that higher eState, remaining calm and living in that more powerful eMotion. What would you say and do if you could relive that moment in the higher eState? How will you behave differently next time?

Like an Olympic athlete, use visualization to train the brain how to operate more effectively when the stress occurs again. For example, the client feeling anxiety over a sales call, who found that it triggered an eState of anger for being stuck in such a job, might instead visualize responding to the task with the courage it takes to carry out the call despite fear.

Repeat for all three pings. Keep your eyes closed and your palm on your forehead. Take time to relax and feel the TURN ON eState at work in your mind and body. Train the brain to be calm and emotionally resilient next time the ping occurs.

The final step is to **RESOLVE** the three most significant pings of the day in your mind. Mentally step into courage and ask what is necessary to put the ping away. You will find that when you RAISE a ping to a higher eState you will neutralize the charged thoughts associated with it. If necessary, make plans to positively RESOLVE the stressful challenge. Courageously place a to-do in your calendar and visualize yourself being willing to accomplish it. You can also choose to RAISE the eState to acceptance and forgive the person, or seek to be more understanding of the situation. Forgiving, understanding and loving yourself are always good TURN ONs. Give yourself lots of room to grow. Like everything, practice makes perfect. You will learn more about this methodology in the days to come.

End the day's journal entry by completing the GRATITUDE box. Simply REMEMBER and REFLECT three people, places or events you are thankful for. For the next 21 days, challenge yourself to come up with something new every day. You'll be surprised how much there is to be grateful for.

The Odyssey Quest

Appreciate that what pings one person may not ping another. Every Odyssey client came with a unique set of pings and life experiences. You will undoubtedly bring your own collection of challenges to this program. Like others, you will learn to reflect and resolve your stress triggers in your own unique way, in the moment when they occur. Although I cannot tell you what will ping you, or how to resolve each ping, here are some common pings to look for.

Most people will experience a ping to their pride when they make a mistake, or when someone corrects them. (Those in an eState of pride easily fall into anger and resentment.) When you find yourself craving for something you do not have, you experience a ping of desire. Wishing for a new job or partner, or wanting something are all desire pings. You will experience pings of shame and guilt when you do something that disconnects you from others. Apathy will ping you when you feel emotionally exhausted and unable to take on new tasks. You may feel a ping of grief when you lose something or someone close to you. The key improvement strategy here is to TUNE IN negative pings and TURN ON a more empowering way of dealing with them permanently.

This is more than a rational exercise. It's an emotional experience. It's not enough just to read about feeling better or write in your pings. You must live the methodology. For example, one client was going through a divorce and experienced pings each time she contacted her former partner. To grow stronger, she had to TUNE IN feelings of blame, fear and regret, and TURN ON an eState of courage to trust relationships again. In time, she worked her way up to experiencing optimism, acceptance and reason. Today, she reports that she is able to love again.

Another client routinely experienced pings triggered by the people he managed. On a typical day, he would experience pings of fear, desire and anger. "Sam failed to get the report in," or, "The revenue figures fell short again," were typical pings for him. With a TUNE IN, he learned to TURN ON courage to become a leader of people and deal directly with the hard stuff when it occurred. Soon, he built trust and a sense of optimism filled his work environment.

Pings will occur commonly while living life. An unexpected email or phone call might ping anxiety. In your exchanges with sales clerks, customer service representatives and people living their lives unaware of your own needs and feelings, you will inevitably be subject to pings. You may be going through a difficult period. While reflecting on your day, simply concentrate on the people, places or events that disturb your energy. Typically, you can expect pings of anger, desire and fear, as they are a natural part of life. The goal here is to teach your rational brain what your emotional brain is doing, and eventually improve what you find.

As mentioned, we will learn more about this in the days to come. Now, if you haven't done so, simply follow the Odyssey Methodology to complete today's Quest Journal entry.

If you would like to complete the Odyssey Program without writing in this book, copies of the forms may be downloaded from odysseythelivingmoment.com.

odyssey

The Odyssey Methodology

1. TUNE IN

Remember your day	Close your eyes and mentally review your day. Remember the pings—the people, places or events—that caused you stress, then determine the eMotion triggered by the ping. - *A ping is a significant emotional experience that shifts your energy.* - *You remember pings because of their emotional energy.*
Record your pings	Pick the three most impactful pings of the day and record. [PING - box 1] For each ping, choose the eState that best suits how you responded to the eMotion experienced and record. [TUNE IN - box 2]
Reflect your energy	Focus on how the ping affected your energetic state. Teach your brain what the ping feels like (i.e. grief, anxiety, apathy, etc.). Mentally label the feelings with a rational understanding of the eMotion.

2. TURN ON

Raise your eState	Choose an eState higher than the one experienced for each ping and record. [TURN ON - box 3]
Replay your day	Close your eyes and with palm on forehead, visualize reliving each ping in the higher eState. Imagine the same people, place or event ping in the new eState. - *Include all aspects of the more empowering eMotion. See yourself being confident, responding authentically with pleasant gestures, facial expressions, calm voice, etc.*
Resolve your pings	Set action to neutralize the ping-energy. Ask yourself: What task or solution is necessary to fix a problem? Reconnect with a person? What steps are required to repair what is broken / disconnected? In courage, take action! - *Set an intention to follow through on the commitment. With palm on forehead, mentally rehearse being courageous / optimistic / accepting of the situation. Visualize the new behavior. Train the brain for a high-energy response to stress.*

odyssey

The Quest Journal
- Day One -

Date: Day: S — M — T — W — Th — F — S

eState	eMotion	
Experience	*Feeling*	*Energy*
Enlightenment	Nirvana	1000
Peace	Bliss	600
Joy	Serenity	540
Love	Reverence	500
Reason	Understanding	400
Acceptance	Forgiveness	350
Optimism	Willingness	310
Trust	Neutrality	250
Courage	Affirmation	200
Pride	Scorn	175
Anger	Resentment	150
Desire	Craving	125
Fear	Anxiety	100
Grief	Regret	75
Apathy	Despair	50
Guilt	Blame	30
Shame	Humiliation	20

PING—a significant emotional experience

[box 1]

Duration: ___hr. ___min.

TUNE IN [box 2]

TURN ON [box 3]

PING—a significant emotional experience

Duration: ___hr. ___min.

TUNE IN

TURN ON

GRATITUDE
1.
2.
3.

If the only prayer you say in your whole life is 'thank you' that should suffice.—Meister Eckhart

PING—a significant emotional experience

Duration: ___hr. ___min.

TUNE IN

TURN ON

Emotion hierarchy adapted from Map of Consciousness: *Power vs. Force.* David R. Hawkins, M.D. Ph.D., 1995.

People say that what we're looking for is a meaning for life. I don't think that's what we're really seeking. I think what we're seeking is an experience of being alive, so that our life experiences on the purely physical plane will have resonance within our own innermost being and reality, so that we actually feel the rapture of being alive.

Joseph Campbell (1904 - 1987)

Day Two—Dynamics of Feeling Alive

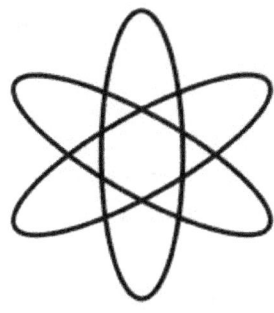

Life is stressful by nature. From the moment we pop out of our mother's womb, life is filled with uncertainty and doubt. Food, water, air, a safe environment and positive social interactions all become essential elements to our health and happiness. Obtaining these amidst unpredictable obstacles and challenges becomes our instinctual quest. In our pursuit of survival, we will meet with disappointment and loss—expectations not fulfilled. As a result, we develop feelings of anxiety and aggression, becoming addicted to external sources of pleasure to fill the void of despair within.

Yet, the same unknowable future holds the potential for a completely opposite life experience. When our survival needs are met, and our stresses neutralized, we thrive. Without the emotional weight, we feel lighter. More energized and motivated. On this path, life is filled with optimism and understanding, powered by undaunted strength and self-confidence. Rather than play victim to circumstance, we make things happen. Life becomes an adventure, a pursuit to TURN ON the essential ingredients that make life worth living. At this enlightened state of mind, we become so empowered that pain and sorrow take their proper place in the background.

Odds are, this is not exactly what you're feeling right now. However, whatever feelings you are experiencing right now, they are just feelings. And in time, feelings change. They always do.

Feelings are perhaps the most dynamic aspect of being alive. The question is, are you controlling your feelings or are they controlling you?

In my past, I experienced what I now consider a self-created living hell. I distinctly remember how on my 'dark days,' I'd wake up and feel disappointed it was morning. It was agony to realize another stressful day lay ahead. Rather than facing the world and its challenges, I'd sooner shut off my brain and zone back to the void of nothingness. There were months where I felt lifeless, rudderless and at odds with the people around me. Oftentimes it took tremendous effort just to drag myself out of bed. This is the realm of apathy and despair, a place too many experience in today's fast-paced world.

Since then, I've reached an altogether different level of living and I am glad I stuck with self-improvement. It's a level we all know. You've been there too. It's a place where you feel so connected, so 'in tune' with yourself and others that a song and smile come naturally. This is a place where the brain neutralizes the energetic impacts of stress automatically. Where your actions and decisions are made with authority and confidence. Here you feel alive, profoundly in the moment with whatever comes your way.

In this program, you'll 'get it,' both slowly and abruptly. You'll begin to understand how life can be a freer paradigm, where stress isn't something to be feared, but taken on as a call to adventure.

So how do you get back to or reach such a place? Begin by observing what weighs you down and keeps you trapped in negative thoughts and emotion. Ask: What are the current stresses that ping my energy? How is my energy being affected by what I think and feel? As an intelligent individual, you have a right to a clear mind and body. Learning to manage your energy is key to claiming that clarity.

A Constant Energy Crisis

In every respect, we are energy beings—creatures dependent on energy to function. The living systems within us consume an exorbitant amount of energy to feed the hungry cells repairing and manufacturing *you*. This active living process is called metabolism. Your brain alone requires the energy that can power a 20-watt light bulb. And the more you use your brain, the more energy you burn. To the chronically stressed, being alive is a constant energy drain. So how do we quiet our minds and gain more energy?

Energy is drawn from the food we eat, metabolized by the water we drink and liberated by the air we breathe. Our body—without conscious effort—converts this energy to work, each cell acting as a molecular factory that maintains the operations that keep us alive. Even if we are busy and forget to eat, our primal intelligence will inform us to do so. As a core competency, we are instinctually driven to be hungry for energy, both physically and psychologically.

Energy is also drawn from the emotional energy we receive. If people around us are happy and healthy, having fun and enjoying life, we tend to 'top up' our energy reserves by hanging out with them. Unfortunately, such positively powered people are hard to come by. Many are in survival mode; defensive, angry and anxious. Their negative energy can rapidly drain our own. For our health and happiness, we need to better manage our energy by becoming mindful of the energy drainers around us.

Fortunately for us, our primal intelligence in our subconscious has automated many of the instincts that keep our energy in check. Our stomach growls when we're hungry. We breathe rhythmically to take in oxygen automatically. We feel anxious when danger is near. Too much stress and we get depressed—a telltale sign we need to retreat and recharge our energy. If we listen to our instincts, many times our *spirit of life* will tell us exactly what is needed to boost our energy levels. Let me convey what this means in everyday life.

In terms of energy, our brains and bodies are in a constant energy crisis. Starving for energy, like young chicks peeping for the mother hen for food, our living system is on constant alert for energy sources. Be it a juicy steak or a beautiful blond, our subconscious is on the continual lookout for food, safety and positive social intercourse. While we are alive, our primal intelligence will always ping our minds with mental reminders to eat the next metaphorical meal.

If you don't listen to your primal intelligence, your brain and body experience stress. An energy crisis ensues as the internal flow of energy is misdirected. Mental and emotional processes become imbalanced and you feel drained. The key is the free flow of higher, more powerful energy, or as I like to think of it, 'high-octane life-energy.' This allows our spirit to run the self-organizing living process more efficiently.

Managing the Living Process

Today scientists have a solid idea of the physical properties of life—the 'what' of being alive. However, the 'why' remains a great mystery. Why life exists in the first place and how it executes the mechanisms necessary to keep our hearts beating and lungs breathing are questions that remain open to speculation.

If we stop and focus on the smallest operations of life, we find something truly remarkable. Taking a microscopic look at our body 'in motion' and zooming down to the size of cells and molecules, we witness a seemingly magical process termed self-organization. At the atomic scale of life, what we see is molecular bits and pieces moving around by themselves in endless self-construction and repair. This is your DNA in action. An active self-organizing living process orchestrated by a mysterious spirit that requires energy to operate.

There are an estimated 70 trillion cells in your body. At the center of each cell, we find a nucleus, the brain of the cell itself. It's the hub of intellectual activity much like a queen bee that commands a hive. Each individual cell is alive, supplying both the basic building blocks and instructions for how to build and repair itself. Truly, each cell is a microscopic living factory. Multiplied by 70 trillion, that extensive web of life constitutes the 'what' of who you are. With 300 million cells dying each minute, this continuous manufacturing and self-organization consumes a tremendous amount of energy.

Similarly, the complex neural web of the brain requires a constant flow of energy. With over 100 billion neurons, your brain is in constant energetic activity and is always hungry. 'Firing off' with every thought or movement, the brain is the body's biggest energy consumer. Without oxygen for example, even for a few minutes, your brain will perish.

If we step back and look at our brain and body from a greater holistic perspective, we find that 70 trillion cells have organized themselves together to form specialized tissues and organs. The heart, lungs, liver, kidneys, brain and every muscle and nerve fiber within you, all require energy to keep things self-organized. In fact, your entire self-organizing living process is alive with biochemical activity using energy as the catalyst.

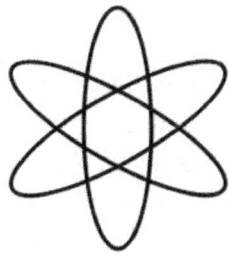

Biochemical Reactivity

When we distill and disseminate the essential elements of which we're made, we find there are only four basic building blocks to our bodies: carbon, hydrogen, oxygen and nitrogen, otherwise known as CHON. Beyond being the foundational elements of your body, CHON are the most common molecules found in the entire universe. Two elements we know quite well—hydrogen and oxygen—which together form water, the single greatest component to the human body. Without water, there would be no 'soup' in which life performs its operations. No water. No life.

In terms of energy, CHON molecular structures are highly reactive with one another. When exposed to a flow of energy, these four organic elements come alive and are electrically excited—connecting, combining, separating and recombining with one another in seemingly limitless designs.

From only four molecules, scientists have identified over 90,000 different protein structures within the human body, all produced following the central instruction manual of our DNA. Using 90,000 proteins made from four energy-excitable elements, your *spirit* creates *you*. This requires (again) a tremendous amount of energy. Here within this active living process, the great mystery reveals something of itself. Every living component is using energy to communicate with every other living component. Your brain and body are alive with energy, using the biochemical activity to self-organize into the living creature that you are. To improve the living process, begin to eavesdrop on the conversation between the brain and body. Better yet, learn the language your spirit is speaking.

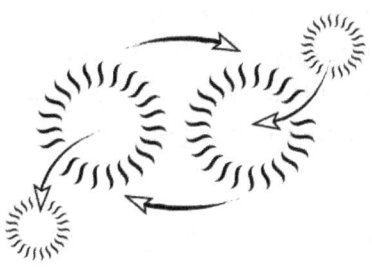

Energy: The Currency of Communication

Living things need one another to survive. Left alone, a single cell soon withers and dies. So too does an abandoned infant or a socially isolated individual. Only in a collective community life truly thrives. Life united is stronger. With a competency of sex, connecting intimately to others is paramount to the survival process. The more comfortable we are in openly exchanging energy with people the more love and joy we experience. The freer life-energy flows.

As such, it's no wonder that in our deepest instincts, we are energetically 'excited' to self-organize with one another to be social, have sex, make friends and form families, communities and cultures. Positive energy is experienced when we create trustworthy relationships. As social creatures, we are attracted to charismatic individuals and are drawn to their energy. We pay celebrities and sports stars big money to radiate their energy our way. Seems we are indeed happiest when our web of life is filled with positively-fueled people.

Expanding on this, our greatest human achievements come from the successful self-organization of our civilization. When our community assures health and safety, we thrive as a society. We experience the 'highs' of the emotional spectrum when connected to a steady supply of positive energy. As our brains have developed, this social cohesion via energy exchanges has increased. When someone full of energy walks into a room, people's energy is aroused. As 'high-octane life-energy' is injected, the more open, relaxed and connected we feel. The positive energy flow benefits everyone.

The same is true with the self-organization of our physical body. When the living elements within us are communicating effectively with one another, and energy is plentiful, we feel relaxed and content. Stress is at a minimum. There is little to block the flow of life-energy and we feel happy. However, when we become stressed, energy flow is blocked and we experience anxiety. The energy drain manifests as tension and emotional angst. For health and happiness, aim to reduce stressful emotional pings so that your energy is freed up to flow and self-organize the 70 trillion cells that make up your internal living community.

Remember that your state of mind is 'powered' at the cellular level. As energy beings, every cell, every fiber, every living organ is alive and in constant energy communication with every other cell, fiber and living organ. At every living moment, energy is either being drained or gained somewhere within you. If you are feeling depressed, energy is low. When energy is high, you feel enthused and motivated. Energetically speaking, feeling 'balanced' means the gain-drain exchange is neutral. Experiencing a neutral state of mind comes with a feeling that 'all is okay'. When energy is balanced, you feel neither manic nor depressed. Rather, a 'can-do' attitude permeates all you do.

In your quest, it's increasingly important to TUNE IN to your energy levels and actively manage what you find. Pay close attention to the self-organizing living process within. Beyond brain and body, your life-energy is a lot smarter than you think.

How Intelligent is Spirit?

In an astonishing experiment conducted in 2000, Japanese scientists studying simple life forms were surprised to find that a gooey mass of single-cell organisms showed remarkable intelligence when placed together in a maze and given food as a common goal.

The life form—the common slime mold, found in every backyard and responsible for the decay of dead material—is remarkably simple. Made up of mostly water, a few proteins and a fatty membrane to hold everything together, this low-level organism took on the intelligence assumed only by animals higher up the food chain. Mysteriously, the slime mold is neither plant nor animal, but possesses characteristics of both. And despite its simplicity, slime mold is surprisingly smart at staying alive.

In the experiment, the scientists watched in amazement as individual slime mold cells came together to form one sludge-like worm that successfully plotted its way through the shortest route of a complex maze to reach food at the other end.

The scientists wondered how this fusion of gooey slimy cells, with no brain and no nervous system, knew how to communicate, self-organize, specialize (some cells became 'head' cells while others became 'tail' cells), make decisions and mobilize. With no brain and a watery body, how did this multi-cell creature come to behave as one single body and unify toward a common goal? Where exactly did the unified intelligence come from? Who is the conductor of the biological symphony?

The source of the intelligence remains a great mystery. However, this remarkable intellect is readily apparent in all life forms, from the bacteria in the soil or in our guts to the cells in your head and heart to that single sperm that successfully navigates its way to unite with the egg which, in its manifestation and self-development, becomes a human being like you. This means that your innate intelligence, the source of your core competencies, is not found in the brain and nervous system, but in *you*—in the unique life form you are.

Indeed, your spirit is profoundly brilliant at keeping you alive. Your quest is to trust it to do its job.

Day Two Exercise

Have you noticed that understanding is a high-energy eMotion? For the next 20 days, aim to better appreciate and learn from what pings you. Gaining a greater reason and understanding of your emotional triggers can and will improve your self-organizing living process.

When improving the efficiency of a process, you should not attempt to tweak the machine without first gathering sufficient data on what the process produces. On Day Two, continue to TUNE IN and gather data on your pings. Soon you'll discover the underlying emotional patterns that are driving your behavior.

Again, simply follow the Odyssey Methodology to complete the Quest Journal.

odyssey

The Odyssey Methodology

1. TUNE IN

Remember your day	Close your eyes and mentally review your day. Remember the pings—the people, places or events—that caused you stress, then determine the eMotion triggered by the ping. - *A ping is a significant emotional experience that shifts your energy.* - *You remember pings because of their emotional energy.*
Record your pings	Pick the three most impactful pings of the day and record. [PING - box 1] For each ping, choose the eState that best suits how you responded to the eMotion experienced and record. [TUNE IN - box 2]
Reflect your energy	Focus on how the ping affected your energetic state. Teach your brain what the ping feels like (i.e. grief, anxiety, apathy, etc.). Mentally label the feelings with a rational understanding of the eMotion.

2. TURN ON

Raise your eState	Choose an eState higher than the one experienced for each ping and record. [TURN ON - box 3]
Replay your day	Close your eyes and with palm on forehead, visualize reliving each ping in the higher eState. Imagine the same people, place or event ping in the new eState. - *Include all aspects of the more empowering eMotion. See yourself being confident, responding authentically with pleasant gestures, facial expressions, calm voice, etc.*
Resolve your pings	Set action to neutralize the ping-energy. Ask yourself: What task or solution is necessary to fix a problem? Reconnect with a person? What steps are required to repair what is broken / disconnected? In courage, take action! - *Set an intention to follow through on the commitment. With palm on forehead, mentally rehearse being courageous / optimistic / accepting of the situation. Visualize the new behavior. Train the brain for a high-energy response to stress.*

odyssey

The Quest Journal
- Day Two -

Date: Day: S — M — T — W — Th — F — S

eState	eMotion	
Experience	*Feeling*	*Energy*
Enlightenment	Nirvana	1000
Peace	Bliss	600
Joy	Serenity	540
Love	Reverence	500
Reason	Understanding	400
Acceptance	Forgiveness	350
Optimism	Willingness	310
Trust	Neutrality	250
Courage	Affirmation	200
Pride	Scorn	175
Anger	Resentment	150
Desire	Craving	125
Fear	Anxiety	100
Grief	Regret	75
Apathy	Despair	50
Guilt	Blame	30
Shame	Humiliation	20

PING—a significant emotional experience
[box 1]

Duration: ___hr. ___min.

TUNE IN [box 2]

TURN ON [box 3]

PING—a significant emotional experience

Duration: ___hr. ___min.

TUNE IN

TURN ON

GRATITUDE
1.
2.
3.

If the only prayer you say in your whole life is 'thank you' that should suffice.—Meister Eckhart

PING—a significant emotional experience

Duration: ___hr. ___min.

TUNE IN

TURN ON

Emotion hierarchy adapted from Map of Consciousness: *Power vs. Force*. David R. Hawkins, M.D. Ph.D., 1995.

Human beings are accustomed to think of intellect as the power of having and controlling ideas and of ability to learn as synonymous with ability to have ideas. But learning by having ideas is really one of the rare and isolated events in nature.

Edward Thorndike (1874—1949)

Day Three—Primal Intelligence

Every living thing, in whatever shape or form, comes fully equipped with the innate instinctual intelligence to use energy, self-organize, adapt and reproduce. To further understand how your spirit knows what to do to survive, consider that all living things do not exist alone, but rather in a vast web of life.

Since your body contains the essential components and genetic instructions required to produce every part of you, you are considered organizationally closed. Being a self-contained unique life form means that your inner world is sufficient at keeping you alive, only interacting with the outer world in an exchange of energy. With no external influences to direct internal self-organization, the intelligence driving your inner processes appears to originate directly from *you*—the self-organizing living process itself.

If we contemplate that intelligence is a primal aspect to our being alive, we may do well to begin considering the mind not as a thing, but as a living process, the key function of life. When the *spirit of life* leaves our body, self-organization stops and decay immediately begins. What was once a "tendency toward order", powered and contained, immediately falls apart.

Without the mysterious spirit, the ghost in the machine, the mind and body no longer function as one interdependent living process. Perhaps the energetic aspect of our spirit is the essential spark of our mind. Like the slime mold, it may indeed be an *intelligent energy* that unifies our individual cells and organs into one vast living organism. This means that our conscious mind may only be the tip of a much bigger intellectual iceberg.

While you are alive, your primal intelligence provides direction, coordination and competition—subconscious activities that originate from your core competencies. As such, what we think of as the subconscious mind may well be the essence of being alive—the *spirit of life* itself. In this arena, being alive and being innately intelligent are inseparable. By your very nature, intelligence ensures your ongoing survival. In short, you're a lot smarter at staying alive than you think.

Begin to consider that being alive is based on a mind that envelops much more than just thinking. Primal intelligence spans much more than the cognitive chatter in our head—our ideas and their words and language—much more than the key attributes of human consciousness. Primal intelligence includes perceptions, emotions, body movement and physiological responses. Even now, your very own primal intelligence is controlling your heartbeat, respiration, blood pressure and flow, digestion and neural activities. Your *spirit* drives this activity automatically, all without conscious thought or intentional effort.

At every moment of every day, your primal intelligence is in tune with the living activity in and around you. The question then beckons: Are you in tune with your primal intelligence?

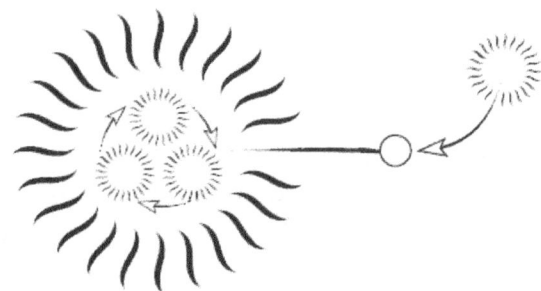

The Attention System

Every life form, no matter how simple or complex, is aware of both its inner and outer world. Scientists have clearly observed creatures without brains operating intelligently, perceiving changes in their surroundings and noticing the difference between good energy and bad energy. Every organism knows the difference between hot and cold, light and dark, the higher and lower of chemical concentrations. And yet, without brains or nervous systems, they are attentive and intelligent, and they respond instinctually, automatically doing what they need to do to survive.

Likewise, your primal intelligence comes fully equipped with a highly developed attention system which includes not only this rudimentary level of awareness, but the utilization of the entire spectrum of sights, sounds, smells, touch and tastes captured and processed by your senses—all energy exchanges your primal intelligence uses to monitor and remain in sync with the reality going on in and around you.

Your primal intelligence is always in tune to the constant exchanges of energy and continually on alert. Even while asleep, your primal intelligence is filtering your sensory energy for signs of distress, listening for things that could threaten your survival. Like a vigilant sentinel, your spirit never sleeps. Its continuously monitors every nerve impulse, every incoming sound or smell for signs of danger. Your spirit is a part of every thought, every emotion, and every movement. When a stressor is recognized, your subconscious primal intelligence pings your conscious mind to attend to the source of stress, and a thought is created.

At every moment, your spirit is scrutinizing the life-energy in and around you. Your spirit uses that energy as information to keep it in tune with the outer world. If you have a busy mind that's cluttered with thought, there's little doubt that your primal intelligence already knows your troubles, and is informing your higher rational intelligence with emotionally-charged mental reminders of what's not right. Over time, survival-driven thinking habits are formed. As a result, we wire our brains to think constantly about what can go wrong. A cognitive-emotive feedback loop begins without end. Without intervention, no wonder so many experience anxiety and attention-deficit disorders. Fearful thoughts generated by their primal intelligence commandeer their rational thinking process.

Instead of attending to the cognitive chatter, begin to listen and TUNE IN to what your primal intelligence is telling you. This is where your process re-engineering begins: putting self-conceived notions aside and beginning to use your energy as information. There's gold in reflecting on how your life-energy is being consumed.

Energy as Information

Your primal intelligence is especially sensitive to the ebbs and flows of emotional energy. With millions of electrical impulses firing off every living moment, your mind is constantly inundated by the inflow and outflow of sensory energy originating both externally (perception) and internally (proprioception).

> **Perception (The Outer World).**
> Sensory input, which includes sights, sounds, smells, tastes and touch (pressures, temperatures, etc.). This also includes the higher levels of communication including language, meanings, physical gestures and facial expressions.
>
> **Proprioception (The Inner World).**
> Perceived as feelings, this is the awareness of the energetic communication going on within the brain and body, including thoughts, biochemical reactions, nerve activity, immune responses, blood pressure, balance and muscle coordination.

To hear your spirit, your conscious mind must listen to two different sources of energy at the same time. Being in tune to your spirit in this manner from now on will be referred to as *in-tune-ition*. Learning to trust your in-tune-ition means strengthening self-awareness by developing a clear interpretation of your energy as information. In-tune-ition begins by training the conscious brain to become more informed by subconscious energy states. Considering life-energy as intelligent, learning to trust your spirit is a valuable leadership skill that greatly improves decision making and the ability to navigate stressful challenges effectively.

By utilizing energy as information, your primal intelligence distinguishes positive energy from negative energy all the time. Positive energy is from sources helpful or constructive in maintaining self-organization, whereas negative energy originates from sources deemed harmful or destructive to self-organization. In terms of feelings, we associate positive energy with pleasurable sources, and negative energy with painful ones.

Whether we focus attention on the positive or negative aspects of life is not necessarily a rational choice, but an emotionally-charged one. As human beings, our attention system is rather complex, existing in both our conscious and subconscious awareness. Energy exchanges are combined and cumulative, creating a collective energetic charge that manifests as your ongoing state of mind.

The States of Mind

Your spirit is often instantly impacted by the subtlest shifts in energy. When your primal intelligence senses danger, say when someone is angry or when something goes wrong, the ping of negative energy instantly shifts the living process of your brain and body to instinctually respond to the stressful event. This ping is an emotional impact, or known in scientific terms as a stress response. It's why we immediately fight, flee or freeze without having to think about it. *Primal intelligence shifts or pings our state of mind automatically, without rational thought.*

Your brain is intimately involved in the energy ping process. Depending on the degree of emotional impact from an event, your mental processes are also affected. You may find yourself having trouble clearing your mind or feeling relaxed. Experiencing a stress response, you can easily forget what you wanted to say, or fail to react in the way you would have liked. Tension and anxiety builds if we do not consciously stop it.

Have you ever become snappy without warning, having been pinged by bad news or circumstance, although only moments before you've been enjoying a peaceful relaxing afternoon? This is primal intelligence commandeering your state of mind—*energy that must be consciously managed.* Although being emotional is generally frowned upon in most civilized societies, and no matter how hard we may try not to be emotional, we often are.

An unfocused unmanaged mind is likely to change its energy state without notice. One moment, you can be feeling stress-free and happy, optimistic and energized, and the next, your attention system picks up that something is wrong, pinging you into a defensive mindset without warning. The fact that your state of mind is dynamic and continually changing is testament to the primal intelligence alive within you—a powerful living *spirit* that requires energy management. The secret then to health and happiness is to become more acquainted with your ever-changing state of mind.

> TUNE IN: Knowing the state of mind you're in is the first step to changing it.

The Feeling Spectrum

As the world and people around you change, so too does your state of mind. Your emotional states span a broad spectrum of emotion, from stress-free to stress-full. On the lower end of the spectrum, when energy is low, your state of mind falls into negative emotions—feelings of anger, anxiety, sadness and envy. Conversely, on the upper level, when energy is high, your state of mind rises into positive emotions—feelings of joy, happiness, understanding and acceptance.

It is within this spectrum of positive and negative emotions where the experience of life occurs. When our energy is drained, we feel anxious, depressed, sad and guilty. When our energy is full, we do feel high—trustful, optimistic, accepting of things and are less emotional when presented with a conflict. The regulation of our emotions is based on primal instinct, the core operating system within us all that we, for obvious benefits, should become familiar with more intimately.

> What is your energy state right now?
> From 1 meaning 'dead' to 10 meaning 'alive,' how are you feeling?

Primal Energy States

The most basic states of mind are the same for everyone on the planet. We all fight, flee or freeze many times without rational intent. The genetic instruction of what to do under stress is systematically encoded within our instincts, and their energetic expression is honed deep within our DNA.

When a conflict appears before you, it's the strength of your state of mind that dictates how you react under pressure. Without self-awareness of your eState, these fundamental responses to stressors become your habitual behaviors in routine challenges and everyday circumstance.

Our primal states of mind are most essential to our survival. The three most fundamental states of mind are fear, desire and anger. That means that being anxious, addicted or aggressive is natural. They are our most common survival programs. Dogs, cats, kangaroos and cockatoos all have these primal emotions. If earlier you had thoughts of worry, obsessions, or resentment, know this is normal in the sense that your primal intelligence is powering those emotional energies thus creating those thoughts. Simply put, the energy of your body (emotions) powers your mind (thoughts) and vice versa.

How do you become "wise and brave" when your conscious mind is scattered? You start at the beginning—knowing what pings you into a primal state of mind.

As we have learned, despite a perceived lack of self-confidence, we are all powered by an intelligent living process. Both our physical hardware and our mental software are based on a 100+ million year evolutionary journey, where our instincts evolved to keep us alive automatically. How truly smart can our conscious mind be if our subconscious mind isn't taken into account? What aspect of our intelligence can we really count on to survive when the proverbial shit hits the fan?

> TURN ON: Who can you trust if you cannot trust your own instincts?

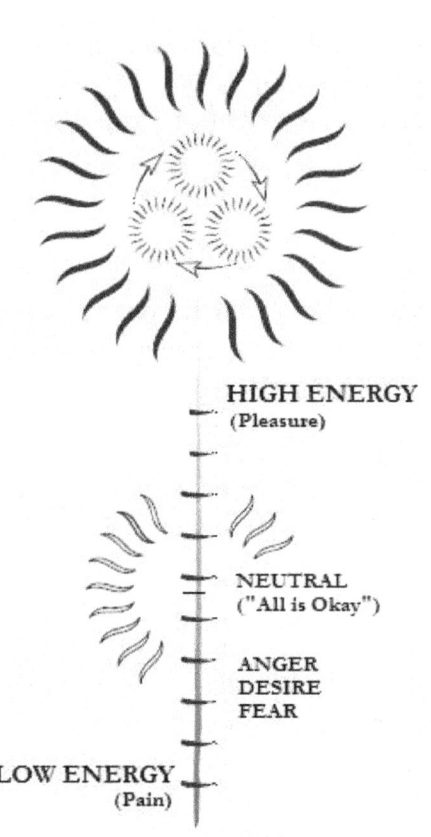

It is always easier to ignore what we do not understand rather than investigate it, examine it, experience and embrace it. This brings us to the very core of our courage. On our quest, we must learn to rise above our life experiences and be brave, not only to examine our primal nature but also to put into practice what we learn each and every day. The dimension of our self that we call on for this focus-strengthening activity is the *Experiencer*.

The Experiencer Consciousness

Ongoing states of mind are experienced as feelings. And like our states of mind, our feelings are dynamic and may change in the blink of an eye. Our states of mind span the entire spectrum of feeling alive, from pleasure and joy to pain and shame. From an evolutionary perspective, feelings represent an intellectual heritage we all share, but few of us have ever mastered their feelings or felt truly comfortable embracing their full spectrum. With knowledge and practice however, you can become more truly comfortable at *feeling alive*.

Pleasure: Energy-Gaining Experiences

When there is an abundant, free-flow of positive energy, physical tension in our body is released and we experience rest and relaxation. In these high-energy pleasure states, our spirit is free to soar and enjoy the elevated feelings of being alive. Such experiences normally occur in an energetically positive environment, where you feel accepted and loved, and experience a healthy connection to work, family and friends. When positive experiences occur, your brain and blood stream are flooded with feel-good biochemicals that produce the high-energy feelings of bliss, happiness and contentment. Pleasure is a biochemical reaction in your body. The question then: How can we create more of the good stuff in the mind-body system?

When your life is intimately connected to positive energy sources—happy people, purposeful work and a secure financial future—a powerful state of mind emerges. This consciousness allows you to take on more with less effort, or recognize solutions where you only saw hardship before. The trick then to having more pleasure in your life when life isn't perfect is to learn to maintain a higher, more positive consciousness in dealing with challenges or unexpected conflict. To achieve this, we must first strengthen our ability to deal with stress when it happens. This means that before we can truly enjoy more pleasure in our lives, we need to first befriend and effectively understand and neutralize its opposite state of mind: pain.

Pain: Energy-Draining Experiences

When energy is low, say due to chronic worry over financial debt, concern over a dysfunctional relationship or misgivings about a challenging conflict, the brain responds by shutting down its higher rational functions. With low-energy reserves, you easily become anxious, addicted or agitated. Under stress, our primal intelligence forces us to react as our primitive ancestors did: instinctively driven by fear, desire and anger. In short, we go primal.

If we're not careful, the pain associated with the active energy drain will be noted in our higher brain functions, and we are forced to think about and remember the sources of stress. Our conscious mind is then inundated with over-analysis and worry: negative thoughts of what's not right and what needs doing. If the stress-full situation continues unabated, the experience of anxiety becomes chronic. Experienced over time, life-energy is drained and a depressed state of mind is formed. With such low-energy, constant worry and negative thought, your brain can easily become wired to be anxious and depressed all the time. Truly, through self-created habits of thinking, you become addicted to those ill-fated states of mind.

The pain associated with enduring chronic energy-drains is all too common. Addictions, anxiety and aggression are each painful conditions that ping us when things aren't right. With chronic stress, we soon feel energetically exhausted and depressed, drained of life-energy. Even with enough sleep, people still feel sluggish and tired. In such stress-full states of mind, creativity disappears. People force themselves through their day, using artificial stimulants such as caffeine, energy drinks and drugs to boost energy levels that temporarily engage higher energy.

As the Experiencer to our feelings and states of mind, we can use our higher brain functions to acknowledge the primal emotional energy and use it to inform our process improvement. Instead of reliving the emotion, we simply reflect upon the experience and examine the emotional energy produced. At this enlightened perspective of experiencing a painful emotion, we become empowered to change it.

As you may know, if there's too much pain, you struggle to get out of bed. But too much pleasure may result in non-productive bliss. Somewhere in the middle is where you want to be. The remedy is managing a neutral state of mind.

Neutrality: Trusting That All is Okay

Stress is a vital component of life. As living creatures, stresses play a key role in keeping you functioning. Without stress, in the scientific sense of the word, the body's healthy physical self-organization would atrophy, and the living system would fall apart. Without pressure, there'd be no reason for movement and growth. Despite the associated painful experience, stress keeps you on your toes and makes you attend to your survival requirements. For the most part, stress is there to keep us alive.

How then can we reduce the feelings of pain in our lives? Simple—by intentionally growing from it.

By consciously attending to your primal intelligence and intentionally learning from the pings of life, we adapt and grow stronger. No pain, no gain. Similar to how our immune system builds resistance when a dead virus is injected into our blood stream, our emotional system gets tougher with the vaccine of experiencing a stressful experience. Use it or lose it— the old adage is more than that: It maintains and increases the strength of our living system to ward off enemies that may attack us. What can we take away from this? Intentionally stepping into pain makes us smarter and stronger.

As you have learned, adaptation—growing and becoming better at something—is a core competency. Just as you can grow physically stronger by lifting weights, you can intentionally develop your core strength by the lifting of emotional weight. Similar to a physical fitness program that improves your muscles, a structured program of mental-emotional improvement, which strengthens mental focus and stamina, will help you combat life's never ending battles. This neutrality exercise is important in fine-tuning your attention. In my experience, this process re-engineering method is much more effective than medication or meditation. Let me explain.

Training the brain to remain neutral in stressful situations (beyond the meditation room) is the quest. To become smarter and stronger in dealing with stress means becoming better at neutralizing pings as they occur in the moment. Use the TUNE IN – TURN ON process in moments of stress to quiet charged thoughts or ill feelings that may be present. As you gain cognitive strength in deflecting stress in the moment, your energy naturally increases. You think more clearly using higher brain functions that are empowered to reason solutions. When cognitive energy drains are systematically reduced and eliminated, the buoyancy of your spirit elevates into a balanced energy state. This naturally occurring neutral state of mind engenders a calm feeling that all is okay. Operating in the emotional energy of trust, you are relaxed and present, confident in your ability to survive.

> TURN ON: *In courage, train your brain to trust all is okay in the moments of anxiety and aggression. This intentional TURN ON practice helps neutralize the energy drains of stressful thoughts by empowering higher brain functions to better understand and tackle the challenge.*

Actively managing your own energy state in the moment is paramount to this process. As we've learned, knowing your state of mind at any moment is key to this quest. You are already learning this self-knowledge by recording your three most significant pings each day. Continue this TUNE IN exercise with conviction. A TURN ON of "all is okay" will improve the performance of your brain.

The Adaptable Brain

Like fingers on a pulse, your *spirit* is constantly in tune with your state of mind. As a vital component to your physiology, your brain is an intricate part of this ongoing living process. Your brain adapts continually, with every ping of pleasure and pain. By learning from everything you do, you begin using your modern intelligence to help manage the primal living process.

Right now, your brain is taking in information, interpreting it and creating your experience of feeling alive. With over 100 billion neurons, your brain is one complex living process. But with conscious effort, you can train your brain to improve upon itself. If you put your mind to it, the possibilities for improvement are immense. Becoming emotionally stronger requires the creation of new neural pathways that help you remain strong in stressful situations. With practice, this adaptation will ensure that you succeed in everything you do.

Start considering pings as unique learning opportunities. Continuous improvement of your state of mind will turn self-doubt into self-confidence, and transform self-criticism into self-actualization. This is not a rational exercise but an experiential one. Truly, you will learn to be confident by understanding how to TURN ON confidence.

This leads me to a very important point. *It is not enough to merely read about training the brain—you must actually do it. You must stop thinking and concentrate on remembering and replaying the ping in a higher energetic state.* **To get results, be sure to close your eyes, and place a palm on your forehead. With the brain relaxed, use the power of imagination in all its energetic glory to relive the moment and build emotional resiliency in the brain. When the ping next occurs, the brain will now have the option to operate within a new eState.**

This ability does not happen overnight. Practice makes perfect. New neural pathways take time to grow. Go easy on yourself as you learn to respond to daily stresses in a more powerful, high-energy state. Intentionally teach your modern rational brain what your primitive emotional brain is doing when subjected to stress. In time, you will develop a true leadership mindset—a heightened self-awareness and control that effectively deals with the pings of life in the moment.

Perhaps you've never thought the brain can be changed, or at least not changed for the better. Instead, we unknowingly teach our brains habitual states of anger, desire or fear—reactions that are often unnecessary. On a beautiful sunny day, an optimist will see blue skies, while someone in the throngs of depression will shield his or her eyes from the bright light. Unconsciously, and without a better understanding of what we're doing to ourselves, our brains become wired to maintain certain negative states of mind that eventually become our personalities.

The very real impetus for change is this: You have nowhere to hide if you have a negative personality. James Borg states that human communication consists of 93 percent body language and paralinguistic cues, while only 7% of communication consist of words.[3] This means that people can pick up on our negative energy through our actions and behaviors alone. If you're feeling angry, addicted, anxious or depressed, people will know.

The good news is that our brains have the capacity and flexibility to learn, including learning how to change our state of mind at will. Being powered by such an enlightened spirit gives us the freedom to continuously develop and improve our mindsets.

With continuous improvement, our brain can go from being a feared enemy to a cherished asset. Just as we can teach ourselves to skip rope, drive a car, speak Italian or play tennis, we can also learn to be better at dealing with conflict, handling difficult people or staying sane in the midst of chaos. We just need to set a conscious intention to do so.

As you will discover tomorrow, the only impediment to living with a stronger, courageous spirit is your own rational intelligence and the beliefs therein.

Day Three Exercise

As you gather more data on your day, become fascinated by the emotional reactions you are experiencing in the moment. As you learn what pings your energy, acknowledge and appreciate that your primal intelligence is actively keeping you alive with every stress response. Accept every ping as an opportunity to grow. Aim to better understand its impetus of survival.

Again, use the Odyssey Methodology to complete the Quest Journal.

---

[3] Borg, James. *Body Language: 7 Easy Lessons to Master the Silent Language.* FT Press, 2010.

odyssey

The Odyssey Methodology

1. TUNE IN

Remember your day	Close your eyes and mentally review your day.
	Remember the pings—the people, places or events—that caused you stress, then determine the eMotion triggered by the ping.
	  - *A ping is a significant emotional experience that shifts your energy.*
	  - *You remember pings because of their emotional energy.*

Record your pings	Pick the three most impactful pings of the day and record. [PING - box 1] For each ping, choose the eState that best suits how you responded to the eMotion experienced and record. [TUNE IN - box 2]
Reflect your energy	Focus on how the ping affected your energetic state. Teach your brain what the ping feels like (i.e. grief, anxiety, apathy, etc.). Mentally label the feelings with a rational understanding of the eMotion.

1. TURN ON

Raise your eState	Choose an eState higher than the one experienced for each ping and record. [TURN ON - box 3]
Replay your day	Close your eyes and with palm on forehead, visualize reliving each ping in the higher eState. Imagine the same people, place or event ping in the new eState. - *Include all aspects of the more empowering eMotion. See yourself being confident, responding authentically with pleasant gestures, facial expressions, calm voice, etc.*
Resolve your pings	Set action to neutralize the ping-energy. Ask yourself: What task or solution is necessary to fix a problem? Reconnect with a person? What steps are required to repair what is broken / disconnected? In courage, take action! - *Set an intention to follow through on the commitment. With palm on forehead, mentally rehearse being courageous / optimistic / accepting of the situation. Visualize the new behavior. Train the brain for a high-energy response to stress.*

odyssey

The Quest Journal
- Day Three -

Date: Day: S — M — T — W — Th — F — S

eState	eMotion	
Experience	*Feeling*	*Energy*
Enlightenment	Nirvana	1000
Peace	Bliss	600
Joy	Serenity	540
Love	Reverence	500
Reason	Understanding	400
Acceptance	Forgiveness	350
Optimism	Willingness	310
Trust	Neutrality	250
Courage	Affirmation	200
Pride	Scorn	175
Anger	Resentment	150
Desire	Craving	125
Fear	Anxiety	100
Grief	Regret	75
Apathy	Despair	50
Guilt	Blame	30
Shame	Humiliation	20

PING—a significant emotional experience

Duration: ___hr. ___min.

TUNE IN

TURN ON

PING—a significant emotional experience

Duration: ___hr. ___min.

TUNE IN

TURN ON

PING—a significant emotional experience

Duration: ___hr. ___min.

TUNE IN

TURN ON

GRATITUDE
1.
2.
3.

If the only prayer you say in your whole life is 'thank you' that should suffice.— Meister Eckhart

Emotion hierarchy adapted from Map of Consciousness: *Power vs. Force*. David R. Hawkins, M.D. Ph.D., 1995

Perhaps the kind of mind you get when you add language to it is so different from the kind of mind you can have without language that calling them both minds is a mistake.

Daniel C. Dennett, Director of Cognitive Studies, Tufts University

Day Four—The Human Condition, Part 1

Somewhere, perhaps on an African plain hundreds of thousands of years ago, our ancestors evolved to a new level of intelligence. Having lived for millennia with just primal intelligence to guide their actions, our distant relatives woke up to a whole new way of communicating with themselves and the world around them. Using an intellect that was so profoundly different from that of animals, they left behind a simpler way of life. Where their actions were once dictated by their emotional intelligence, their life now was directed instead by a superior rational intellect.

In the paradigm shift that occurred, our ancestors forever separated themselves from the animal kingdom. Humans began thinking in symbolic terms, associating noises with distinct images and creating first languages. With a new rational perspective to emotional experiences, our ancestor's became self-conscious. Breaking free from a primitive perception of the world, they became increasingly self-aware. In terms of evolution, this was a massive breakthrough. Life could now *know itself*.

In becoming what we now recognize as modern human beings, our far distant relatives began utilizing the tool of speech to create a new way to coordinate behavior. Instead of using primal energy solely to communicate (i.e. grunts, growls and gestures), they learned to voice their opinions using specific verbal sounds in what we now recognize as language. With their newfound rational intelligence, our ancestors quickly associated symbols of positive energy to pleasurable events, and symbols of negative energy to painful events. Today, in everyday conversation, we still convey this primal energy exchange in the words we use. In a subtle yet distinct way, everything we say involves the giving (or taking) of energy.

Consider the energy-drain that occurs when someone criticizes you. The emotional impact from an argument or verbal assault can certainly ping your state of mind and leave it disturbed for hours. The use of profanity, harsh judgments and other cutting remarks act as bullets of negatively charged energy meant to disable the recipient by placing them into an eState of shame. To protect your energy, train your brain to respond in a higher eState when bad energy is shot your way. Be wary: Words are like weapons—they wound sometimes.

Likewise, when you tell others of your difficulties, the negatively charged words (complaints) assault the listener with the same stress-full energy as you may be experiencing. Dumping your problems on someone may seem like a good way to share your burden and gain sympathy, but in the energy-exchange, you are sparking the same pain stressors in their brain as your own. No one likes a whiner. Complainers drain energy and we subconsciously learn to avoid them. Everybody, however, likes a leader. We are subconsciously attracted to their 'can-do' attitudes and are inspired by them. So, when troubles arise, TURN ON courage and resolve the conflict positively without dragging others down in the self-improvement process.

Indeed, our own state of mind can be dynamically affected by the states of minds of others and the words they use. We need to remain aware that the prehistoric notions of stress are still encoded into our modern brains. Despite an educated rational intellect, primal intelligence remains a sentinel for survival, listening to every word for potential threat. Sensitive types may too often find themselves easily pinged by negative remarks and judgments of others. An unfriendly tone of voice can itself ping our defenses. Remember it's not the words used, but the associated emotionally charged energy that triggers the stress response within your brain. If you've ever reacted negatively to criticism, the defensive reaction is an automatic stress response, encoded into your emotional memory. Such forceful emotional programs can, with continuous improvement, be updated to instead respond in more inspiring, authoritative energy.

There is significant reward for your effort. With 90% of communication being non-verbal, it's not what you say, but how you say it that shifts other people's state of mind and influences their behavior. Ultimately, emotions distinguish a leader from a manager. A life manager is forceful and reacts defensively to stress. A life leader is powerful and responds in high-energy personal authority. Confident leaders are attractive because of their ability to inspire others to take action. They have energy people want and people will follow them to get it. If you want to positively influence an outcome, learn to maintain high-energy in the words you use. Practice the TUNE IN—TURN ON process when true leadership is needed. Again, not what you say (rational intelligence) but how you say it (emotional intelligence) gets the point across. It's why life leadership—remaining high under stress—is so important for a healthy and happy existence.

Mastery of the Human Condition

Rational knowledge without emotional experience is perhaps the most negative consequence of the human condition. Armed with rational intelligence, most of us will negate experiencing pain by simply reasoning that something that is painful should be avoided. Emotionally speaking, this lack of pain exposure makes us less resilient when subjected to it. Although uncomfortable, experiencing pain is necessary to keep our primal intelligence in touch with reality. For example, we can rationally know the stove is hot but we really do not understand what hot is until we emotionally experience the burning sensation. Once our primal intelligence learns the true meaning of hot, our emotional programming keeps us aware and away from it automatically. With no pain, there can be no gain in primal intelligence. Our spirit learns by doing the hard stuff.

Like exposure to a virus strengthens the immune system, gaining resistance to emotional stress means exposing yourself to stressful challenges. Bouncing back from stress quickly requires that our emotional system must have prior experience in how to handle the challenge. It's not enough to just tell you how to think and feel about an experience; you need to live it.

In today's sophisticated educational system, we sit comfortably in classrooms while studying foreign cultures, wars and tragic histories without ever experiencing the anxieties and courage that made individuals heroic. To be emotionally intelligent and resilient—qualities of a life leader—means taking an intentional step into stressful challenges and learning from the experience, as potentially painful as it may be. Assuming you survive, you will be wiser and braver for the effort.

In the pursuit of emotional intelligence, we should aim to teach both our brains—one rational (conscious), the other emotional (subconscious)—how to deal with the stresses that occur in the world we live in. This is the essence of wisdom—rational knowledge augmented with emotional experience.

> *Imagination is more important than knowledge.* Albert Einstein

As humans with big brains, there are ways to teach neurons new tricks without harming ourselves in the self-improvement process. Instead of taking physical action, take positive mental action. Simply begin using your higher brain functions to actively imagine positive strategies to deal with negative pings as they occur. Positive-solution visualization has proven we can make great discoveries if we just TURN ON the courage to think beyond our neural network.

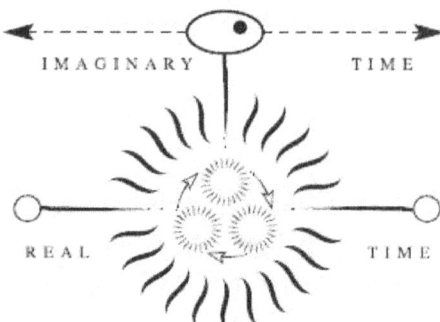

The Realm of Imagination

The most rapid evolution of our ancestors' intelligence was in the exponential learning of symbols and their associated meanings. This included the advent of cave paintings and drawings, along with the resulting development of reading and writing. Our ancestors expanded their rational intelligence to imagine life and experience it in a completely new way. They could now visualize and communicate things that weren't immediately in front of them.

The miracle of self-awareness has provided humans with a brand-new ability to think beyond the living moment. We can use our rational intelligence to imagine what tomorrow brings or what yesterday did to us. With active imagination, we can dwell upon past misfortunes or spur thoughts of potential catastrophes waiting to happen. With our 'intelligence' of self-awareness, stress takes on a whole new meaning: *Pain is avoidable if we're smart enough.*

Observing the road of life from this higher consciousness made our ancestors increasingly brilliant at staying alive. Rational intelligence gave them an evolutionary advantage in dealing with the pains that do disrupt our lives. They learned to store food for the winter. They stockpiled firewood for cold nights. With self-awareness, life became a whole lot better, but it also became a lot more complicated.

The Observer Consciousness

As humans, not only are we aware of our immediate environment and the outer world, but we can contemplate our place within, particularly in relation to our community. We can also observe the goings-on within our inner world. The thoughts and feelings we find can be examined and improved upon. For the emotionally aloof, emotions can become something to fear. The skilled life leader, however, understands how to learn from fear and not get lost in imagined emotional experiences.

Evolution has decreed that not only do we have an Experiencer consciousness (an awareness of feelings we experience moment-to-moment) but we also possess an *Observer* consciousness—an ability to observe those feelings in time and space. Our Observer consciousness provides us with the self-awareness of the vast pleasures and pains both in the imagined future and the remembered past. Putting our rational intelligence to constructive use, we can begin to observe thoughts and feelings without getting overwhelmed by their intensity. With rational awareness, we can TUNE IN the incumbent energy and TURN ON our imagination and observe good things happening to us in the future. This has a positive impact on our spirit. By imagining ourselves in high-energy, our brain's biochemistry shifts and we feel energized. Energy is gained when we enact courage to give the hard stuff a go, if only in our imagination.

Using our higher Observer consciousness, we can learn to TUNE IN energy-draining people, places and events and place them in a brighter light. If we use this rational analysis wisely, we can consider solutions for tomorrow as we contemplate and learn from the mistakes made today. In doing so, we can keep our feelings in check by grounding the spirit on optimistic outcomes. This takes practice but with persistent effort, the new neural network created will subconsciously empower your mind-body system when pings do occur.

In contrast, and without self-governance, we instead often let our Observer consciousness run wild and habitually imagine all the misfortunes seemingly destined for our lives. With such chronic stress, our minds become locked in endless rational analysis, a desperate attempt to use words and thoughts to think our way out of the mess. By doing so, we suppress our primal intelligence which is at the source of our survival-driven emotions. We begin to experience anxiety, addiction and aggression in imagined rational realities. This only compounds the problem in resolving stressful challenges by undermining our ability to make the smart decisions or take purposeful action that would resolve pings permanently.

Here we need to stop and contemplate an important point: Our primal emotions remain a foundational aspect of our ongoing state of mind, without which we would not survive. Before we possessed rational intelligence, we existed in whatever state of mind our primal intelligence applied to the stressors. That animalistic emotional energy still operates within us. If we dismiss our primal animal intelligence in favor of operating solely on modern rational thought, we risk allowing our minds to become bombarded with negative thoughts and emotions, whereas the integration of both rational and primal intelligence will allow us to identify our natural emotions and direct that energy to a higher level. Remember that the human condition represents two different minds—one conscious, the other subconscious. As we will discover, thoughts and emotions are inextricably interdependent. One affects the other. To know something is to feel it. Therefore, for health and happiness, intentionally integrate the two. The TUNE IN—TURN ON process is helping you do just that.

> *"...but from the tree of knowledge of good and evil you shall not eat, for in the day you eat from it you shall surely die."* Genesis 2:17

The Crux of Rational Intelligence

Ignorance is bliss, they say. While the personalities of our primitive ancestors were driven solely by their primal intelligence, our modern relatives became increasingly smart and cognitively sophisticated. They soon found their thoughts were easily addicted to pleasurable sources, and more often, overly anxious to avoid painful ones. Using their new smart way of thinking, they schemed to obtain positive energy—sex, food, money and shelter—while contemplating the stressful consequences of surviving without them. With fear fueling their imagination, pain sources became the things to worry about. With big brains, there are no limits to our fears. We can funnel huge amounts of life-energy into cognitive processing what's not right. As worry burns an enormous amount of energy, maintaining vigilance for constant and never-ending evil exhausts even the most courageous.

From an early age, we were taught to use our rational intelligence to navigate life's obstacles—to be smart in making decisions and thinking constructively. You were more than likely taught what is "good" or "bad", and perhaps were scolded (pain experienced) when you considered a new alternative. Growing up, you were naturally indoctrinated into whatever belief system or mindset was provided to you, leaving your brain and emotions wired for a certain way of experiencing the world.

Take politics and religion for example. We become so habituated into certain perspectives of life that such emotionally-charged topics are banned at dinner tables. The neural networks created in our brains lock us into virtual realities made real by the visceral emotions that charge our memories. Veer too far from your comfort zone of beliefs and behaviors, and emotional distress ensues. Once our thought and emotional processes become wired in our brain and body, it's hard to think or behave differently. Our brain pushes back on our efforts to change it, mainly because it requires energy to grow new ones. That's why it takes acts of courage to change your mind. Literally.

Remember that adaption is a core competency. Given enough pressure, the brain will adapt to new ways of behaving by growing new neural pathways. Creating a neural habit takes effort—an intentional effort that encodes new emotional programming into memory. The 'fake-it-till-you-make-it' approach may not be bad advice. Practice makes perfect. Mastery involves repeating a new behavior over and over until it becomes subconscious. Routinely TURN ON your higher brain functions when you TUNE IN a ping and keep at it until the process becomes wired. Consider pings as "tests of the Universe" until you master high-energy responses.

Millions of us have been taught to ignore our primal intelligence in order to be smart. We learned that emotions are something to fear, leading us to feel isolated as we struggle to keep our agitations to ourselves. Considering the brain as an adaptable resource, the path to an empowered consciousness begins with a greater appreciation of the underlying emotional engine.

With a higher human consciousness, we can rationalize anything. We can come up with reasons why we should attend a pleasurable event while avoiding a painful one, or why we should disregard feelings of guilt and shame by using rationality to dissect the way we feel. Using rational intelligence, we can weigh the pros and cons of a situation and make decisions that are counteractive to our primal instincts. With so much cognitive pressure, it's no wonder that so many are struggling with distressed states of mind. Even though the United Nations Council has placed Australia as one of the top 10 happiest countries in the world, one in five Australians will experience mental illness at some point every year—that's 20% of the population![4] With anxiety and depression so prevalent in even the happiest countries, what chance do other, less happy countries have? For enduring happiness, aim to develop a leadership mindset no matter where you are or what you may be doing.

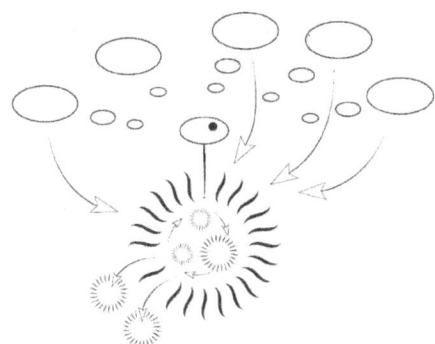

A Sea of Complexity

In the heyday of my corporate career in the United States, I used my rational intelligence for everything. At meetings, I placed competitive pressure on myself to be smarter and cleverer than my counterparts. I overproduced and prayed I'd get noticed. I schmoozed and networked, strutting my stuff for all to see, then punishing myself for being too out there and up myself. I analyzed and fretted over my behavior, and wired my brain to perform like a circus monkey every moment of every day. It was exhausting.

The cognitive chatter of self-doubt and judgment was so overwhelming and excessive that I sought anti-anxiety medication and sleeping pills to help quiet the noise. Energetically drained, I downed antidepressants to power up my apathetic state of mind. In hindsight, I ran like a hamster on a wheel, never stopping to charge my batteries, or appreciate the material things I was accumulating. I reacted angrily to conflict, then cowered in shame for having been so forceful. I used my prideful brilliance to make excuses and snake my way of trouble. Over time, my brain adapted to this forceful way of living and I became trapped in the neural network of

---

[4] *National Survey of Mental Health and Wellbeing*, Australian Bureau of Statistics, 2007.

my rational intelligence. Put simply, I had lost connection with my primal intelligence, the source of feeling alive.

Despite the fact that many of us live with wealth and professional success that would be unimaginable to our ancestors, true feelings of joy and happiness still elude most of us. People remain locked in cycles of despair, thinking self-destructive thoughts that prevent them from engaging their basic selves and live life authentically. If we would just stop and TUNE IN and observe reality with our negative emotive drivers noted and neutralized, we would find ourselves in a much more productive, happier space.

Instead, the negative consequences of the human condition—the mental-emotional imbalance discussed above—will get the best of us. We end up in states of anxiety and melancholy without legitimate reasons. Attention deficient disorders, social phobias, anxiety and states of chronic depression are now at epidemic proportions. It's as if our jaded consciousness is being tossed about like a cork on a stormy sea. Even when we're off the clock and away from the responsibilities of our professional lives, rest often eludes us. When sleep is desired, our primal intelligence is so stirred up from the onslaught of stressors created by our rational intelligence that we are forced to relive the pings of the day over and over again. Is there no rest for the weary?

How do we quiet such unnecessary mental chatter and grow emotionally stronger? The answer lies in developing a mind that is more consciously attentive to feeling alive. More of this tomorrow.

Day Four Exercise

Your brain is a living organ, adapting and learning from every significant experience. A current theory of why we dream is so that the brain can incorporate the events of the day into memory. The more impactful the event, the more emotional energy is encoded. Capitalizing on the core competency of adaptation, in today's exercise you will continue to strengthen self-awareness by learning what pings your primal intelligence (TUNE IN) and begin to move forward.

Again, follow the Odyssey Methodology to complete the Quest Journal.

odyssey

The Odyssey Methodology

1. TUNE IN

Remember
your day

Close your eyes and mentally review your day.
Remember the pings—the people, places or events—that caused you stress, then determine the eMotion triggered by the ping.
- *A ping is a significant emotional experience that shifts your energy.*
- *You remember pings because of their emotional energy.*

Record
your pings

Pick the three most impactful pings of the day and record. [PING - box 1]
For each ping, choose the eState that best suits how you responded to the eMotion experienced and record. [TUNE IN - box 2]

Reflect
your energy

Focus on how the ping affected your energetic state.
Teach your brain what the ping feels like (i.e. grief, anxiety, apathy, etc.).
Mentally label the feelings with a rational understanding of the eMotion.

2. TURN ON

Raise
your eState

Choose an eState higher than the one experienced for each ping and record. [TURN ON - box 3]

Replay
your day

Close your eyes and with palm on forehead, visualize reliving each ping in the higher eState. Imagine the same people, place or event ping in the new eState.
- *Include all aspects of the more empowering eMotion. See yourself being confident, responding authentically with pleasant gestures, facial expressions, calm voice, etc.*

Resolve
your pings

Set action to neutralize the ping-energy. Ask yourself: What task or solution is necessary to fix a problem? Reconnect with a person? What steps are required to repair what is broken / disconnected? In courage, take action!
- *Set an intention to follow through on the commitment. With palm on forehead, mentally rehearse being courageous / optimistic / accepting of the situation. Visualize the new behavior. Train the brain for a high-energy response to stress.*

odyssey

The Quest Journal
- Day Four -

Date: _____ Day: S — M — T — W — Th — F — S

eState	eMotion	
Experience	*Feeling*	*Energy*
Enlightenment	Nirvana	1000
Peace	Bliss	600
Joy	Serenity	540
Love	Reverence	500
Reason	Understanding	400
Acceptance	Forgiveness	350
Optimism	Willingness	310
Trust	Neutrality	250
Courage	Affirmation	200
Pride	Scorn	175
Anger	Resentment	150
Desire	Craving	125
Fear	Anxiety	100
Grief	Regret	75
Apathy	Despair	50
Guilt	Blame	30
Shame	Humiliation	20

PING—a significant emotional experience

Duration: ___hr. ___min.

TUNE IN

TURN ON

PING—a significant emotional experience

Duration: ___hr. ___min.

TUNE IN

TURN ON

PING—a significant emotional experience

Duration: ___hr. ___min.

TUNE IN

TURN ON

GRATITUDE
1.
2.
3.

If the only prayer you say in your whole life is 'thank you' that should suffice.— Meister Eckhart

Emotion hierarchy adapted from Map of Consciousness: *Power vs. Force*. David R. Hawkins, M.D. Ph.D., 1995.

There is nothing lacking in you and you yourself are no different from the Buddha. There is no other way of achieving Buddhahood than letting your mind be free to be itself.

Tao-hsin

Day Five—Becoming Consciously Attentive

Doug, my professional client who had lost his core confidence, had actually lost connection to his primal intelligence. His self-conscious mind was caught up in a feedback loop of negative self-talk. Like so many of us, he was obsessed with what is wrong rather than what is right. In survival mode, he had become addicted to feeling and thinking defensively. This unfortunate failure had developed automatically, as a habitual way of thinking because Doug had simply allowed his thoughts to become powered by his fear and anxiety—primal emotions running amok without conscious control.

Doug's convoluted conscious mind was trying hard to gain distance from his painful subconscious mind because of fear—but in fact, fear was not something to avoid. Instead, it was a signal, a warning to Doug that he was disconnected from his primal intelligence. It was this disconnection that left him feeling alone and alienated—and the further he pushed the fear away, the worse it became. The paranoid chatter he experienced in his rational mind kept Doug in a disassociated state of social phobia. The resulting survival state caused his real panic attacks.

Doug did not realize at the time that, within him, he had, an enlightened state—what Buddhists refer to as the "Buddha Mind." I like to think of that as a peaceful primal intelligence. The same courageous spirit that was keeping Doug's heart beating and his blood pumping was also very capable of calming him down.

Funny how, with such potential, we instead create for ourselves a living hell. Imagine living in the Stone Age and feeling depressed. Without the use of language, you wouldn't rationalize the low-energy state. And you certainly wouldn't ask a doctor for antidepressants. You would simply stay in your cave until you recharged your energy. Without rational intelligence, our ancestors did a much better job listening to their primal intelligence.

A genuine rest away from stressful triggers may be what is needed should pings become chronic. Even though, in secret, I would have admitted to being chronically depressed years ago, I limped forward with great effort, failing to listen to my primal intelligence and take on what my apathy communicated. I was in defense of my spirit, my true intelligent nature, which was telling me mainly to lie down and have a good rest. Not just sleep, but use the depression to really relax my anxious state of mind. Instead of feeling depressed about being depressed, I learned to TURN ON acceptance of the eState and began to embrace my apathy and despair as an intelligent instinct—namely, to take a real break from the stressful challenges at work and recharge my batteries. Engaging the ritual, I inadvertently learned to manage my life-energy by connecting with my living power source.

Today, those diagnosed with chronic depression are given special empathy. They may use the label to justify their low-energy levels and all but surrender to the dysfunction. Certainly there are those whose biochemistry does not function properly and trudge through life with a curse they must live with. However, armed with a core competency of adaptation, I truly believe that those in the dark depths of an emotional canyon can get themselves out. Their willpower all but exhausted, they may not feel capable. But a glimpse into the pings that drain their energy may prove insightful in the continuous energy-gaining effort.

What throws many people into a depressed state of mind is a sense of alienation from the world around them. They feel separate, disconnected and alone. With an overly analytical mind, they conjure up imaginary problems and judgments that psychologically separate themselves from others. In the great mystery of their own minds, they construct walls and barriers that keep make-believe enemies at bay. In doing so, they unknowingly extend this fragmented perception to friends, family and colleagues. We end up worrying about how others think and perceive us.

Instead of living in unity and cooperation, we compete with one another and ourselves in an endless rational analysis of the world. We become afraid of our own neighbors and strangers lurking around the corner. We argue with our partners instead of accepting and understanding their differences. All this negative mental activity alienates us further from the collective web of life and the pleasure that life offers, even craves! With energy flow cut off from others, it's no wonder people feel anxious and alone. To truly master the human condition, a new paradigm of thinking with feeling is required, if we are to resolve this issue at its source—a rational fragmenting of mind from body.

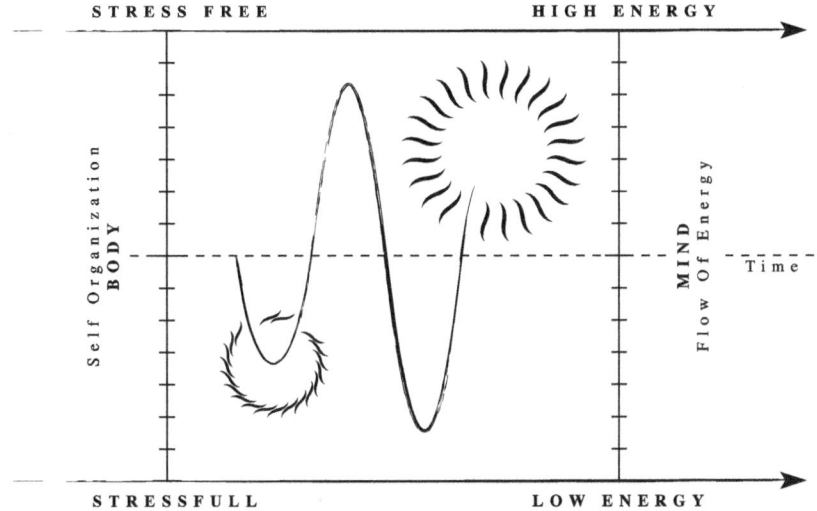

The Mind-Body Connection

Recent research into the emerging field of psycho-neuro-immunology strongly illuminates how our mind and body are intimately interdependent. Primal intelligence includes not only the brain and nervous system, but the extensive biochemistry of our emotional, immune and endocrine systems as well. This means that the energetic state of your subconscious mind directly affects and influences your conscious mind. In stress-filled environments, this conscious-subconscious balance can prove fragile. Within the self-organization of your world, your spirit can easily be forgotten, lost in the worries of what can or will occur.

The philosophy of Buddhism holds some of the oldest wisdom about the human condition, especially its roots in language and consciousness. In the Buddhist view, existential human suffering is called *dukkha*. The central importance of *dukkha* in Buddhist philosophy is not intended to present a pessimistic view of life, but rather to present a realistic practical assessment of the human condition—that all beings must experience suffering and pain at some point in their lives, including the inevitable sufferings of illness, aging, and death.[5]

To mentally detach from *dukkha*, Buddhists teach that the physical forms we see and touch are nothing but *maya*—an intellectual concept that has no reality. As Westerners, perhaps our biggest challenge in grasping such a concept is letting go of the attachments we have to the things we think will make us happy. Certainly, many of us would experience greater peace of mind and serenity if we surrendered our expectations of the people around us and became emotionally detached from the stressful realities of life. Is this practical? How can we live in harmony with the intensities and insensitivities that are required in our professional and personal life? Are we to become cold and emotionless?

The answer lies in feeling alive.

---

[5] Gethin, Rupert (1998), *Foundations of Buddhism*, Oxford University Press p. 61.

TUNE IN: The Pleasure Principle

There is a real pragmatic reward for your effort. By becoming more in tune to your primal intelligence, you actively strengthen your self-awareness by becoming better at managing your energy. By becoming better at controlling your feelings, you create a pleasurable response to stress. Indeed, when you stop and sync up with your self-organizing living process (like, for example, in meditation or yoga), your spirit recharges its energy and regains motivation. Tension is genuinely released and you begin to feel calm and more focused. In this higher state of mind, we better understand the stress source and can reason solutions. Indeed, taking time out to TUNE IN is a discipline we all should actively develop for optimal health and happiness.

Many spiritual practices deal with reconnecting mind (thoughts) and body (emotions). Yoga (Sanskrit, *yunakti*, to yoke) and many martial arts are ancient disciplines aimed at training the brain to be in better control of the mind-body system. Even the word 'religion' originates in the Latin verb *ligare* meaning 'to tie or fasten.' In all aspects, whatever your spiritual practice, it's best to use the spirit-strengthening exercises wisely to reconnect the conscious aspects of life to the subconscious realms we often forget.

As living beings, we need energy to survive. As physical creatures with physical needs, movement is essential in the energy-gaining process. Physical exercise is a courageous state by which we TURN ON our biochemical engine by taking action *despite* the lack of energy. When you're depressed, it takes willpower to get out of bed. In time, atrophy can take hold and you can become habitually wired to be depressed. But to those who are awake to their thoughts and emotions, apathy is a wakeup call to get up and get moving. A good sweaty exertion is the prescription to rid apathy. So is reconnecting with friends, family and relatives. Everyone needs the emotional energies of life that excite our spirit. This includes the good, the bad, and the ugly.

Certainly, it's easier to lie in bed and not face the day's challenges. I know I become imbalanced when I do not actively balance my thoughts with my emotions. Positive experiences come when the mind (thoughts) and body (emotions) act as one. Much like white-water rafting, you can be lost in the moment—in control, having fun navigating through the chaos—or be in a panic thinking of everything that can go wrong. What's needed is a systematic approach to feeling more courageous, remaining strong in moments of stress by taking mindful control of challenging situations in the moment when you need it most. This is the true path to enlightenment. The Odyssey we all must take for health and happiness.

Here's your motivation: The body and brain have a pleasurable response to a more focused mind. An intentional integration of the primal and rational self allows for a release of the body's own feel-good biochemicals that neutralize negative and stressful emotions. This permits the body to recharge the energy levels required to resurrect our feelings of motivation and self-confidence.

A clearer conscious mind and improved focus allow the nervous system to better self-organize the flow of energy. Relaxing the body intentionally conserves energy by being less tense. In meditation, metabolism slows. Heart rate, blood pressure and breathing rates fall, while the electrical transmission of the skin decreases. As a result, a lot less energy is drained by primal emotions and we feel happier. Living less on the defense, our health and well-being benefit. To accomplish this, we need to simply keep learning from the pings of life.

The Pings of Continuous Improvement

The more knowledge we extract and accumulate, the more rationally intelligent we become. This is especially true when it comes to improving processes, be it a manufacturing operation or your own self-organizing living system.

After graduating from college, I worked as a quality control specialist in the manufacturing industry. It was my job to go into production plants and help improve their processes. I assisted in the quality improvement of everything from toothbrushes to jet engine parts. When I first stepped onto the manufacturing floor, I never started by tweaking the machines themselves. Instead, I listened to the machines by simply observing what they were doing. I would start by collecting data on the quality of products each machine was producing.

Similarly, to begin improving a living process, such as your own state of mind, you need to begin collecting data. Begin observing your mind-body machine and its product, your ongoing state of mind. You have been doing this already by noting three daily pings that disrupted your last few days. Continue with the daily exercises. Recording data on your pings is critical to improved energy management.

Ping—a Significant Emotional Experience

A ping is something stressful that has impacted your energy. In clinical terms, it's a stress response. If a ping is impactful enough, it will charge your living system and you will be overwhelmed by the associated emotion. You won't be able to get the charged thought out of your mind. A ping can be energy-gaining (a positive ping) or more often, energy-draining (a negative ping). For your quest, may I suggest you increasingly direct your attention on recording the negative pings (i.e. emotional defects) impacting your life.

> TUNE IN: Recognizing negative pings is the first step to neutralizing their disruptive energy.

A ping can be subtle or dramatic. A ping occurs when your primal intelligence perceives a threat—real or imaginary—and alerts your conscious mind to wake up to the stress. A ping is identified with an ill feeling or an overly active thought. As you know, step one is to identify a ping by reflecting what you remember about your day. Since memories are encoded with emotional energy, mentally reviewing what pings you can provide a wealth of self-aware wisdom.

If you've been under constant stress, you may be chronically pinged. When life is one big mess, it may take a bit of dissection to identify the individual pings in a pinged state of mind. For the most part, pings are happening all the time. Someone bumps you at the market and doesn't apologize. Rain puts a damper on your hike. The toilet backs up. The proposal was rejected. All these stressful experiences drain energy and ping our consciousness to attend to the stress. Despite creating a negative feeling within us, from an evolutionary perspective, a ping moves us to become aware of and resolve the problem. For health and happiness, begin to see pings simply as data points in a continuously improving living process.

Pings come in three forms: people, places or events.

People Pings. Most pings you will receive will be from people. Your people pings will provide important insights into your deepest values. How you react automatically to others tells of the beliefs you hold most dear. To make recording people pings easy, begin observing people and their behavior as opportunities to learn about what makes you tick. Without question, people can be our best teachers if we have the courage to drop our prideful defenses and learn about ourselves from the social stresses encountered.

Place Pings. Many pings will be associated with a place and time. A place ping links an emotion to an environment or location. You can have a place ping when entering a dysfunctional office or crowded freeway—places that contain negative energy. Place pings include experiencing low-energy moods or replaying a significant emotional episode repeatedly. A place ping may also impact your state of mind by revisiting the setting where an emotional experience took place. If you experience anxiety at staff meetings, feel fear speaking in front of an audience, or get angry in traffic jams, the place and time receives a negative association in your consciousness. Like people pings, place pings can go on automatic replay in your conscious mind until you intentionally TURN ON high-energy and turn off the survival response. Many times, place pings are at the root of post-traumatic stress disorders (PTSD).

Event Pings. Some pings are the result of things that happen unexpectedly. Event pings include specific circumstances, conditions or situations that are outside your control—things that have happened to you that made you feel a certain way. You get fired and feel ashamed. Your picnic gets rained on. You receive bad news from the doctor and experience fear. Your financial portfolio takes a tumble and you panic. If your health is less than perfect, the pre-existing condition is also an event ping. Contrary to your negative self-assessment of the experience, event pings can also be a good source to examine your values and beliefs.

Learning From a Ping

The most important aspect to note about recognizing a ping is this: *You remember what you remember because an emotional charge is attached. If there is no emotion, there will be little if any memory, no thought remembered of the occurrence.* The thoughts you have and dwell upon are there because they are being moved by the energy of an emotion. The question then arises: Which emotion was activated by the ping?

Without emotive energy to move or activate the thought, you wouldn't have one. For example, if you had a boring uneventful day, your primal intelligence would remember very little. On the other hand, if you had a harsh quarrel with your partner, you'll remember because it was emotionally significant. This is also why you remember your first date, your first day at a job, or a traumatic event. If you vividly remember a car wreck, an accident, a battle, or a painful separation, you do so because the associated negative emotion has encoded the memory into your brain. The more impactful an emotional experience, the more emotional energy is encoded. Luckily, this post-trauma emotional programming can be actively improved upon.

> TURN ON: You remember what you remember because emotion powers the memory.

A downside of this emotional encoding is that negative pings and their associated thoughts ALWAYS outweigh positive ones. It's as if nature has dictated that it is more important for you to auto-remember your bad experiences rather than the good ones so as to avoid repeating the experience. Optimists aside, this is the reason why, left unmanaged, our conscious minds become inundated with negative thinking patterns. We become wired to habitually remember the stressful times in order to remind us to survive them. Soldiers who have come back from war still remember the stressful events in an unfortunate cognitive-emotive process known as post-traumatic stress disorder (PTSD). In many ways, we all experience PTSD to some degree when we can't get impactful pings out of our head. Again, with the core competency of adaptation, we can improve the living process and regain a clearer, more focused state of mind.

If you become lost in your own cognitive chatter, the voices that keep you awake at night are simply saying that the mind-body system is imbalanced. Mastery of the human condition means re-integrating thoughts with their emotions. This TUNE IN—TURN ON process is vital in quieting an overly active mind by bringing you back to the living moment.

There is no magic cure to instantly silence negative thinking patterns. Like lifting weights, focused attention requires persistent mental exercise. In my opinion and experience, no psychologist, no natural therapist, and no religious leader can zap your mind clean. What is required is a systematic and intentional de-cluttering of your mental desktop—an applied continuous improvement methodology. Ping by ping—that's how you will improve the process.

The first step is the collection of ping data, a step you have been taking for the last few days. I suggest that those of you with an active intellectual perspective of life take a Thought Inventory periodically. By taking time to review and record what you're thinking about, you can discover what life-energy your primal intelligence is charged with. This is a meta-thinking exercise. It requires you to observe what your mind is thinking.

TUNE IN—The Thought Inventory Exercise

We unwittingly ping ourselves all the time. For example, the daily Odyssey Methodology exercise focuses on external pings. Someone looks at what you're wearing with judgment and this triggers shame. There are internal pings as well. The Thought Inventory instead focuses on internal pings like waking up and realizing that you're anxious about a conversation you will have at work that morning. Becoming aware of thinking patterns helps plug energy leaks and elevate your eState.

With every negative thought, you can self-ping your emotions and a feedback loops begins. With an unbridled rational intelligence galloping at full speed, you can experience endless pings played repeatedly in the open-air theater of your active imagination. Every thought you think unknowingly can ping your emotional processes, which will keep you energetically tied to that way of thinking. If you think about nothing but the stresses in life, your brain will become wired to think about pings all the time automatically. When negative habits of thinking and feeling become who you are, best to find who you've become in the ping adaptation process.

> TUNE IN: Like a magnet, you attract into your life what you think about moment-to-moment.

Every negative thought you may dwell upon siphons energy from your living system. Energy management and the plugging of energy leaks is essential for health and happiness. What you may find is that most of the stress you deal with is a creation of your imagination. Don't sweat it. It's just a negative consequence of the human condition. And all it needs is energy management.

To quiet the mind, continue to collect and thus better understand what is pinging the self-organizing living process.

The Path to Enlightenment

As I just mentioned, the Thought Inventory exercise is a good way to gain a better understanding of how your brain and body—your primal intelligence—are unconsciously processing your daily activities. The more data you initially collect on your pings, the more informed you become on the sources of stress in your life. We will then use this self-knowledge going forward to improve upon the entire living process by balancing the human condition. With a better harmony of thoughts and emotions, your mind will go surprisingly quiet. Your body will be more relaxed. Your life will become a whole lot healthier. And happier.

Patience and persistence are important in this continuous improvement process. Avoid pinging yourself! No self-flagellation, please. Aim to love yourself unconditionally in your quest of self-improvement. Nothing is a mistake. Consider every ping for your learning.

Continue to use the **Quest Journal** to record your pings every day. In the following week, we will build upon what you have learned here, and systematically uncover the biological mechanisms that keep you from being your best.

Day Five Exercise

We unknowingly ping ourselves all the time. Negative thoughts and feelings often sabotage our potential. Knowing what pings you helps identify emotional patterns that may be blocking energy in your daily efforts. Remember, acceptance and understanding are high eStates, especially if they include loving and enjoying your own self-organizing living process.

Pings can create a stress response in the body. When stress hits the brain, the frontal cortex—the seat of our rational intelligence—shuts down due to a lack of blood. In a ping, blood can be diverted in an instant, super-charging your emotional brain. Without intent, you go primal. That's why you may have difficulty thinking in the eState of reason when under stress—there's no energy to fuel the rational neurons. To think straight, intentionally bring blood flow back into your higher brain functions using the palm-on-forehead technique.

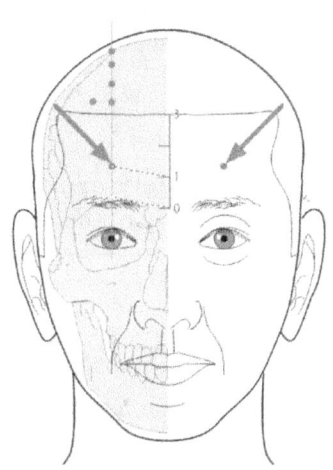

PALM ON FOREHEAD:
There are two acupressure points located on the forehead which act as arousal triggers, easing tension by bringing blood flow back in the frontal cortex—the executive center of the brain. Placing a palm on the forehead is an instinctual response of stress, instigating a generalized feeling of calm and relaxation. With more blood flow, the brain is better able to learn and adapt to the stress.

To calm the brain from a ping, and improve its overall cognitive performance, close your eyes and intentionally relax the body, placing a palm on your forehead and bringing the ping on line. After you TUNE IN to the ping, TURN ON your imagination and visualize reliving the ping in a high-energy eState. Choose any eState higher than the one experienced, ideally starting with courage. Use your imagination to replay the ping in a more empowering energy. Practice makes perfect in training the brain to be "wise and brave" in stress.

For today, use the Odyssey Methodology to complete the Quest Journal.

odyssey
The Odyssey Methodology

1. TUNE IN

Remember your day	Close your eyes and mentally review your day. Remember the pings—the people, places or events—that caused you stress, then determine the eMotion triggered by the ping. - *A ping is a significant emotional experience that shifts your energy.* - *You remember pings because of their emotional energy.*
Record your pings	Pick the three most impactful pings of the day and record. [PING - box 1] For each ping, choose the eState that best suits how you responded to the eMotion experienced and record. [TUNE IN - box 2]
Reflect your energy	Focus on how the ping affected your energetic state. Teach your brain what the ping feels like (i.e. grief, anxiety, apathy, etc.). Mentally label the feelings with a rational understanding of the eMotion.

2. TURN ON

Raise your eState	Choose an eState higher than the one experienced for each ping and record. [TURN ON - box 3]
Replay your day	Close your eyes and with palm on forehead, visualize reliving each ping in the higher eState. Imagine the same people, place or event ping in the new eState. - *Include all aspects of the more empowering eMotion. See yourself being confident, responding authentically with pleasant gestures, facial expressions, calm voice, etc.*
Resolve your pings	Set action to neutralize the ping-energy. Ask yourself: What task or solution is necessary to fix a problem? Reconnect with a person? What steps are required to repair what is broken / disconnected? In courage, take action! - *Set an intention to follow through on the commitment. With palm on forehead, mentally rehearse being courageous / optimistic / accepting of the situation. Visualize the new behavior. Train the brain for a high-energy response to stress.*

odyssey

The Quest Journal
- Day Five -

Date: _____ Day: S — M — T — W — Th — F — S

eState	eMotion	
Experience	*Feeling*	*Energy*
Enlightenment	Nirvana	1000
Peace	Bliss	600
Joy	Serenity	540
Love	Reverence	500
Reason	Understanding	400
Acceptance	Forgiveness	350
Optimism	Willingness	310
Trust	Neutrality	250
Courage	Affirmation	200
Pride	Scorn	175
Anger	Resentment	150
Desire	Craving	125
Fear	Anxiety	100
Grief	Regret	75
Apathy	Despair	50
Guilt	Blame	30
Shame	Humiliation	20

PING—a significant emotional experience

Duration: ___hr. ___min.

TUNE IN

TURN ON

PING—a significant emotional experience

Duration: ___hr. ___min.

TUNE IN

TURN ON

GRATITUDE
1.
2.
3.

If the only prayer you say in your whole life is 'thank you' that should suffice.— Meister Eckhart

PING—a significant emotional experience

Duration: ___hr. ___min.

TUNE IN

TURN ON

Emotion hierarchy adapted from Map of Consciousness: *Power vs. Force*. David R. Hawkins, M.D. Ph.D., 1995.

Day Six—The Thought Inventory Exercise

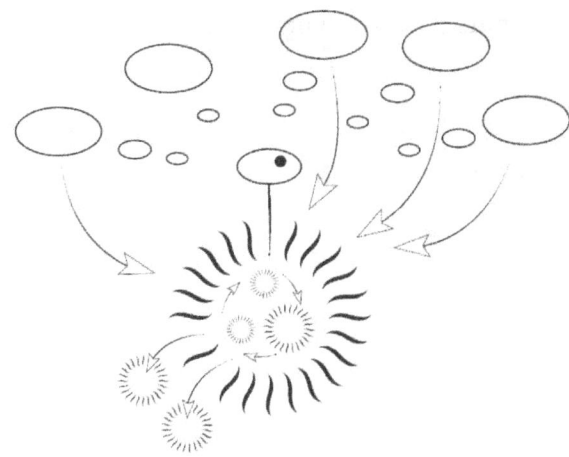

What's on your Mind?

While our subconscious primal intelligence can attend to millions of neuro-energy signals at any given moment, our rational intelligence can only hold one conscious thought at a time. You may be able to multi-task—switching from one thought to another—but no matter how hard you try, you will only be able to consciously think of one thing at any one time. You can use this to your advantage and begin to inventory the emotionally-charged thoughts (active thoughts) that may be unknowingly impacting your state of mind.

First, find a quiet place where you won't be disturbed.
Have the Thought Inventory form close by. Allow 5-10 minutes.

Second, sit in a comfortable position, and begin counting your breath.
Pay special attention to the in-and-out of your diaphragm. Attempt to count sixty breaths without distraction. Inevitably your conscious mind will be pulled to think about something else.

Third, TUNE IN.
Use your Observer consciousness to find out what the subconscious mind is up to. Observe the potential variety of active thoughts that distract you from counting your breath. Become aware

of their charged eState. Ask, what eMotion is fueling the persistent thought? How is the emotional energy impacting your state of mind? The health of your body? Focus on identifying the ping (stress trigger) of each unwanted thought. This meta-thinking exercise allows you to better understand the incumbent pings that are impacting your living process. Observe the tension, the upset or pain points. Be curious and accept what you find.

Fourth, record the active thought.
Using the form, write down your active thoughts. Use enough words to jog your memory about the person, place or event that is currently charged in your mind-body system.

Finally, ask yourself, "What eState is powering the active thought?"
Active thoughts are moved by eMotion. TUNE IN and identify the eState generated by the cognitive ping. For example, resentful thoughts are fueled by an angry state of mind, despairing thoughts stir from an apathetic state, while fearful thoughts stem from an anxious mind and so on.

In an eState of courage, ask what action is needed to RESOLVE the ping. Set an intention to follow through on your plan and grow stronger from the ping experience.

odyssey

The Thought Inventory

Date: _____

eState	eMotion	
Experience	*Feeling*	*Energy*
Enlightenment	Nirvana	1000
Peace	Bliss	600
Joy	Serenity	540
Love	Reverence	500
Reason	Understanding	400
Acceptance	Forgiveness	350
Optimism	Willingness	310
Trust	Neutrality	250
Courage	Affirmation	200
Pride	Scorn	175
Anger	Resentment	150
Desire	Craving	125
Fear	Anxiety	100
Grief	Regret	75
Apathy	Despair	50
Guilt	Blame	30
Shame	Humiliation	20

My Active Thoughts	eState
1.	
Action needed:	
2.	
Action needed:	
3.	
Action needed:	
4.	
Action needed:	
5.	
Action needed:	
6.	
Action needed:	
7.	
Action needed:	
8.	
Action needed:	

Observations: _____

_____

_____

Emotion hierarchy adapted from Map of Consciousness: *Power vs. Force*. David R. Hawkins, M.D. Ph.D., 1995.

Day Seven—Rest and Reflect Upon Your Week

Look back at the daily exercises and transcribe your pings in the boxes below. Note any commonalities and group accordingly. This exercise is not to assign blame, but to elevate your awareness of the people, places or events that are disturbing your energy. Observe any patterns. Consider high-energy strategies that would help neutralize the ping. Plan any action necessary.

Day One Pings	Common Pings—People, Places & Events
1.	
2.	
3.	
Day Two Pings	
1.	
2.	
3.	
Day Three Pings	
1.	**Strategies for Improvement**
2.	
3.	
Day Four Pings	
1.	
2.	
3.	
Day Five Pings	**Action Items:**
1.	
2.	
3.	

odyssey

The most beautiful and most profound emotion we can experience is the sensation of the mystical. It is the sower of all true science.

He to whom this emotion is a stranger, who can no longer wonder and stand rapt in awe, is as good as dead.

To know what is impenetrable to us really exists, manifesting itself as the highest wisdom and the most radiant beauty which our dull faculties can comprehend only in the most primitive form.

This knowledge—this feeling—is at the center of all true religiousness. The cosmic religious experience is the strongest and oldest mainspring of scientific research.

My religion consists of a humble admiration of the illimitable, superior Spirit who manifests itself in the slight details we are able to perceive with our minds.

That deeply emotional conviction of the presence of a superior reasoning power, which is revealed in the incomprehensible Universe, forms my idea of God.

Albert Einstein

odyssey

WEEK TWO—THE ROAD OF LIFE

Stress & Defensive Force

Throughout our lives, we have a lifetime of opportunity to experience the full spectrum of emotion, from the highest joys to the deepest despairs and all the pleasures and pains in between.

The road of life is not marked with minutes or hours; rather, it is painted with experiences that become etched into the very fabric of our being.

To truly lead our lives and feel alive, recognize pings as they occur—those moments of emotion that impact your state of mind. Understanding these triggers and their source will assist you in seeking solutions that neutralize negative thoughts and emotions.

odyssey

The Quest Objectives

At the end of Week Two, you'll be able to…

1. Recognize how your rational intelligence and the human condition exacerbate stress by falsely engaging the survival response.

2. Understand how stress responses instinctually move our body and thoughts by producing energy for motion automatically.

3. Review your past life experiences in a change-centric context that will spur insights into your present state of mind.

As I have always held it a crime to anticipate evils, I will believe it a good comfortable road until I am compelled to believe differently.

Meriwether Lewis, American Explorer (1774-1809)

Day Eight—The Road of Life

O - - - - O————————O————————O - - - - O
         BIRTH   DEATH

On the road of life, your spirit will inevitably experience a broad spectrum of emotion—from the pains of grief and loss, to the exhilarations of joy and happiness. As we travel down life's path, we grow and adapt to the challenges placed before us. Many times, we strive forward with good intentions, navigating the world and its complexities, sometimes with success, but many times without. Along the way, our primal intelligence remembers every pain and misfortune. At the same time, our rational intellect attempts to comprehend the significant emotional experiences and understand their impact on our lives. The journey molds you into the unique person you are today. For health and happiness, it's best to continually improve yourself every step of the way.

As much as we may fret about the woes we have met and worry about what lies ahead, our spirit remains in the present moment—converting our mental imagery into emotional energy. We know now that it's not what you think but how you think it that gives you the motivation to go forward. Think optimistically about the future, and feel-good biochemicals will flood your bloodstream. Think fearfully and your body reacts differently, giving you an altogether different, negative life experience. Because our brain is fear-oriented, thinking about what can go wrong comes naturally. Thinking negatively about life is programmed in our instincts because it's important for us to remain aware of the dangers that lurk around the corner. But constant thinking about the evils that lie ahead can harm us emotionally and lead to an ongoing march of apathy and aggression. Traveling today's super highways requires high-octane life-energy.

As a living being, your spirit will continually strive for health until you take your last breath. The best inoculant to help survive an anxiety-riddled future is the mastery of feeling alive—trusting your spirit to navigate the road blocks that will come your way. The road of life can undoubtedly be one of mundane repetition and survival. The key to thriving and creating more joy in life is to wire the brain to feel alive in everything you do, from washing dishes to orchestrating a corporate takeover. Learning to step forward in courage and embrace the entire spectrum of being alive is the path to an enlightened existence. If negative life experiences are outweighing the positive, it's time to pull over and tune up the self-organizing living process that is driving your thoughts and feelings right now.

"The mass of men lead lives of quiet desperation." This statement by Henry David Thoreau is as current today as it was a century ago. It's unfortunate how many are out of touch with their primal intelligence and are failing to live their life fully. People have never been smarter yet more bogged down by their own thinking process. Despite good intentions, smart people develop attention deficit disorders, react emotionally or fall into energy-draining black holes. When we fail to turn off our thoughts or listen to our instincts, primal intelligence can become a demanding inner demon.

This was true of another exceptionally bright client—I'll call him Greg. Greg's road of life had become difficult for him to navigate. With a lack of trusted intuition to guide him, Greg had no gut navigational system to help inform his decisions. Greg needed to upgrade his mental software and reengage his internal GPS.

When I first met Greg, he was sitting alone in a Sydney beachside cafe early one overcast morning, smoking a cigarette and looking like someone who was suffering a hangover. I had known Greg's father, the owner of a mid-sized manufacturing firm, for some time. Greg, who was head of sales for his father's business, had the enormous responsibility of bringing in millions of dollars to keep the company alive.

I had heard about Greg's anger management issues long before I met him. He was notorious at work for slamming doors, stomping down hallways, and throwing things. Many of his colleagues had learned to move aside if they saw him coming. A week earlier, Greg had, in a fit of rage, punched his fist through an office wall. After a talk with his father, Greg agreed to meet me. Unbeknownst to Greg, hitting the wall started him on a new path of improvement.

At the café that early autumn morning, Greg and I exchanged introductions and started chatting about his life. With a little investigation, I learned that Greg was often angry because of what he called "stupid people" who "weren't doing what they were supposed to do." During our talk, I also learned that Greg drank every night and indulged in cocaine on a semi-regular basis. Often, and for no other reason than fear of being alone, he had casual sex with women. Further inquiry revealed that Greg was scared of commitment and was at a crossroads. He told me he just wanted to be happy, settled, and enjoy life. Fair enough.

Another great mystery sat before me. How could a nice looking smart chap in his late 30s, by all accounts a successful executive living near one of Sydney's best beaches, fall so far? Where was his rage coming from? And why was he in such a destructive state of mind?

Odds are you too have experienced bouts of emotional misalignment. You may have felt guilty, depressed, anxious, ashamed, sad and angry for times longer than you wanted. These are all life experiences we'd rather do without, but despite success and material riches, we end up experiencing them anyway. During such emotionally critical moments, remember that your primal intelligence still operates in your subconscious, learning and adapting from everything you experience. Every thought, word or action molds your brain and creates your reality. The important question to ask then is: What are you teaching it? Is your primal intelligence growing smarter and stronger in stress? Or are you letting it atrophy, subjected to destructive thoughts and emotions.

To improve the self-organizing living process, begin to see the road of life as a camouflaged teacher. Begin to appreciate the stress and challenges you encounter as life lessons you can actively learn from. By stepping in and acknowledging the pain in our lives, we can grow in our capabilities to deal with it. In this learning process, it is important to keep in mind that what we remember when we reflect on our day says a lot about the operations of our subconscious. If you've been challenged emotionally, you'll remember it. So will your subconscious. The critical step is to put aside rational analysis, and instead consciously TUNE IN to the emotional impact these experiences have on your primal intelligence. As I've said now many times, becoming more self-aware to the underlying emotional energy powering your thinking process is the first step to improving it.

Without energy management, we can—and often do—lock ourselves into destructive states of mind that sabotage our life experience and imprison us in a self-created living hell. How do we get out of such horrible places?

The answer is: learning by doing. Not simply reading about improvement, but living it. Adaption is a core competency. Your brain and body are always learning every moment of every day. How about intentional positive adaptation? What if you began applying a continuous improvement strategy that places you on the proverbial path to enlightenment? By embracing the road of life as your teacher, you'll begin seeing roadblocks as opportunities for improvement. In this heightened consciousness, when the sun rises, you'll wake up enthused to go out and make a difference in the world. This is a true leadership mindset.

The very real impetus for adopting this attitude of self-development is this: Stress isn't going away; it will forever be part of our lives.

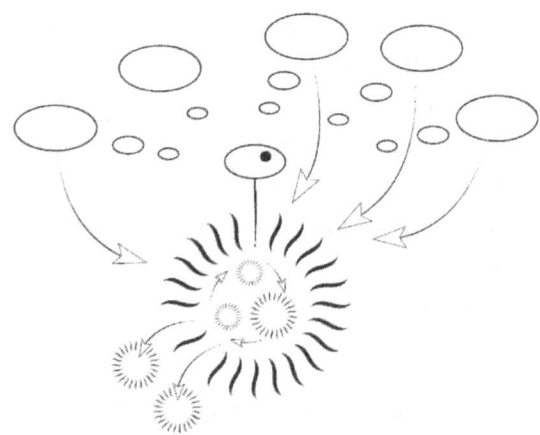

Constant and Never-Ending Stress

It was just over 100 years ago that Edison installed the first electric lights in lower Manhattan. Suddenly, nights became brighter. So too has our intelligence and understanding of the world around us. As a result of Edison's revolutionary leadership, and the contributions from hundreds of thousands of others, humankind is seeing the light like never before. With the world of information at our fingertips, we are smarter than ever. Or are we?

The road of scientific discovery has been difficult but impressive. From our ancient ancestors' first discovery of fire to the brightening of our nights with electric light, to the harnessing of atomic energy, humanity has come a long way in improving the world and ensuring ongoing survival. We have never lived longer, eaten better, and enjoyed more comfort and conveniences. On a basic level, we are very fortunate that we do not suffer the cold and hunger our predecessors endured. Could you imagine primitive ancestors visiting us in a modern suburban home? Our comforts would be beyond their wildest imagination.

Today, if hundreds of thousands of people lose electrical power because of a storm, it's front page news. Just over a hundred years ago, people didn't even know what electricity was! Compared to our ancestors, we have incredible lives. Today, we no longer have to go to bed at sunset. With electricity, we can stay up all night long—and do what we want, when we want. But why don't we feel free?

We have so much freedom to live as we please, yet there is more mental illness in our society than ever before. Researchers say that in the next 20 years, we will experience a rate of change that is equivalent to that of the last 100 years. More than half of the world's population is now living in urban areas, which are hotbeds for increased levels of depression and schizophrenia.[6] New technologies and automated systems will make or break the careers of millions of people, while overpopulation will see humanity competing for shrinking food and fuel supplies. On top of it all, global warming is melting icecaps and flooding low-lying coastal cities. No wonder

---

[6] Scientific American MIND, *Big City Blues*, March/April 2013, p. 58.

depression is slated to become one of the world's leading health problems by 2020.[7] These are real anxieties for a brave new world.

Modern Stress—Primal Intellect

From the dark ages to the technology revolution, human life has changed dramatically. While our physical brain structures have remained the same, the cognitive challenges our primal intelligence faces are massively complex compared to those our ancestors dealt with when roaming the Serengeti. We may have updated software for our computers, but the core operating system of our own psyche hasn't changed in millennia. Even in our modern world, we still operate with a primal intelligence powering our self-organizing living process.

As children, we heard that future technology will improve our lives, yet we are finding life has become a lot more complicated and expensive. How fast do days and years fly by? In a wired information-centric world, we instantly hear about terrorists and tsunamis, earthquakes and psychotic killers, global financial crisis, civil wars, famines, droughts, forest fires and potential pandemics. With so many stressful challenges, it's no wonder we're experiencing psychological distress. It's one ping after another.

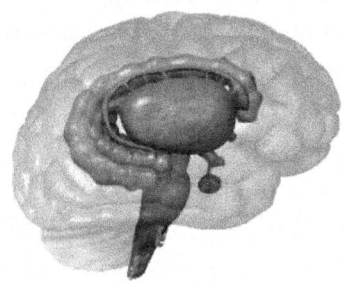

The Stress Response

A stress response occurs when our subconscious primal intelligence senses that something isn't right. In terms of energy, our state of mind shifts in response to changes in our environment with emotions that seem to come out of nowhere. This energy shift then pings our conscious mind to attend to the source of stress and redirects our attention. Left to its own devices, our mind may easily lose focus when facing enough stress responses. No wonder ADHD is so prevalent. Our attention follows our pings.

As we've discovered, significant emotional experiences—pings—generate a stress response automatically. Without awareness, our self-organizing living process is pinged and energy flow is shifted. When we are inundated by stress, we tend to focus on the negative consequences of those experiences. Feeling the stress responses, primal intelligence pings your conscious mind to pay attention to the stress and survive it.

---

[7] *The Global Burden of Disease: A Comprehensive Assessment of Mortality and Disability, Injuries, and Risk Factors in 1990 and Projected to 2020*, World Bank, Harvard School of Public Health, Geneva, 1996.

To our Observer consciousness, active thoughts are simply mental reminders to attend to the source of stress and resolve it. If we're not careful, we can easily wire our brains to over-attend to the thoughts created by stress. We end up analyzing every problem, seeking solutions that we think will help us survive. As a habitual way of thinking, we can lock our minds and emotions into survival mode. We feel anxious. Unsettled. Worse, in the chaos we lose contact with our in-tune-ition, our intuitive navigational system. Without a rudder to steer, a ship can easily veer off course. And if we're not mindful, a spirit may get lost on the road of life.

Our primal intelligence has a subconscious attention system that is very sensitive to shifts of energy. If your spirit is chronically anxious, you can become over-sensitive, and live your life anticipating that something bad will happen. With such a paranoid spirit powering consciousness, it's no wonder that so many fail to truly relax and recharge. We become chronically stressed and susceptible to the mental-emotional imbalance. Our active imagination runs wild with catastrophic thinking. The cognitive chatter and unfocused thoughts then ping our primal intelligence, setting off more stress responses and anxious thoughts, which further drain energy. All this keeps us feeling anxious, resentful and depressed—classic symptoms of mental illness. How do we regain control and get back to where we want to be?

Remember that your subconscious attention system picks up every thought, daydream and fantasy, along with the emotions they elicit. When those mental images are about survival, a stress response is engaged, activating the fight or flight response even though nothing tangible has happened or is about to happen. Your primal attention system is fear-oriented, meaning that your built-in survival instincts will ping your conscious mind automatically with what's not right. That's why you think negative thoughts without conscious effort. The cure? Learn to neutralize the ping's emotionally-charged energy with the TURN ON adaption process. This will free up your energy immensely.

A Living Energy Crisis

MRI scans tell us that when experiencing stress during a stress response, for example, the brain initiates a dynamic and instantaneous diversion of blood flow from the modern rational brain (the frontal cortex) to the primitive emotional (limbic) brain. In evolutionary terms, this makes sense. While your subconscious primal intelligence (with its core competencies) is crucial to your survival, in a stress response it can—and does—commandeer your conscious mind and engage the stress response to fight or flight automatically. In other words, any significant ping can instantly shut down your higher brain functions and force primal emotions upon you. Under stress, and without energy to fuel our rational intelligence, we can and often do become irrational. That's why we go primal—snap and unexpectedly say and do things without thinking.

Our brain burns a tremendous amount of energy, so even the slightest decline of blood flow to your higher reasoning center can cause you to react emotionally. The hungry neurons of your brain crave oxygen provided by blood, which, under stress, can all but disappear. With a ping, blood vessels constrict, blood flow is redirected to the primal brain, and—bang!—you're in fight or flight. In terms of evolution, it appears as if it's better to react to stress automatically than to allow your rational brain time to mull over things and ponder what to do.

Primal-Rational Adversity

This shifting of intelligence is done very quickly, within 1/500th of a second. It's the main reason we can react so forcefully in stressful situations. It's a battle between the two aspects of our human psyche—the conscious and subconscious. Unbalanced, we have made one the enemy. As smart as you may be, when stress occurs, your subconscious mind takes control of your energy and thus your behavior. By increasing your emotional intelligence, you can elevate the subconscious response.

Two brains are at work within our skull. One, the rational brain, is located behind the forefront of your head and is called the frontal cortex. Scientists often refer to this as the executive center, and it's where reasoning, planning and intentional decision making occur. When you're not under stress, this modern brain does an excellent job in analyzing, planning, organizing and constructing solutions. It can also do a great job in keeping primal emotions in check—when we're not stressed.

Your other, more ancient brain, located underneath your modern brain, is much more primal. It's called the limbic or emotional brain and you can think of it as the seat of your primal intelligence. That's where emotions originate; its job is to produce and regulate the biochemicals that generate the energy that powers your brain and moves your body. To make this understanding easier, think of emotions as "energy for motion" or eMotion. Like a car which is powered by petrochemicals, your brain and body are run on biochemicals. For health and happiness, it's best to run your brain and body on "high-octane" eMotion—higher, more positive emotional energy that doesn't wreak havoc on the self-organizing living process.

> **The Two-in-One Brain**
> Your conscious mind is seated in your frontal cortex (i.e the executive center). Your subconscious mind is situated in the limbic brain (the emotional center located deeper) tasked with moving the body. Together, the two brains constitute the mind (thoughts) and the body (emotions). Balancing this dualistic living process is a primary challenge of the human condition.

So how can we get rid of our negative primal reactions? You start by befriending them.

Primal Defensive Force

As we've learned, when you're under stress, your primal instincts step in to help you survive. We react automatically to stressful challenges without having to think about what to do. Even after we become conscious of a ping, our subconscious primal intelligence has long since injected biochemicals into our bloodstream that have shifted our energy and put us in survival mode.

Even if you've been stalwart about thinking positively, which is what present-day cognitive behavioral therapy (CBT) and positive psychology teaches, the intensity of the survival emotions operating in your subconscious may continue to lock down your conscious mind in endless negative thoughts. After all, thoughts are flows of energy. This is why no matter how hard you try to think positive thoughts, you end up being pulled to the negative ones. Your conscious mind becomes a battlefield as you fight your charged primal eMotions with endless rational analysis. How does anyone win such a self-destructive civil war?

The Art of War, an ancient Chinese book written by a high-ranking Chinese military general named Sun Tzu, is commonly considered the definitive work on military strategy and tactics. *The Art of War* is still referred to today, thousands of years later, by many military officials in modern warfare. In particular, I enjoy one proverb distilled from its timeless wisdom:

Know your enemy and know yourself, find naught in fear for 100 battles. Know yourself but not your enemy, find level of loss and victory. Know thy enemy but not yourself, wallow in defeat every time.

I like this proverb, especially in the context of our disregard for the subconscious as if it were an enemy to fear. To win our inner battles, we must first become self-aware of what is driving our most foundational behaviors. To "find naught in fear," we must "know our enemy *and* ourselves". Do you know yourself so well that you have no fear in everyday battles? Before you answer, remember that you already have everything you need within you right now to overcome the pings that come your way. Let's dive deeper into what makes you tick when the stress is on.

If we look at our brains and behaviors from a scientific perspective and begin examining what we discover, what we'll find are three primal instincts which forcibly direct our actions under stress. They are the three fundamental survival eStates found in every mammal—anger, desire and fear. Their energies for motion instinctively engage the body and mind when push comes to shove. The result is behaviors—emotional patterns that drive movement when stress pings the living process. Aggression (anger), addiction (desire) and anxiety (fear) are three survival programs that automatically move us to action. Fear keeps us safe, desire gets us out and looking, anger takes and defends. For improved health and happiness, best to "know yourself" in everyday battles and become better in tune with the primal energetic forces that work within.

Three Primal Behaviors

Aggression

Getting angry is a natural and common stress response. The gamut of behaving aggressively spans from short-tempered road rage to chronic anger management issues and everything in between. When we don't get what we want, we become angry and aggressive, powering up the body to take forceful action to obtain what we believe to be necessary for our survival.

As a cognitive habit, those who are chronically aggressive are unsurprisingly quick to get angry. Because their rational brain shuts down in response to stress so quickly, those in aggressive moods are difficult to reach with reason. Handling aggression will be discussed more in the coming days.

Addiction

The instinctual eState of desire and its craving tendencies drive you to seek out and find things that will appease your brain with pleasure. We are naturally addicted to food, water and air, because they are our primary energy sources. As social creatures, we also crave companionship and feel discomfort when left alone or isolated from others.

With a core competency to form sexual relationships, we are driven by an insatiable desire to obtain the pleasures sex offers. This powerful instinctive directive is what creates lustful thoughts and obsessive desires. This addictive state is natural but can be artificially nurtured by illicit drugs, alcohol, porn and dopamine-fuelled video games. Seen in an evolutionary sense, a preoccupation with sex is vital to the advancement of the human race; however, too much attention on self-pleasure and the emotional habits that form lead to an addictive state of mind.

If presented with the choice, most people would choose pleasure over pain. In our modern world, many artificial sources of pleasure are readily available to appease our desire to feel good. We shop, smoke, drink alcohol, swallow pain killers, take mind-altering drugs, zone out on entertainment and loose ourselves in the Internet. If we're not careful, we may lock our brains into a desirous state of mind that craves pleasure constantly.

An addictive spirit is constantly on the lookout for something better. To the mind and body, a desire energy state is like being hungry but not getting fed. Unlike physical hunger however, addictive minds are never sated, even when the object of their desire is obtained. Instead, addictive minds race after ever better, bigger, faster, stronger... desires.

Anxiety

Perhaps the most uncomfortable of the three primal behaviors is anxiety. Anxiety is an emotion that feels like fear without end. Anxiety may become our default state of mind

> when we have been chronically stressed. Anxiety rapidly drains energy, leading to a state of apathy and depression.
>
> When we experience fear, our primal intelligence forces our minds to pay attention to what may harm us. If then we unknowingly allow our thoughts to dwell on our fears, we set up a mind-body feedback loop where our fear-driven imagination triggers off actual feelings of fear. Left unchecked, anxiety escalates. More about anxiety later.

These instinctual energies for motion are the primal emotive forces that help us survive. These often chronic, energy-draining behaviors reflect how our spirit naturally responds when the stress is on. If we fail to control the primal responses to the stresses of life, the downhill slope may lead to chronic behaviors that deplete our energy. To fight, flight or freeze requires energy. Chronic aggression, addiction and anxiety often precede depression because they burn an exorbitant amount of energy.

Primal eMotions are forceful, meaning they are literally forced upon us. Without energy management, they can easily lock down one's potential. How many people do you know who are really at peace with themselves, and remain cool and collected under pressure? Not many, for sure. However, this life leadership skill is learnable.

You can develop an enlightened spirit by teaching your rational brain which primal eMotions are triggered by stressors. By teaching your rational brain to understand what pings your primal brain, you will gain greater self-knowledge, trust and confidence in your own innate intelligence. In short, you will better know yourself and thy enemy both of which are you. This is accomplished by continuing to collect data on your pings and by gaining greater conscious awareness of their recurring behavioral patterns.

Trusting your Instincts

There is nothing mysterious about primal behavior. Our primary movements are comprised of our survival-driven responses to perceived threats. Without self-improvement, you can easily lose touch with how to regulate your eMotions effectively. This loss of spirit is a negative consequence of the human condition, and that is why energy management needs to play a key role in everything you do.

Undoubtedly, a multitude of things on the road of life will ping us. People annoy us, we say and do stupid things, and find ourselves in the wrong place at the wrong time. Add to that our imaginary analysis of it all and we can easily lose trust in our key navigational aid—our gut intuition.

How many times have you disregarded your initial feelings and instead have rationally justified some awful predicament you could have avoided? We have been taught to be rational, yet being rational often leads us to a place of being emotionally vague and confused. Relying on our rational brain to be brilliant in the moment can give us false hope. The underlying primal eMotions get in the way when we need our higher smarts most. If we are going to navigate the constant and never ending stresses of life with resiliency and strength, then we need to know ourselves and know what we are really made of.

Trusting your instincts means trusting your eMotions to move you. That's something many are terrified of, as we have been taught that eMotions are something to fear or repress. But when stress rears its ugly head and you are faced with a real challenge, how connected are you to your primal power? Do you trust your eMotions to move you to resolve the situation?

If you are to be the hero in your own life story, aim to remain connected to both your primal and rational intelligence, even when the stress is on. When a bully confronts you, stand your ground. When the forecast is grim, be optimistic. When conflict occurs, constructively resolve the situation. In short, a hero mustn't shy away when real courage is needed. This is the quality of a true life leader. After all, if you can't trust your own spirit to move you, who can you trust?

Day Eight Exercise

After a week of recording and resolving your pings, you should now have a better grasp of the energy that is driving your eStates under stress. I would like you to continue this self-improvement process to further train the brain to be resilient when future pings occur. Again, use the Odyssey Methodology to complete the Quest Journal.

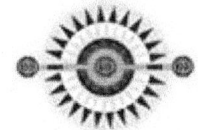

odyssey

The Odyssey Methodology

1. TUNE IN

Remember your day	Close your eyes and mentally review your day. Remember the pings—the people, places or events—that caused you stress, then determine the eMotion triggered by the ping. - *A ping is a significant emotional experience that shifts your energy.* - *You remember pings because of their emotional energy.*
Record your pings	Pick the three most impactful pings of the day and record. [PING - box 1] For each ping, choose the eState that best suits how you responded to the eMotion experienced and record. [TUNE IN - box 2]
Reflect your energy	Focus on how the ping affected your energetic state. Teach your brain what the ping feels like (i.e. grief, anxiety, apathy, etc.). Mentally label the feelings with a rational understanding of the eMotion.

2. TURN ON

Raise your eState	Choose an eState higher than the one experienced for each ping and record. [TURN ON - box 3]
Replay your day	Close your eyes and with palm on forehead, visualize reliving each ping in the higher eState. Imagine the same people, place or event ping in the new eState. - *Include all aspects of the more empowering eMotion. See yourself being confident, responding authentically with pleasant gestures, facial expressions, calm voice, etc.*
Resolve your pings	Set action to neutralize the ping-energy. Ask yourself: What task or solution is necessary to fix a problem? Reconnect with a person? What steps are required to repair what is broken / disconnected? In courage, take action! - *Set an intention to follow through on the commitment. With palm on forehead, mentally rehearse being courageous / optimistic / accepting of the situation. Visualize the new behavior. Train the brain for a high-energy response to stress.*

odyssey

The Quest Journal
- Day Eight -

Date: _____ Day: S — M — T — W — Th — F — S

eState	eMotion	
Experience	*Feeling*	*Energy*
Enlightenment	Nirvana	1000
Peace	Bliss	600
Joy	Serenity	540
Love	Reverence	500
Reason	Understanding	400
Acceptance	Forgiveness	350
Optimism	Willingness	310
Trust	Neutrality	250
Courage	Affirmation	200
Pride	Scorn	175
Anger	Hate	150
Desire	Craving	125
Fear	Anxiety	100
Grief	Regret	75
Apathy	Despair	50
Guilt	Blame	30
Shame	Humiliation	20

PING—a significant emotional experience

Duration: ___hr. ___min.

TUNE IN

TURN ON

PING—a significant emotional experience

Duration: ___hr. ___min.

TUNE IN

TURN ON

PING—a significant emotional experience

Duration: ___hr. ___min.

TUNE IN

TURN ON

GRATITUDE
1.
2.
3.

If the only prayer you say in your whole life is 'thank you' that should suffice.— Meister Eckhart

Emotion hierarchy adapted from Map of Consciousness: *Power vs. Force.* David R. Hawkins, M.D. Ph.D., 1995.

In addition to facial and vocal communication, apes often gesture at each other. Bonobos tend to gesture with their right hands, which hints at a brain specialization similar to the one underlying human language.[8]

Frans De Waal, world-renowned primatologist

Day Nine—eMotions: Energy for Motion

In simple terms, emotions are energy for motion—states of mind that contain energetic impulses that move the mind-body system. To remind ourselves that energy and movement are implicit in every emotion, I will continue using eMotion as a pseudo acronym. This is to emphasize that every state of mind you experience—from the lowest energies of humiliation and blame to the highest energies of serenity and bliss—all have an instinctual purpose to move you, physically and mentally.

Although eMotion is defined as physiological energy that moves you, some eMotions are meant to keep you immobile. In fact, some eMotions depress movement or halt it all together. The energy that is produced by negative eMotions can vary greatly, from the near motionless energies of humiliation and despair to the more active energy of pride and affirmation. The

---

[8] De Waal, Frans, *Bonobo: The Forgotten Ape*, University of California Press, 1977, p. 150.

energy of your spirit is mirrored by the eMotions you experience, again both physically and metaphysically.

The state of energy in your mind-body system can vary greatly depending on the eMotion being experienced. As a rule, the higher the energy, the more positive the emotional experience. For example, guilt has greater life-energy than shame. Where shame is the separation from another's energy, guilt moves you to feel bad and thus reconnect with another's energy. Living in regret has more life-energy than being in despair. When a depressed person begins to cry, we know they are getting better. Being courageous is more powerful than being scornful in that it takes transformative energy to admit you were wrong. Feeling willing and optimistic is more powerful than remaining neutral, and so on up the life-energy spectrum of eStates.

Lowest on the energy scale, in shame we experience a separation from the life-energy of others, as an outcast, disconnected from our living community. In ancient times, being thrown out of the tribe meant death. That's why in shame, many feel like dying. If you feel alone, the emotional energy of shame may be at play. Being punished or bullied as a child sets up emotional disconnections within the mind-body system. This imbalance is especially crippling for a young child who is starving for emotional energy from his parents and peers. If you didn't get fed high-energy as a child, take extra effort to TURN ON higher emotional states, as your brain may simply not have the energy for motion programs on file. This means you will have to teach yourself to trust, to be optimistic, to accept imperfection, and to see and understand another person from their point of view. The path to such enlightened states of mind starts with the TURN ON of courage—stepping into that which is feared and becoming wiser and braver in the process. This is the warrior spirit in all its energetic glory. It takes an act of courage to transform negative energy into positive, and to shift consciousness from a me-pride to a we-trust paradigm. This is why inspirational leaders are ideally courageous and positive in their outlook of life.

Fueled with high-energy, we feel connected to everything and everyone. Nothing is separate, even those who have caused us pain. In such an enlightened energy state, consciousness experiences "all-is-one". Achieving this highest level of energy is the quest of many religious philosophies that promise a Christ-consciousness or the Buddha-mind to its followers. Regardless of the approach, the spectrum of feeling alive spans the emotional realm of "alone" to "all-is-one." With this polarity in mind, begin thinking of eMotions as a connection-indicator to your web of life and the energy sources therein. By becoming better at interpreting your own eMotions and energy needs, the better you'll be at maintaining the health and happiness of the people connections in your web of life. This is a critical quality for a life leader.

With a duality of consciousness—possessing both primal intelligence (the Experiencer) and rational intelligence (the Observer)—human beings can have a dualistic experience of eMotions. To the Observer consciousness, eMotions are interpreted as feelings. Again, consider eMotions as the collective life-energy powering your self-organizing living process. Right now, your spirit's energy is directly reflecting your energy-connection to yourself and others, whether you are high and blissed or low and depressed. The ensuing state of mind is a candid expression of your energy and its emotional connections. For the un-enlightened, eMotions can shift at a moment's notice. If people are emotional, life-energy is constantly changing. Life around such volatile people can be one bumpy ride for those in low-energy states of mind. Best to TURN ON a psychic force field that protects our energy from such erratic sources.

As energy beings, we are intimately tied to our energy levels. As much as we may like to avoid being emotional, we often cannot help ourselves. We react to stress automatically, become defensive, agitated or submissive. So what are we to do? How do we not become victims to our emotional states and the energy states of others? Whether angry or optimistic, happy or sad, understanding what generates your own energy for motion can provide valuable insight into protecting your energy from the shifting eMotions in others.

Biochemical Reactivity

Like gasoline fuels an engine, your biochemistry powers your eMotions. Much like mixing an alcoholic cocktail, your brain causes the release of varying amounts of biochemicals into your bloodstream, producing different states of mind. When you are fuel-injected with high-octane adrenaline, for example, you become aggressive. Inject the living system with serotonin, dopamine, oxytocin and other pleasurable neurotransmitters, and you get an altogether different, happier experience.

Science has discovered multitudes of hormones and neurotransmitters that can shake us awake and get us moving, and has also identified how a lack of these ingredients keeps us down and immobile. Swallowing anti-depressants and anti-anxiety pills may artificially regulate your biochemistry, elevating your energy levels so you feel brighter. But if your intention is to be drug-free, you must learn to master your spirit and its varying energy levels. Begin by believing in your innate ability to train the brain to sustain high-energy under stress—a skill you have been learning with the Odyssey Methodology.

It only takes a few molecules of biochemistry to profoundly impact your state of mind. With our physical body composed of CHON, four highly electro-reactive molecules (carbon, hydrogen, oxygen and nitrogen), even a few grains of a substance can have a profound effect on our energetic state and feelings of self-confidence. Any cocaine user will verify that. When your energy is pinged, a cascade of biochemicals has inundated your living system: your heartbeat changes, your blood pressure increases, your breathing becomes shallow and digestion slows down. Your energy may be lowered and feelings change. Want to stay high without taking drugs? Take greater command and control of this subconscious living process by actively managing your energy. Even if you are atheist, TUNE IN and TURN ON religiously.

Coincidently, party drugs such as cocaine and Ecstasy, by themselves, do not change your state of mind. Rather, they enable the release of the body's own feel good biochemicals that already exist inside you. By eliminating your stress responses, you can enable your brain and body to release more of the good stuff, so that you feel high-energy naturally without the nasty side-effects of a drug.

It is interesting to speculate that before language existed, our primitive ancestors didn't have names like guilt, anger, desire or fear. Because they relied so heavily on their primal intelligence, they lived their eMotions and absorbed them as part of their everyday life experiences. If you will, they were one with their primal intelligence. As modern humans with a dual brain (conscious and subconscious), our mission should be to incorporate the best of both worlds, so that we don't fight or fright ourselves. Being truly comfortable in one's own skin is the birthright of every human being. To govern ourselves with such finesse, our modern quest should be to become more intimately familiar with the subconscious processes beneath our conscious awareness. In stress, learn to TURN ON your higher brain functions and let the feel-good endorphins flow.

An Intuitive Notion

For many, living a stress-free life, surrounded by luxuries is the holy grail of existence. With a beautiful home and a hefty bank account, many people believe they would have a good life that is free of pain and social conflicts that plague the less fortunate. How many times, however, do we hear that those who seemingly have it all—celebrities, sports stars or lottery winners—go through emotional meltdowns for the whole world to see? Why don't they know better?

As we learned last week (The Human Condition, Part 1), without emotional resilience, many easily buckle and break under the slightest stress. Instead of facing the stress head on and becoming emotionally stronger in the stress-growth process, many mask tension with distractions such as gaming, shopping, alcohol, drugs and promiscuous sex. In our pleasure-centric world, many take the easy road—shying away from the hard work and becoming emotionally weaker in the process.

It is not a question of physical strength. I have known body builders who are physically strong but emotionally fragile. They could leg-press four times their body weight, yet on the inside, they experienced insecurity and a lack of self-confidence, and consequently reacted aggressively at the slightest provocation. As we've read, like a weakened immune system, our emotional system can become diseased by stress. The problem is not the stress itself, but the incumbent energy and emotional programming that dictate the way we respond.

We all have an internal guidance system that tells us what's right or wrong. But this enlightened realm of self-knowledge can be easily masked by the self-doubting cognitive chatter and endless analysis, causing us to lose sight of who we really are in the moment. Genuine self-confidence comes when we learn to navigate the road of life with a solid connection to our most personal, emotionally-charged values. This means listening to your spirit rather than the voices in your head.

> Enlightenment happens when you continually TUNE IN and TURN ON your life-energy.

The TUNE IN process of in-tune-ition helps us to recognize and improve upon what is already there. If you are to truly trust your spirit, TURN ON the courage to know yourself at a deeper emotional level. Ask yourself: What is really important when all hell breaks loose? What's real and valuable in the moment? As I've mentioned, dealing proactively with negative states of mind requires that you learn to better listen to what your instincts are telling you when the stress is on. TUNE IN by asking, "What am I feeling right now?" "What do I intuit to be true?" Then TURN ON a high-energy resolution to neutralize the ping. This will help manage your energy and better equip you to deal with your future daily challenges.

Again paraphrasing *The Art of War*: Knowing thy enemy but not yourself, wallow in defeat every time. Take time to lift the emotional weight off your spirit and get stronger at resolving pings as they occur in the moment. Begin winning your ping battles. A good place to begin is with the fundamentals, that is, the six universal eMotions we all deal with on a regular basis. In the quest, get to know the following intimately, in particular when they are pinged and become dominate in your behavior.

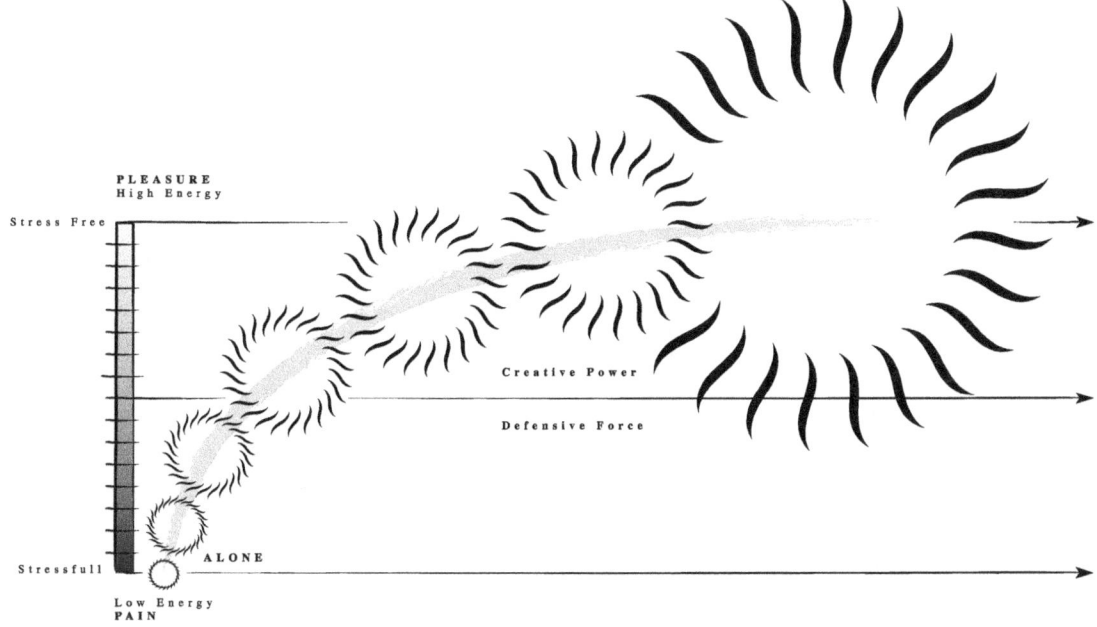

Six Universal eMotions

The hereditary components of our emotional nature are the same for everyone, everywhere. No matter where you go, you can easily recognize eMotions in others, and the eStates in which they operate by simply watching how they move. The most obvious emotional behaviors—happiness, sadness and aggression—are instantly identifiable in every culture. The instinctual movements, facial expressions and body language are all similarly encoded into our common genetic programming. In other words, eMotions are in everyone. They are a natural aspect of being alive.

Recognizing other people's emotional states is essential for our survival. Being able to distinguish whether the person approaching is a friend or foe can mean the difference between life and death. For the most part, we make these distinctions automatically using mirror neurons, or specialized brain cells that mirror the emotional states of those around us. These highly sensitive neurons allow us to subconsciously pick up the emotional intentions of others without thought. In this manner, our primal intelligence is always in tune to the exchanges of emotional energy emanating from other people.

So, how do you accurately identify the state of mind in others? Simple—by becoming more aware of your own state of mind. Before you can successfully recognize the emotional state of friends and strangers, you must first master the TUNE IN process of reflecting on your own significant life experiences. The intimate self-knowledge of your own eMotions and the eStates they generate, will then teach you everything you need to know about recognizing the emotional states of others.

Six Universal eMotions

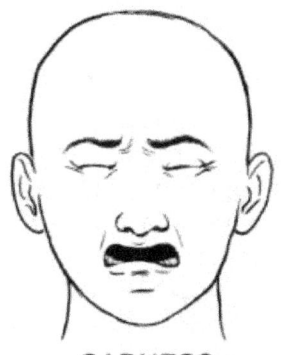

SADNESS

Sadness
(Includes Regret, Despair, Blame and Humiliation.)

Instinctual movement:
Immobile, sluggish, tired, depressed.

When we experience a loss, death or separation, the stress response of sadness and grief slows our metabolism and through tears, we release the associated biochemistry. When we are sad or continually disappointed, feelings of despair shut down our movement to allow us to rest and recharge from the loss.

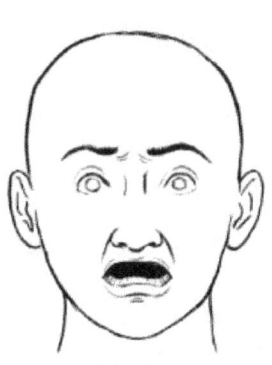

FEAR

Anxiety
(Fear)

Instinctual movement:
Fearful, nervous, reactive, tense

As we experience fear, our muscles become spring-loaded with tension. Wound tight, we brace in a defensive posture as our conscious minds attend to the source of fear. If a fearful mind continues unabated, chronic worry and anxiety develops, leaving our brains wired in a fear-feedback loop. A heightened state of fear quickly drains energy as our metabolism works overtime in a fight or flight stress response, many times related to an imaginary fear-filled reality.

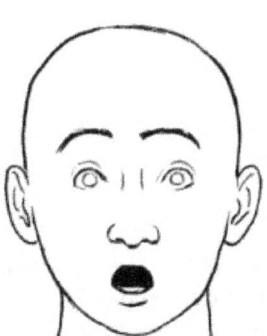

CRAVING

Craving
(Desire)

Instinctual movement:
Hunger, desirous, obsessive behavior

Desire is the most powerful instinctual directive of life. It's the reason why we're all here. The core competency of sex manifests in a continual pursuit of the pleasures found in the higher eMotions. Desire gets us motivated to eat, drink and breathe, to be social and have sex—in short, to take the necessary action and achieve the objects of our desire. The downside of desire is obsessive tendencies or addictions to external sources of pleasure such as food, alcohol, drugs, or sex. Smart phones and the Internet provide a dopamine-rich experience, which is why many today are addicted to their electronic gadgets.

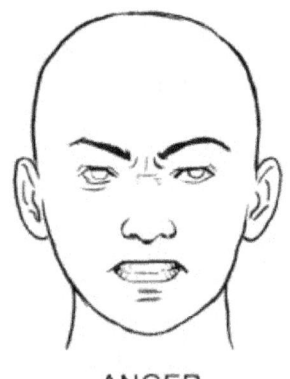

ANGER

Resentment
(Anger)

Instinctual movement:
Charged, aggressive action, enraged

The stress response of anger powers up the body for aggressive, competitive action. With adrenaline pumping through our veins, we experience an energy that is strong enough to prompt us to take forceful action. In unbridled anger, our rational intelligence all but shuts down, leaving a potentially hostile primal intelligence in charge. Anger redirects blood flow (energy) to the large muscle groups, prompting us to take aggressive action. Annoyance, irritability and resentment are conscious reminders that our spirit is operating in anger.

Happiness
(Includes Neutrality, Willingness, Forgiveness and Understanding.)

Instinctual Movement:
Energetic, excited, full of life

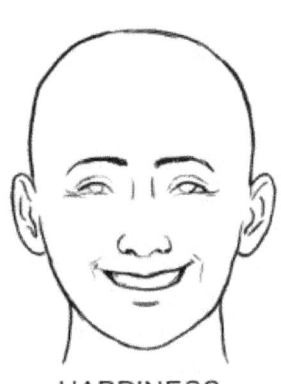

HAPPINESS

With minimized stress and our survival needs met, feel-good biochemicals flood our bloodstream, leaving us feeling happy and content. We feel happiest when we are involved in positive social relationships and satisfying work, and feel empowered to live uninhibited by external factors. Without emotional tension to weigh us down, our energy soars. We experience carefree feelings and an authentic enjoyment of life. Being happy inhibits our anxiety, providing a genuine rest for the body and brain.

Love
(Includes Serenity & Bliss.)

Instinctual movement:
Electrified, weightless, ecstatic

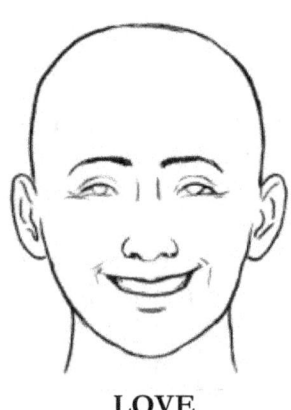

LOVE

Love electrifies both body and brain. Like a psychedelic drug, the magical experience of love elevates consciousness above the stressful realities of life. When we are in love, anxiety and social tension is reduced by the connection with another's energy. The intense sensations of love and sex are so pleasurable and so powerful that we are innately drawn to return to love when we're not experiencing its electrifying state. Indeed, the happiest people around are those in loving, mutually-satisfying relationships.

These six universal eMotions are instinctual and are integral to our basic behaviors. Their expression and movements play an important role in surviving everyday challenges. In their purest form, there is beauty to each type of life experience. As infants, we are pure eMotion. As we travel down the road of life, we pick up both trash and treasure, and our primal intelligence adapts as a result of our significant emotional experiences. We become wiser or weaker as a result of the pleasures and pains we encounter. This energy programming—or eMemory—is how each remembered ping is encoded into our emotional software.

eMemory: eMotion Fine-Tuned with Experience

As mentioned earlier, when we experience something that is genuinely frightening or stressful, our primal intelligence learns from the experience. At a minimum, we subconsciously learn to avoid it. As adaption is a core competency, the encoding of emotional energy is a living process: Our brain and body are continually updated with every significant emotional experience we encounter. This is the role of emotional memory, or what I call eMemory.

While your rational intelligence is prone to forget, your primal intelligence remembers everything. For example, when you encounter negative energy (such as an angry person or a stressful situation), your primal intelligence remembers the associated factors (the tone of voice, the body language, the facial expression) and records them in an attempt to avoid the same situation in the future.

As children, we learned by example. If you had high-energy role models, you more than likely respond to stress in a positive, healthy manner. If you experienced emotionally dysfunctional role models, those negative behaviors were encoded and may now be triggering eMemory programs that inform your eMotions. As we've learned, most pings—those significant experiences that impact our energy levels—originate from our interactions with people. Understanding our people pings, managing their impacts and ensuring that the eMemories we encode are memories of controlled and responsive behavior, lie in our ability to read the eMotions of others. Like it or not, we are social creatures, caught in a tightly spun web of life, continually impacted by the energy of those around us. To remain high around low-energy people, TUNE IN to their energy and TURN ON a strategy for dealing positively with them.

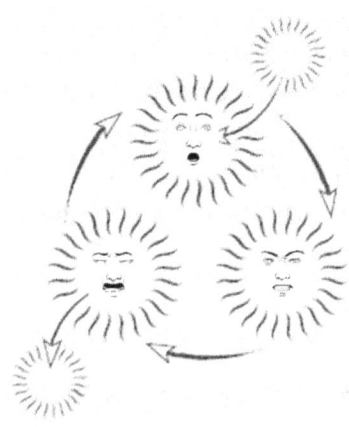

Emotional Ecology

As we make our way along the road of life, our environment naturally changes. People come and go, providing our lives with a broad spectrum of life experience. Our web of life is electric—energy flows continually to us through the emotional energy of others. We connect and disconnect constantly with our fellow man. We make friends and fight enemies. We bond with coworkers and condemn the neighbors. We give our energy to suitors then take it away. This network of energetic communication—the exchanges of energy with other people—is called *emotional ecology*. In terms of spirit, it's the unseen web of life that tightly connects all living things. And as it's an energetic extension of who you are, best to pay attention to its state of health and well-being. If people in your web of life are not healthy and happy, energy management is in order.

We must remember that eMotions are not an isolated function of primal intelligence. Our eMotions are physical and mental expressions of our energetic state of mind—our eState. As mentioned earlier, upwards of 90% of communication is non-verbal. That means there is a lot of energetic communication going on around us and our brain is in on the conversation.

We are more likely to recognize these ecological moments when there is a direct interaction with another person. A glare, a terse conversation, or an inappropriate gesture and we're pinged. However, not only face-to-face interactions can cause us grief. In today's world, our emotional ecology expands onto the highways (with road rage) and into cyberspace. We get pings from posts and are subject to cyber-bullying. With instant messaging, texts and social media sites we try to convey our eMotions (with rational intelligence), gain sympathy from others or be publically ridiculed by our enemies. In the end, gaining emotional intelligence about others requires that we use our in-tune-ition to access our primal intelligence to gain the rational awareness as to what state of mind they're in.

The odds are that your primal intelligence already knows what mood your partner or boss is in. TUNE IN and trust your intuition to tell you what eState they are operating in. The mirror neurons in our brain replicate the eMotions of those around us automatically, so there's a good chance you can accurately identify another's eMotion. Your conscious awareness helps in rationally connecting you to their emotional energy without being drained by their negativity.

For example, if you TUNE IN and intuit that someone is angry, use that information to understand how to best deal with the aggressive energy, even if it takes a TURN ON of courage to walk away.

As we learned, our primal intelligence has already identified that emotional energy in others. If we're not mindful, this subconscious awareness can shift our energy and we may find ourselves in a defensive state of mind. Around all people, there is a constant onslaught of energetic signals that can prove pervasive. All this incoming energy needs to be filtered and interpreted by our primal intelligence to keep us in tune to our emotional ecology.

> For health and happiness, TUNE IN to both your state and the energy state of others.

Likewise, your own emotional state of mind can affect those around you. If your energy is aggressive, anxious or depressed, people can feel your emotional weight. People may tend to avoid you in an effort to protect their own energy levels. If you sense that your energy is drained, you are most likely draining the energy in others. In contrast, if you feel happy and optimistic, the positive flow of energy will lift the spirits of those around you. In a high spirit, we inspire others. To improve our interactions with other people, our eMemories must be updated (TURN ON) as our primal intelligence learns to survive in social environments effectively.

No matter how rationally intelligent you are, your primal intelligence remains busy orchestrating the living processes that help you survive. To be successful at surviving any social interaction, embed in your consciousness positive eMemories that auto-generate high emotional energy around people. Continue to befriend your primal intelligence every day and TURN ON the person you know you can be.

Tomorrow we will examine how powerful your spirit can really be in keeping you alive.

Day Nine Exercise

Today you have learned the six universal eMotions. It is not surprising that you may have found much of the same basic energies powering your reactions to stress in the past week. Learning to TURN ON and train the brain to resolve pings as they occur is the next focus of your quest. This week, concentrate on keeping your energy high, specifically around those who are notoriously negative. TUNE IN and identify not only your eState, but the eState of others who ping you in the moment.

Continue strengthening your brain by using the Odyssey Methodology to complete the Quest Journal.

odyssey

The Odyssey Methodology

1. TUNE IN

Remember
your day

Close your eyes and mentally review your day.
Remember the pings—the people, places or events—that caused you stress, then determine the eMotion that was triggered by the ping.
- *A ping is a significant emotional experience that shifts your energy.*
- *You remember pings because of their emotional energy.*

Record
your pings

Pick the three most impactful pings of the day and record. [PING – box 1]
For each ping, choose the eState that best suits how you responded to the eMotion experienced and record. [TUNE IN – box 2]

Reflect
your energy

Focus on how the ping affected your energetic state.
Teach your brain what the ping feels like (i.e. tension, anxiety, etc.).
Mentally label the feelings with a rational understanding of the eMotion.

2. TURN ON

Raise
your eState

Choose an eState higher than the one experienced for each ping and record. [TURN ON - box 3]

Replay
your day

Close your eyes and with palm on forehead, visualize reliving each ping in the higher eState. Imagine the same people, place or event ping in the new eState.
- *Include all aspects of the more empowering eMotion. See yourself being confident, responding authentically with pleasant gestures, facial expressions, calm voice, etc.*

Resolve
your pings

Set action to neutralize the ping-energy. Ask yourself: What task or solution is necessary to fix a problem? Reconnect with a person? What steps are required to repair what is broken / disconnected? In courage, take action!
- *Set an intention to follow through on the commitment. With palm on forehead, mentally rehearse being courageous / optimistic / accepting of the situation. Visualize the new behavior. Train the brain for a high-energy response to stress.*

odyssey

The Quest Journal
- Day Nine -

Date: _____ Day: S — M — T — W — Th — F — S

eState	eMotion	
Experience	*Feeling*	*Energy*
Enlightenment	Nirvana	1000
Peace	Bliss	600
Joy	Serenity	540
Love	Reverence	500
Reason	Understanding	400
Acceptance	Forgiveness	350
Optimism	Willingness	310
Trust	Neutrality	250
Courage	Affirmation	200
Pride	Scorn	175
Anger	Hate	150
Desire	Craving	125
Fear	Anxiety	100
Grief	Regret	75
Apathy	Despair	50
Guilt	Blame	30
Shame	Humiliation	20

GRATITUDE
1.
2.
3.

If the only prayer you say in your whole life is 'thank you' that should suffice.— Meister Eckhart

PING—a significant emotional experience

Duration: ___hr. ___min.

TUNE IN

TURN ON

PING—a significant emotional experience

Duration: ___hr. ___min.

TUNE IN

TURN ON

PING—a significant emotional experience

Duration: ___hr. ___min.

TUNE IN

TURN ON

Emotion hierarchy adapted from Map of Consciousness: *Power vs. Force.* David R. Hawkins, M.D. Ph.D., 1995.

It has yet to be proven that intelligence has any survival value.

Arthur C. Clarke

Day Ten—#1 Road Rule: SURVIVE!

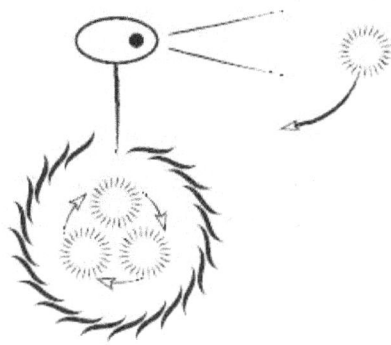

Our eMotions keep us alive by prompting us to act. The energy for motion produced by our brain and body are auto-responses that are fine-tuned as a result of life experiences. As primal survival instincts, being aggressive, addictive or anxious is normal in the sense that they are the basic traits of being alive. However, on a daily basis, these primitive energies can cause real harm, leading to emotional, mental and physical disorders. To a modern human consciousness, chronic primal eMotions are a sign that not all is right.

Our most primal emotional energies can easily lock our consciousness into survival mode. Here, constant thoughts of worry, lust or resentment disrupt our inner lives. Left unmanaged, anyone can design a self-created living hell. Alienation, social phobia, anxiety and depression leave us feeling alone, completely unaware that our primal intelligence is simply trying to help us survive the challenges and stressors we may be facing.

It is important to reiterate that, as well as moving your own body, your eMotions can move other people. As the primal communication mechanism, the emotional energy we give out and exchange with others helps us coordinate behavior. Despite the challenges and frustrations we may experience with our family, friends and fellow man, we need a community around us to survive. eMotions help us do that.

Remember that eons before language evolved, our early ancestors used only non-verbal mechanisms to communicate with others to get things done. Even though we now harness the power of language, the grunts and groans of non-verbal communication remain core to our interactions with the people around us. As stated earlier, our emotional ecology is a tightly-knit energy-exchange network, where eMotions—specifically emotional behaviors—are used to coordinate action with others so that we survive. That's why communication is often cited as being 90% non-verbal—our life-energy speaks much louder than words to express our true intention.

For leaders, managers, parents and partners, it is the grunts, groans, growls and gestures that remain the dominant communication method heard and acted upon by others, not the words and intellectual reasoning we so cleverly speak. If you are to survive—and effectively influence other people to your way of thinking—become effective at thriving in your emotional ecology. Begin to treat others as you would have them treat you. Actively strengthen your ability to positively communicate in order to cut through the emotional barriers that do exist. Providing high-energy to the energy-needy can and does disarm potential conflicts. Continue to train the brain (TUNE IN—TURN ON) to actively elevate your energy when confronted by people in low-energy eStates.

As social creatures with primal survival instincts, we naturally favor positive social interactions over social conflict. While friends bring us pleasure, foes mean pain. (A momentary glance into a stranger's eyes can tell us if there is need for concern.) Without this friend or foe awareness, the human race would not survive. Driven by primal intelligence, our social relationships are part of what makes us the dominant species on the planet. Life connected is strong.

In today's world, without dinosaurs to worry about, surviving is primarily defined in a social context. Our partner, parents, family, friends, co-workers, neighbors and strangers can all trigger a ping and instantly become potential enemies to our primal intelligence. An aggressive tone of voice or a demeaning look and—ping!—we're on the defensive. If we're not careful, we can end up with brains wired with a competitive mindset. We become hyper-aware of people and their problems to the point of paranoia. We begin thinking too much about other people's opinions and judgments, and compete cognitively in response to their negative eMotions. This is why it's difficult at times to get certain people out of your mind: He or she has pinged you and is now a threat to your survival.

> TUNE IN: When your spirit is in survival mode, you are aggressive, addicted and anxious, competing with others on the road of life.

As negative as this all may sound, the survival directive is an evolutionary gift. Being competitive is perfectly natural, the spirit of which we must embrace and take very seriously. Survival is primal to your spirit.

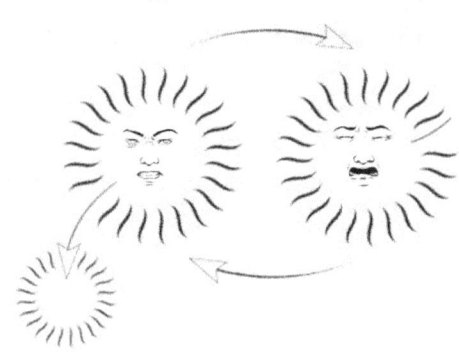

The Competitive Spirit

Being competitive is considered a valuable attribute in today's fast-paced world. It's also a key component to our survival. Without it, enemies would have long ago wiped out our ancestors. However, a competitive spirit—one that brings competitive energy into your interactions and pits you against the people around you—is also a spirit born of defensive eMotions that can leave you locked in survival mode. Being competitive may make you attractive in a business or athletic setting, but it can wreak havoc on your energy levels, directly affecting your state of health. Again, the key is to be energetically higher than your competitors.

For people in psychologically demanding roles, a constant competitive spirit can cause a serious energy drain. Taxing your brain to continuously analyze, organize and systemize in order to stay on top of your work and the competition means burning the midnight oil. This also requires your modern brain to be on 24/7. Like an engine running incessantly, you will inevitably run out of fuel. As we have discovered, a lack of energy will see both brain and body fall into an anxious or depressed state of mind. Again, energy management is the answer to thriving around your competitors.

Like everything in life, the energy-draining aspects of having a competitive spirit can be improved upon and fine-tuned. All that is needed is an improved self-awareness of the emotional energies generated moment-to-moment. Knowing yourself to such a heightened degree of consciousness immediately enables a more proactive approach that keeps energy high when pings do occur.

Again, practice makes perfect. Avoid becoming competitive with your spirit by pressuring it to be perfect all the time. Allow plenty of room to grow and adapt to this enlightened way of thinking. In the quest to develop charisma when it's needed most, continue learning from your people pings, treating them as life lessons. In time, your high-energy will be noticed by others. Your ability to TURN ON others with your more powerful energy will prove incredibly helpful in leading others to your way of thinking. This is what inspirational leadership is all about—getting people on your side. A true competitive advantage!

For now, and for your own health and happiness, continue to get to know yourself at a deeper emotional level. For the quest, let's further examine how the three most powerful and primitive instinctual programs can erode your well-being. This is repetitious, but the better you know your eMotions, the better in tune you will be to your own primal behaviors out in the real world. In time, you'll be able to recognize and neutralize pings in the moment as they occur, both in yourself and in others.

Here again, in more detail, we continue to explore the basic instinctual movements; the primal behaviors of aggression (anger), addiction (desire) and anxiety (fear), as seen from a spirit perspective.

The Spirit of Anger

The experience of anger oscillates on a spectrum between annoyance on one end and rage on the other. In between are sensations such as hatred, resentment, irritation, animosity, impatience and aggression, which are all components of an angry spirit. Experiencing anger is very common. Every one of my clients has reported anger in one form or another. I am still amazed that nearly everyone experiences road rage, or gets into arguments with loved ones over silly things, all because their state of mind is charged unknowingly by eMemories of anger.

As a child, I grew up around what is now referred to as anger management issues. My firsthand experience of anger instilled equally enraged eMemories in me, and led me to use anger as a dominant survival response to stressful challenges in my own life. I would routinely feel resentful of others, and fume over silly things. I didn't want to be angry—*my eMemories were just encoded with aggression*. With anger survival programming instilled in my biology, I would find myself getting angry about being angry. How neurotic is that!

Through a journey of self-discovery and improvement, I came to understand that my anger wasn't my own authentic state— like second-hand clothes, anger had been passed on to the next generation. Realizing that adaption is a core competency, and that the brain and body could learn how to be and do anything, I set out to change my angry state of mind to one of courage and trust. The continuous improvement worked! I became much less upset over the little things and came to understand myself at a deeper emotional level.

In scientific terms, anger occurs when the pituitary gland produces and releases large amounts of andrenocorticotropic hormone, which causes the adrenal cortex to release corticosteroids throughout the body and brain.[9] By noting my pings, I found this biochemical chain reaction

---

[9] Jezova et al., 1995; Sapolsky, 1992.

can occur quickly when I faced a stressful situation. Without learning to shake it off with the TUNE IN—TURN ON process, I would have remained stuck in anger's aggressive energy.

A Loss of Reason

Rage is perhaps the most destructive form of anger. Rage is thought to be an emergency reaction based on deep instinctual programming. We tend to express rage when we face a threat to our pride, position, status or dignity.

An enraged person may lose much of his or her capacity for rational thought and reasoning, and may act, sometimes violently, on his or her impulses. An enraged person may also experience a form of tunnel vision, muffled hearing, increased heart rate and hyperventilation. Attention is often focused solely on the source of anger. Some research suggests that an individual is more susceptible to feelings of depression and anxiety if he or she experiences anger on a frequent basis. However, health implications become much worse if an individual represses their feelings of rage. Cardiac stress and hypertension are key health complications that can occur in people who stifle their emotional engine on a regular basis.

Self-esteem is a key factor in angry behavior.[10] Evidence has shown that individuals who suffer from low self-esteem may compensate by inflicting physical harm onto others. Some psychologists see rage as being internally focused—as an attack on one's self rather than on others. They also believe such self-inflicted rage is a narcissistic response to one's past experience of pain and trauma.[11]

The good news is that as a primary instinctual eState, anger plays an important role in our survival. Anger instigates riots, wars, cultural and personal change. When we mindfully utilize anger in a positive manner (i.e. without rage and with rational intention), we can influence change in the behavior of others and motivate them for a better good. Remember, even Jesus got angry. Upturning the merchant tables in the temple communicated just how serious he was about his values. The key to healthy change management is to inspire rather than expire those in your path of progress.

---

[10] Walker & Bright, 2009.
[11] King, R., 2007.

The Spirit of Desire

As another deep-seated survival instinct, the eState of desire permeates everything we do. As a core competency, our need for energy is constant and never ending, which means we constantly crave food, water, air, safety and sex—the key elements of survival.

As sexual creatures, social desires are often at the forefront of our minds. As a result, we are always interested in sources of social pleasantries and friendships. We crave spending time with family and friends, constantly on the lookout for the next energy-positive social connection.

Desire keeps us hungry for our next energy-rich meal. To our human consciousness, desire manifests as a continual yearning for pleasure. While our attention fixates on energy-positive opportunities, our hunger pains compel us to get up and get it. In a spirit of desire, we can easily become the donkey teased forward by a dangling carrot. Being in a state of constant craving is in many ways natural. However, when a desire-state becomes chronic, addictions and obsessions are again a sign that not all is right.

Like anger, desire has its own sub-spectrum of feelings. On one end we find momentary daydreams of something you want, while on the opposite end we find is lust—a powerful psychological force that produces intense obsessions. In between, we can experience attraction, aspiration, fascination, motivation and passion.

At the more forceful end of the scale, lust is an intense feeling of desire. Lust can take on many forms, such as the lust for knowledge, the lust for wealth, power, sex, and food.[12] Lust is similar to rage in that an extreme desire can shut down the higher brain functions.

Many religions separate the definitions of passion and lust by categorizing lust as a passion for something forbidden. In Roman Catholicism, lust is one of the Seven Deadly Sins. In Islam, intentional lascivious glances are forbidden and are considered the first step toward adultery, rape and other antisocial behavior. In Hinduism, the Bhagavad Gita declares that lust is one of the gates to *Naraka*, or hell.

As we learned earlier, the negative consequence of desire is endless wants. Desire begets desire. When we get what we think will make us happy, happiness itself often eludes us. When we get that new job, we want more money. When we get that new car, we notice the newer models. When we secure a perfect partner, we may lust over complete strangers. In a spirit of desire, we constantly want more and are rarely satisfied. That's why, in order to attain health and happiness, we must mindfully manage desires by the TURN ON of high-energy acceptance of what we have right now.

---

[12] Richard Lazarus with Bernice N Lazarus, *Passion and Reason: Making Sense of Our Emotions*, 1994, New York: Oxford University Press.

The Spirit of Fear

Every one of my clients, at some point in their quest, woke up to the fact that fear dominated their state of mind. By our primal nature, our brain is fear-conditioned; meaning our state of mind will always remember stressful experiences and keep us on alert to avoid them. Without energy management, the older we get, the more anxious we can become.

This isn't surprising. For millions of years our ancestors feared just about everything—where the next meal was coming from, what changes lurked around the corner, what darkness meant. Those who were oblivious to the dangers were killed, their DNA removed from the gene pool.

As living creatures, our fundamental state of mind is always a bit anxious. Fear is normal in the sense that we must remain permanently alert to things that might harm us. But while our ancestors dealt with real fears, many of the fears we face today are created by our active imagination. Hence, the more fear we feel, the more we worry. The more we worry, the more our rational mind informs us of the fears we need to avoid. In a spirit of fear, anything can become a source of harm.

Anxiety often precedes depression. If you question those who've experienced depression and discuss their trigger points, the answers are remarkably similar. Many depressed people find they were first afraid of something that loomed ahead. For each person experiencing anxiety, there is a real personal challenge on the line that needs to be tackled. With avoidance, the anxiety only escalates and they consequently find it difficult to resolve the source of fear.

This is an important point. A fear response is healthy because it motivates you to take action and survive the threat, be it perceived or real. But a continuous state of fear can wire your brain to be chronically anxious. In today's complex society, if you question people in private, you'll find everyone is anxious to some degree. Persistent anxiety is the most common mental illness in America, with approximately 40 million adults affected.

Generalized Anxiety

Anxiety can be adapted into your biology as a generalized state of mind that occurs without identifiable pings, or emotional triggers. It is a feeling of tension, worry and concern even though all may be okay.

Generalized anxiety is not the same as acute fear. Fear is an appropriate cognitive and emotional response to a perceived threat and is concerned with escape and avoidance (the fight or flight response). Anxiety, on the other hand, can create feelings of fear, worry, uneasiness and dread no matter whether there actually is any tangible stressor. Those who have suffered from it know how terrible it feels—anxiety genuinely motivates people to drink alcohol, smoke cigarettes or end their lives.

Anxiety can appear on many levels of the fear spectrum, and can manifest as phobia, social anxiety, obsessive-compulsive behaviors and post-traumatic stress. The physical effects of anxiety may include heart palpitations, tachycardia, muscle weakness and tension, fatigue, nausea, chest pains, shortness of breath, headache, stomach aches, or tension headaches.

As the body prepares to deal with a threat, blood pressure, heart rate, perspiration, blood flow to the major muscle groups are increased, while immune and digestive functions are inhibited (via the fight or flight response). External signs of anxiety may include pallor, sweating, trembling and papillary dilation. For someone who suffers anxiety this can lead to a panic attack.

Panic Attacks

Although not everyone who has anxiety experiences panic attacks, they are a common symptom. Panic attacks usually come without warning and although the fear is generally irrational, the subjective perception of danger is very real. A person experiencing a panic attack will often feel as if he or she is about to die or lose consciousness. Between panic attacks, people with panic disorder tend to suffer from anticipated anxiety, or a fear of having a panic attack. This can lead to the development of phobias.

Social Anxiety

Social phobia is also a common symptom of someone diagnosed with generalized anxiety and depression. Humans are, naturally, a social species who generally require social acceptance. Because of the importance of being accepted among society and conforming to its rules and norms, we dread the disapproval of others. It is this apprehension of being judged by others that is the basic cause of the anxiety we may feel in a social environment. Without self-knowledge and improvement, social anxiety can keep us isolated in our metaphorical cave.

Decision Anxiety

Decision anxiety is an inability to make decisions and is generally accompanied by an overly active rational intelligence. In a decision-making context, unpredictability or uncertainty may trigger emotional responses in anxious individuals, which reinforce the underlying feeling of low self-confidence. Again, without the strength of self-knowledge, we can become insecure and afraid of making decisions.

Surviving Survival Mode

I cannot emphasize enough that the anxieties, aggressions and addictions you may experience are all natural, primal auto-responses to stress. Without effective energy management, your thinking process can easily become powered by one of these primal energies. The only reason why these primal behaviors can become chronic is that our brain literally becomes wired in a cognitive-emotive feedback loop. If you continuously think about a certain resentment or fear, the neurons in your brain form habitual ways of thinking in a survival-based paradigm—your brain becomes hard-wired to survival mode.

As humans, we can become aware of our survival-based triggers. In a quest for high-energy states, we can use our Observer consciousness to TUNE IN to our pings. We can reflect on the underlying emotional processes before it turns into a dysfunctional personality. The corrective action will be discussed in more detail, but for now, continue to focus and learn your pings each and every day.

From an unknown author:

> *Be careful of your thoughts, for your thoughts become your words.*
> *Be careful of your words, for your words become your actions.*
> *Be careful of your actions, for your actions become your habits.*
> *Be careful of your habits, for your habits become your character.*
> *Be careful of your character, for your character becomes your destiny.*

As we will find in tomorrow's reading, the human condition is both a blessing and a burden. The good news is that unlike animals, we can raise our state of mind and remove ourselves from a self-created living hell.

Day Ten Exercise

The TURN ON step of the Odyssey Methodology is now becoming increasingly important in our quest. The visualization exercise trains the brain to replay a higher, more empowering eMotion when a ping occurs. Think of TURN ON as a weight lifting exercise. To get emotionally stronger, you must lift the emotional weight. Use your active imagination to visualize reliving the ping in high-energy or better yet, be courageous in taking action to resolve the challenge.

Continue to use the Odyssey Methodology to complete the Quest Journal.

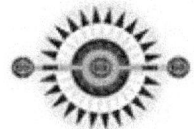

odyssey

The Odyssey Methodology

1. TUNE IN

Remember
your day

Close your eyes and mentally review your day.
Remember the pings—the people, places or events—that caused you stress, then determine the eMotion that was triggered by the ping.
- *A ping is a significant emotional experience that shifts your energy.*
- *You remember pings because of their emotional energy.*

Record
your pings

Pick the three most impactful pings of the day and record. [PING]
For each ping, choose the eState that best suits how you responded to the eMotion experienced and record. [TUNE IN]

Reflect
your energy

Focus on how the ping affected your energetic state.
Teach your brain what the ping feels like (i.e. tension, anxiety, etc.).
Mentally label the feelings with a rational understanding of the eMotion.

2. TURN ON

Raise
your eState

Choose an eState higher than the one experienced for each ping and record. [TURN ON - box 3]

Replay
your day

Close your eyes and with palm on forehead, visualize reliving each ping in the higher eState. Imagine the same people, place or event ping in the new eState.
- *Include all aspects of the more empowering eMotion. See yourself being confident, responding authentically with pleasant gestures, facial expressions, calm voice, etc.*

Resolve
your pings

Set action to neutralize the ping-energy. Ask yourself: What task or solution is necessary to fix a problem? Reconnect with a person? What steps are required to repair what is broken / disconnected? In courage, take action!
- *Set an intention to follow through on the commitment. With palm on forehead, mentally rehearse being courageous / optimistic / accepting of the situation. Visualize the new behavior. Train the brain for a high-energy response to stress.*

odyssey

The Quest Journal
- Day Ten -

Date: ___ Day: S — M — T — W — Th — F — S

eState	eMotion	
Experience	*Feeling*	*Energy*
Enlightenment	Nirvana	1000
Peace	Bliss	600
Joy	Serenity	540
Love	Reverence	500
Reason	Understanding	400
Acceptance	Forgiveness	350
Optimism	Willingness	310
Trust	Neutrality	250
Courage	Affirmation	200
Pride	Scorn	175
Anger	Hate	150
Desire	Craving	125
Fear	Anxiety	100
Grief	Regret	75
Apathy	Despair	50
Guilt	Blame	30
Shame	Humiliation	20

PING—a significant emotional experience

Duration: ___hr. ___min.

TUNE IN

TURN ON

PING—a significant emotional experience

Duration: ___hr. ___min.

TUNE IN

TURN ON

PING—a significant emotional experience

Duration: ___hr. ___min.

TUNE IN

TURN ON

GRATITUDE
1.
2.
3.

If the only prayer you say in your whole life is 'thank you' that should suffice.—Meister Eckhart

Emotion hierarchy adapted from Map of Consciousness: *Power vs. Force*. David R. Hawkins, M.D. Ph.D., 1995.

Most of our strong emotions arise from assuming the reality of something that is unreal.

The Dalai Lama

Day Eleven—The Human Condition, Part 2

At times, our eMotions seem to come out of nowhere. In an instant, we can be bursting with happiness, paralyzed with anxiety, or boiling with resentment. As you've experienced in the quest so far, eStates are automatic responses, pre-programmed in our DNA and fine-tuned with life experience.

By helping us survive, eMotions provide us with the automatic instinctual reactions to a range of events or circumstance. These include both real physical dangers and imagined threats. Our rational intelligence allows us to envision ourselves outside the here and now, placing us in situations that may not occur until the future. Yet, and this is an important point, our primal intelligence doesn't know the future—our spirit lives in the right here right now.

This can turn into a real handicap because in memory, negative emotional memories can easily outweigh positive ones. This can be a real hindrance because the fear-orientation keeps attention focused on what's not right. Soon, neural habits of worry, guilt and regret lock our consciousness in negative thinking processes.

Have you ever woken up at 3 a.m. with something stressful on your mind? Or, does your consciousness replay the pings of the day at bedtime, holding the restfulness of sleep at gunpoint by endless analysis and debate?

At a pinnacle of my corporate career, I remember replaying the events of the day over and over again in my head. I vividly recall lying awake late at night, scheming and challenging my peers in my mind. I analyzed what I had said and did in an ill attempt to protect myself in the competitive jungle at work. To my primal intelligence, I was still in the Serengeti, but to my rational intelligence, the modern dangers were a lot more complex. And frightening.

If you use your brain professionally, you can wire your brain to be on all the time, creating cognitive habits of thinking that are difficult to turn off. Working in a psychologically demanding role, it's not surprising that your brain has adapted to analyze, decipher, judge, create and move thoughts around. Being rational creatures, we easily forget that with every cognitive action, energy flows and is consumed.

On the road of life, keeping you alive is the number one priority of your primal intelligence. Even if you are plotting a takeover of a competitor six months in the future, your primal intelligence can power up your defenses right now—preparing you for the battle ahead. Back in the Serengeti, this made sense. Living 100,000 years ago, you would be hiding behind a bush as you prepared to kill your dinner. In anticipation of the attack, your primal intelligence has already powered up your body for action. Your heart rate has increased, your blood has been diverted to your muscles, your digestion has slowed and your attention has focused on the object of desire, all before the attack has even taken place.

The same thing happens when you wake you up at 3 a.m. Your subconscious pings you awake because it knows the importance of that presentation you'll give tomorrow or of that call you have to make. To your primal intelligence, such stresses are not only in your imagination, but right now, in the same way that the stress of killing your dinner occurs in the anticipation of the event. Remember, your spirit operates right here right now, even as your higher intelligence is plotting a corporate takeover that won't happen for weeks.

So the next time you are awakened with an active conscious mind, say thank you to your primal intelligence for keeping you alive, but TURN ON the strengthened self-awareness to understand what your spirit is telling you, namely to take action to survive the threat. Listening to your spirit is the key to domesticating its insistent survival-driven nature.

Taming the Intelligent Spirit

With the capacity for self-awareness, we can actively visualize ourselves travelling along an imaginary road of life. We can visualize ourselves getting promoted or fired, see ourselves fail or succeed. With eMemories, we can relive a mistake repeatedly in Technicolor brilliance.

If you have been subject to an extraordinary emotional experience (such as a traumatic relationship breakup, a car wreck, front-line combat, abuse, a critical accident, etc.), you may find yourself reliving the experience automatically. This is commonly referred to as post-traumatic stress disorder (PTSD). PTSD is not only common with severely impaired veterans; other, non-combat related stressful situations can trigger PTSD as well.

Given enough emotional charge of a stressful ping, anyone can experience some form of PTSD by reliving a stressful event over again in our minds. Because of their energetic impact on our psyche, significant emotional experiences can easily become encoded into our physiology. We then may mentally relive an emotional event repeatedly even though it occurred years ago.

We can remember the bad moments of our childhood. We can desire a better house or a different partner. We can imagine tomorrow and stress ourselves with all the things we must do. As animals with higher intelligence, we create mountains out of a mole hill and unwittingly torment ourselves about the daunting tasks that lie ahead.

Possessing both a conscious and subconscious mind, the human condition comes with a particular health challenge: *What we think about and remember has an immediate effect on our state of mind. What we worry about worries our spirit. Without being grounded in self-awareness, the disparity between what we think and what we feel can and does lead to mental illness.*

"Be mindful of your thoughts, as they betray you," said a wise Obi-Wan Kenobi. To tame the animal within, identify the primal energies powering your thinking process. Begin to TUNE IN and label the eState in the moment—be it anger, desire or fear. Begin to tell yourself, "I am angry" or "I am anxious" when pings occur. Keep recording your pings and active thoughts in your Quest Journal. Learn from your pings of life every day. Teach your modern brain what your primal brain is doing under stress.

Fine-Tuning Active Imagination

The same creative process that drives you to imagine negative things can be put to good use. When your spirit is powered positively using eStates such as trust, optimism and acceptance, your mind becomes quiet. With high-energy fueling imagination, you effortlessly think outside the box and visualize yourself doing things that are constructive, rather than destructive. This proactive approach keeps the energy of your spirit naturally high and out of survival mode.

To facilitate the cognitive improvement process, TURN ON your brain by closing your eyes and placing a palm flat on your forehead. This has a calming effect by bringing blood flow back to your brain's executive center. (Again, stress notoriously diverts blood from the higher brain into the primal one.) The palm-on-forehead technique also activates learning. With more energy (i.e. oxygen to the executive center), you're able to think more rationally about a ping without the destructive stress of the eMotion. Mentally raise your eState by imagining yourself reliving the event from a higher, more empowering eMotion. In your mind's eye, see yourself acting, behaving and saying what you truly wanted. Aim to understand the ping and its emotional impact. For Olympic athletes, visualization has been proven to improve performance in the stress of the moment of competition. By visualizing yourself acting in a high-energy state with your partner, parent or colleagues, you are providing your brain a new, more constructive option in dealing with challenging people pings in the future.

In our private mental world, we assume our higher sense of reason is in command. However, our primal intelligence (with its emotional brain that powers the thinking process) is really in control when stress pings our psyche. The subconscious emotional energy that moves your muscles is the same energy that moves your thoughts.

> TURN ON: Manage the underlying emotional energy, and you'll gain greater control of the powerhouse that is your active imagination.

In our conscious minds, we're free to imagine a beautiful peaceful garden or dwell on the horrors of drought and famine. Remember that no matter what you imagine, your primal intelligence will respond in real time. If you think about a fearful situation, you'll feel anxiety. If you anticipate an event optimistically, your state of mind becomes more willing to respond positively. A confident choice is not solely a rational one. It includes a subconscious emotional TUNE IN as well. Learn to integrate the two with strengthened in-tune-ition. Ground indecision and active thoughts on what your intuitive wisdom tells you to be true. In short, learn to trust your instincts to resolve the challenges of life.

What Lies Beneath

Whatever you think or imagine, you must consider that your spirit is in on the conversation. To keep your state of mind in the healthy spectrum of eMotions, actively TUNE IN to the energy operating your thinking process. Ask yourself, "What am I feeling right now? What eState am I operating in?"

Paying attention to a negative thought is like fuelling a fire. For health and happiness, never feed a negative thought with conscious attention. Instead, pay attention to discerning the eMotion that is moving the thought in the first place. Identify the eState your mind is operating in. Again, the initial phase in neutralizing overly-active thoughts is to first TUNE IN to the underlying emotive power. This is what self-awareness is all about: *knowing your state of mind at all times.*

> TURN ON: To conserve energy, instead of repeatedly analyzing a thought, ask, "Which eMotion is powering the thought?" Then act to replace the low-energy thought with a high-energy solution.

While your rational mind is off imagining a virtual reality, your primal intelligence is always in tune with the reality that is immediately around you. When you place attention on your emotional state (TUNE IN), the self-awareness helps you gage the emotional energy you're operating with, and with such self-knowledge, you can TURN ON a higher state of mind.

This TUNE IN—TURN ON process was very beneficial for my client Greg who experienced chronic anger. Instead of telling him he shouldn't experience anger, I suggested he TUNE IN to the resentment he was feeling and TURN ON accepting it fully and wholeheartedly. I even congratulated him on his anger, because it meant he was passionate about something. The upside of anger, as we've discussed, is that it gets things done. We just needed to find out what Greg really wanted to have happen, without killing anyone in the process.

By tuning in and accepting his state of mind, Greg realized there were a few specific anger pings that were running nonstop. We talked about his anger triggers and what the best TURN ON strategies would be for him to neutralize the primal energies he was experiencing. For example, as a sales executive, Greg was out on the road making delivery and quality promises to customers. However, the production and quality managers of the company couldn't meet those deadlines, and Greg's promises looked foolish in the customer's eyes. Seen from Greg's point of view, this was a legitimate reason for becoming angry. To Greg, not keeping promises justified going to battle.

Learning to TUNE IN to his own pings, Greg became better at recognizing the triggers that engaged his anger. He taught himself not to get caught up in the "who" and "what" of his angry thoughts, but instead began observing how the emotional engine was operating his self-organizing living process.

With practice, Greg became better attuned to his primal operating system. When he listened to his in-tune-ition and placed more trust in his primal instincts, he realized he needed to use his emotional intensity to inspire said managers to fulfill his promises. He set an intention to use his aggressive energy for good not evil, and began learning from his anger triggers.

As a multimillion-dollar salesperson, Greg was *the* front-line of the company. His promises and handshake agreements were bringing in the big dollars that kept the business operating. And he was proud of that. The anger he expressed was his warrior cry—an emotional attempt to wake up the managers at the factory to keep the commitments he had made to ensure the sale.

In his Odyssey, Greg found that keeping promises—having integrity—was one of his deepest personal values. Violating integrity spurred Greg to go into battle and defend his integrity. Irritating and destructive as it was, Greg's aggressive sense of urgency played a valuable role in the company as it got things done. In neutralizing the rage response, I had Greg engage the TURN ON process and visualize himself being an inspirational leader—courageous, trustworthy, understanding—whenever integrity was pinged.

With strengthened self-awareness, Greg became motivated to become more of a leader, motivating and inspiring others with his own passion for integrity that lay behind the anger. Instead of letting anger get the best of him, Greg began channeling his passion for integrity, and with a few company speeches, he got the company on board to assist in helping him keep his promises. He became an advocate of honesty as the best policy, and the whole company benefitted from his authenticity. So did Greg's health, as his blood pressure and illicit drug use rapidly declined.

Once Greg started communicating his passion for integrity to his peers, people began helping him live up to his promises instead of running away from his anger. As a result, sales and operations began running more smoothly, and Greg felt more appreciated for the sales he made. In his new state of mind, Greg became a true life leader.

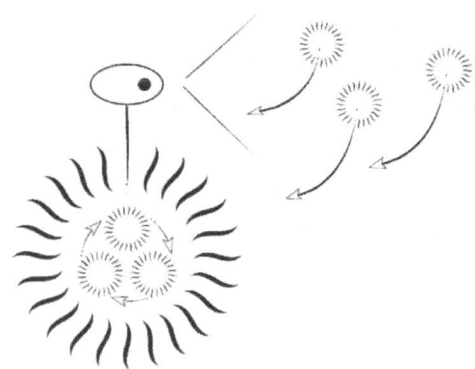

Developing a Leadership Mindset

If you're in an eState of anger, you think angry thoughts. If you're depressed, you dwell on dark thoughts. If you're happy, you find yourself whistling a happy tune. As spirits having a physical experience, we need to fully embrace all the eMotions on the spectrum of feeling alive. Not just the positive eStates, but the negative ones as well. For health and happiness, TUNE IN to the emotional energy that is operating beneath your conscious mind and learn what is valuable in your survival quest.

Modern Mental Stress

Millennia ago, back when our ancestors hunted mastodons and shared space with the mammoths, stress was a bona fide enemy. The stress our ancestors experienced was real. When a lion attacked, they ran. When the gnawing pain of hunger knocked on their consciousness, they hunted and gathered. Back in those times, people were moved to action by eMotion.

Today, life is a lot more complicated. The threats we face are rarely situations that require genuine fight or flight, but rather are self-induced psychological tortures: Will I be on time? Do they like me? Am I good enough? How will I pay for that? Did I make the right decision? Indeed, many of these psychological stresses exist only within our vivid imagination.

Time Pressures
The universal expectation to be on time penetrates everything we do. With time pressuring our daily tasks, it can mean the difference between enjoying the journey or aggressively chastising the slow bastards along our way. Raised in a culture where being first is rewarded, we feel tension and constant competitive pressure when we're not punctual. Add to the race of life perfectionist tendencies, and you find there is never enough time to enjoy what time you have.

Social Inadequacy
A fleeting thought—I'm not good enough—can pack a wallop that instantly zaps your energy and collapses any resident feelings of self-worth. As social creatures, we are instinctively aware of ourselves and our social standing. In our minds, there is always someone smarter, sexier or more cunning we have to look out for, which makes us competitive towards other people.

Professional Insecurity
With daily news of layoffs and redundancies, no one is safe from the fallout of an economic downturn. We remain on guard for signals pointing towards professional instability and experience real panic if our job disappears. In today's highly competitive market, neighbor competes against neighbor in a never-ending battle of survival of the fittest.

Financial Anxiety
Healthy individuals have an instinctive desire to provide the best for themselves and their family. Making it in today's world of luxury means mounting credit card debt, constricting mortgages, shrinking cash reserves and investments forever threatened with economic collapse. We are constantly on alert for downturn in cash flow and higher interest rates, which could send us into a financial abyss.

Cognitive Dysfunction
Cognitive chatter—the endless thoughts of self-doubt, self-blame, self-sabotage and self-regret—does more than cloud our consciousness. Random self-talk creates self-made mental arguments and spurs endless debate in already overly active minds. Decision making and focus becomes difficult in the never-ending analysis. When we desire sleep, we're instead plagued with a self-created hell where decisions and actions are constantly under attack by our insecurities and self-criticism.

All this cognitive stress—whether real or imagined—triggers a very real emotional response in both brain and body. Even the momentary thought of a threat can send a jolt of fear through the entire living system. Be it illusion or reality, an eMemory has the same physiological impact or emotional charge to the body. At every living moment, our brains respond to real, remembered or imagined impulses in the same way—as if the stressor were occurring right here and right now.

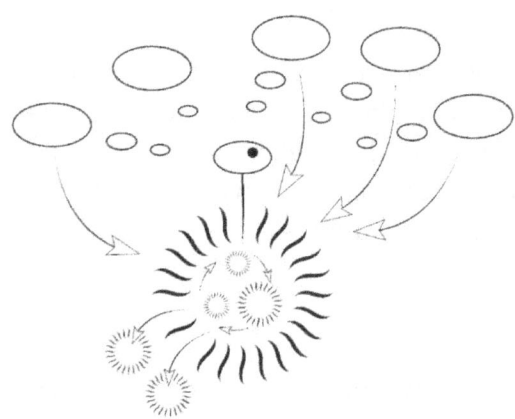

The Challenge with Rational Intelligence

Science has discovered that movement is fundamental to the very existence of the brain. Did you know that only creatures that move (i.e. do not have a root system) have brains? For humankind, however, the brain's frontal cortex has evolved and is now devoted to organizing both physical and psychological action, which includes the movement of thoughts.

When we do anything, a great deal of information—our thoughts, life experiences, eMotions and eMemories—flood into the motor center of the brain, contributing meaning, depth, and complexity to our ongoing movements and actions. If that information is emotionally impactful, we can lose our higher conscious ability to be rational in the stress response. As we have learned, since there are no fat stores (i.e. energy reserves) in the brain, the brain's neurons take a direct hit when stress shuts down the blood flow to our higher reasoning centers. This instantaneous shift in energy causes our emotional brain to step in and steer our behavior. This is why some people can go from being chilled and rational one moment to being aggressive and irrational the next. Strong primal energies such as resentment all but shut down our ability to reason in the moment.

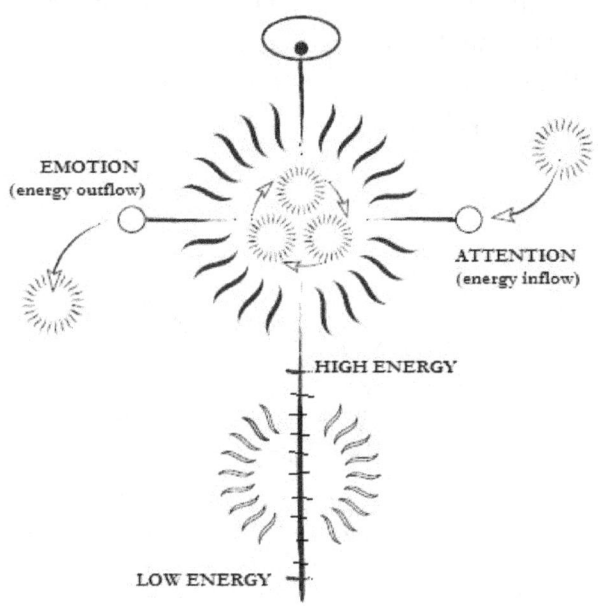

Strengthening Emotional Resilience

Our state of mind is constantly regulating how we experience the world. The decision about what sensory information travels to the higher brain and what is filtered out depends on our eState.

In order for the brain not to be overwhelmed by the constant deluge of sensory input, a cognitive filtering system enables each of us to pay attention to what our conscious mind deems most important and to ignore everything else. Fundamentally, our subconscious mind decides what our conscious mind dwells upon and thinks about.

All my clients have been bright, smart people; many have tertiary degrees and significant professional work experience. However, they all needed to increase their emotional intelligence by becoming more trustful in managing their eMotions in the moment. In short, they needed to TUNE IN and TURN ON a more conscious connection to their subconscious operating system. As such, you are becoming smarter with every ping you TUNE IN and TURN ON.

Out in the everyday world, you should now be increasingly aware of your ongoing eStates. Like a cowboy who has broken a wild stallion, in the end it's up to each one of us to wrangle in our brain and behaviors—both rational and emotional—and have them work as one. "*Know your enemy and know yourself, find naught in fear for 100 battles.*" It's where real strength and confidence originates: continuous improvement of the human condition.

The Odyssey for an enlightened state of mind is a continuous quest. It takes practice to master living in a higher place where your spirit remains calm, cool and collected in chaos. It's a powerful high-energy state where you inspire others with a can-do leadership mindset. In heightened self-awareness, you don't react emotionally but respond to stress rationally and with greater understanding. As a life leader, you keep your wits about you when the shit hits the fan and face stress head on. This undaunted strength doesn't happen overnight. It's a continuously improving growth process you are mastering going forward. Again, practice makes perfect. Never stop improving your eState.

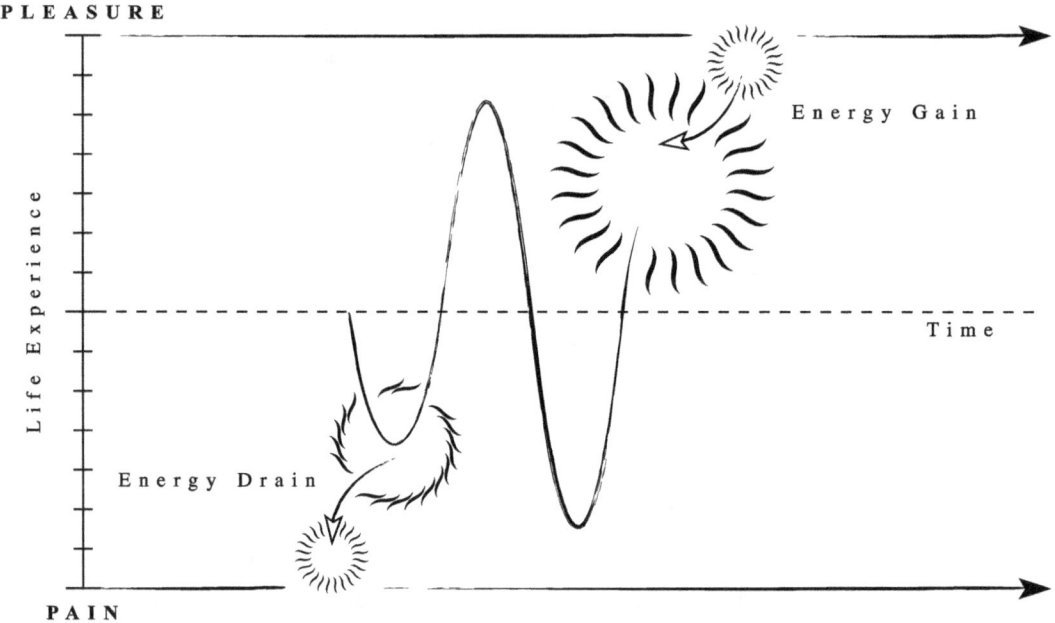

A Continuously Improving Process

With adaption as a core competency of your primal intelligence, your spirit is always learning. Nothing is set in stone as long as a willing spirit resides within you. All you need is reflective learning and an increased self-awareness of the type of energy you're operating in. Like Greg, you may find in your quest that your anger (or fear or depression) has a deeper instinctual purpose, and that it is sending you into battle (or keeping you in bed) for a very good reason.

When you experience a negative eMotion, you're in that state of mind because your rational intelligence is by its instinctual nature, fear-oriented. By gaining a greater understanding and learning from just three pings each day, you're growing wiser and braver by developing a heightened state of self-awareness about what makes you tick. In the courageous pursuit of self-knowledge, you're regaining trust of your primal instincts.

The key to learning this new cognitive skill is the TURN ON of willingness and optimism: Willingness to give it a go and the optimism that better days are ahead. As a living creature, you are adapting all the time, so use that core competency to your advantage by intentionally training your brain to become more emotionally resilient to stress. In time, you will find yourself bouncing back quickly from once distressing pings.

> TURN ON: Have trust in the self-improvement process. Practice and persistence is the key to mastery.

This is your Odyssey—a chance to learn from the pings of life and to manage your energy efficiently. Your journey is to do more with less effort. Work smarter not harder. To better enjoy life and all the experiences the road has to offer.

Day Eleven Exercise

Today concentrate on the TURN ON portion of the methodology. Remember to use the palm-on-forehead technique. Invest time to fully visualize yourself reliving your pings in a higher eState. During the visualization, see and hear the characteristics of the ping, its nuances and resources.

For example, if you had a quarrel with your partner and the feeling of resentment still lingers, TURN ON the courage to go and apologize, or accept them in-the-moment for their differences. Do this for yourself. Aim to keep your eState high and healthy. In the end, you will be of better influence to lead them toward your point of view in a higher energetic state of consciousness.

Again, use the Odyssey Methodology to complete the Quest Journal.

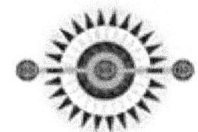

odyssey

The Odyssey Methodology

1. TUNE IN

Remember your day	Close your eyes and mentally review your day. Remember the pings—the people, places or events—that caused you stress, then determine the eMotion triggered by the ping. - *A ping is a significant emotional experience that shifts your energy.* - *You remember pings because of their emotional energy.*
Record your pings	Pick the three most impactful pings of the day and record. [PING - box 1] For each ping, choose the eState that best suits how you responded to the eMotion experienced and record. [TUNE IN - box 2]
Reflect your energy	Focus on how the ping affected your energetic state. Teach your brain what the ping feels like (i.e. grief, anxiety, apathy, etc.). Mentally label the feelings with a rational understanding of the eMotion.

2. TURN ON

Raise your eState	Choose an eState higher than the one experienced for each ping and record. [TURN ON - box 3]
Replay your day	Close your eyes and with palm on forehead, visualize reliving each ping in the higher eState. Imagine the same people, place or event ping in the new eState. - *Include all aspects of the more empowering eMotion. See yourself being confident, responding authentically with pleasant gestures, facial expressions, calm voice, etc.*
Resolve your pings	Set action to neutralize the ping-energy. Ask yourself: What task or solution is necessary to fix a problem? Reconnect with a person? What steps are required to repair what is broken / disconnected? In courage, take action! - *Set an intention to follow through on the commitment. With palm on forehead, mentally rehearse being courageous / optimistic / accepting of the situation. Visualize the new behavior. Train the brain for a high-energy response to stress.*

odyssey

The Quest Journal
- Day Eleven -

Date: Day: S — M — T — W — Th — F — S

eState	eMotion	
Experience	*Feeling*	*Energy*
Enlightenment	Nirvana	1000
Peace	Bliss	600
Joy	Serenity	540
Love	Reverence	500
Reason	Understanding	400
Acceptance	Forgiveness	350
Optimism	Willingness	310
Trust	Neutrality	250
Courage	Affirmation	200
Pride	Scorn	175
Anger	Resentment	150
Desire	Craving	125
Fear	Anxiety	100
Grief	Regret	75
Apathy	Despair	50
Guilt	Blame	30
Shame	Humiliation	20

PING—a significant emotional experience

[box 1]

Duration: ___hr. ___min.

TUNE IN [box 2]

TURN ON [box 3]

PING—a significant emotional experience

Duration: ___hr. ___min.

TUNE IN

TURN ON

PING—a significant emotional experience

Duration: ___hr. ___min.

TUNE IN

TURN ON

GRATITUDE

1.

2.

3.

If the only prayer you say in your whole life is 'thank you' that should suffice.— Meister Eckhart

Emotion hierarchy adapted from Map of Consciousness: *Power vs. Force.* David R. Hawkins, M.D. Ph.D., 1995.

That which does not kill us makes us stronger.

Friedrich Nietzsche (1844-1900)

Day Twelve—Improving Intentional Focus

Think of your attention as a muscle. If you don't use it, you lose it. And, like a muscle, our attention can be sharpened or weakened depending on the workout we give it. You can be in complete control of your attention system like a Buddhist monk, or your attention can be out of your control like an undisciplined child who cannot keep still.

If you've lost your ability to concentrate or pay close attention, you've simply lost the connection with your spirit. Consider that active thoughts are defects in the living process and are simply a result of a primal intelligence that has yet to be tamed. Without continuous improvement, the ability to focus and TUNE IN can grow weak. With the endless distractions in today's world, anyone can easily develop Attention Deficit Disorder (ADD). The time to improve your ability to focus is right now.

> TUNE IN: Close your eyes, and count your breaths to 60.
> TURN ON: How far can you go before your attention is distracted?

Without systematic brain training (like meditation or mindful self-improvement), everyone has ping chatter. At some level, everyone mentally masturbates—stimulated by endless cognitive analysis. So how do we take back control of our attention, and improve our mental focus?

As I've said so many times before, your brain and body possess a core competency of adaption. This means your spirit loves to learn. Used intentionally, this adaption process is what makes the human race an extraordinary species. Even if we're given an ADD diagnosis, there is still the potential to rewire our brain with attention-strengthening exercise.

Researchers have noted we're also happier when we're learning something. When we're willingly learning a new skill such as a new language or sport, we're engaged and passionate, dismissing mistakes and getting on with acquiring the things we don't know.

Ping Neutralization 101

If you truly want to improve your strength and wisdom, you must be willing to put in the time to master the skill. It's not enough to want it, or think it, or to simply read a book and assume your brain will quiet itself down. You must master the technique both emotionally and psychologically—especially when you're under stress.

If this sounds like work, TUNE IN to your spirit right now and sense an eState of apathy. Be aware however, studies do show that we are happier when we're learning something new. So why not learn from your pings? You're having them anyway, so why not improve yourself along the way? The sages call it the path to enlightenment. In terms of health and happiness, continually improving your brain is an empowering road to a life well lived.

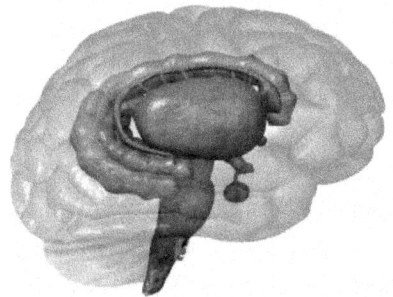

Train the Brain: No Pain, No Gain

It wasn't that long ago in our history that science thought the brain was rigid and stuck in its ways. The you-can't-teach-an-old-dog-new-tricks mentality was the ubiquitous excuse not to change. This fallacy has now been replaced with a more enlightened understanding that no matter how old you are, your brain is fully capable of rewiring itself if you are willing to put in the conscious effort. The trick is to stay with the new thinking process until the brain is permanently rewired to think in a more energy-efficient way.

It's often said that it takes 21 days to form a habit. As our thinking and behavioral processes are habits, let's form a new one: A habit of continuous improvement in which we learn from our pings every day. While we're at it, let's embed the importance of how our spirit is empowering (or disempowering!) us to think and behave. This is why the TUNE IN process of recording your top three pings every day is important: You're teaching your rational brain what your emotional brain is doing under stress.

> "Know your enemy and know yourself, find naught in fear for 100 battles."

With patience and persistence, this heightened self-awareness means installing an increasingly empowered sub-consciousness; an intuitive habit that keeps your spirit feeling lifted automatically, without you having to think about it!

Let's take this healthy vision even further. Let's say that you faithfully record and learn from your pings for 90 days—almost four times longer than it takes for a habit to form. How much stronger and more resilient would you become? How much clearer and focused would your mind be? Imagine being the focused and motivated person you know you can be. Mastery is up to you and your attitude toward rediscovering your spirit—the great mystery running you right now.

Learning by Doing

In sharing this quest with clients that have come to my practice with a wide range of issues (extramarital affairs, illicit drug use, working in toxic environments with sociopathic bosses, etc.), I've become aware that many well-intentioned people exist in self-created hells. How did they get there? Simple. They unconsciously learned by doing.

> TUNE IN: What have you *been unconsciously doing* to get where you are today?

Psychology is about exploring the past: reflecting on your childhood, forgiving your parents and improving the self-love you have of yourself. This is simplified of course, but pragmatically speaking, and in scientific terms, we do know now that your subconscious remembers every emotional experience you've ever had. Over the years (especially during childhood), your primal intelligence has adapted to every pain and pleasure you've ever experienced. That's everything you've ever been emotionally exposed to on your road of life.

So, instead of years of psychotherapy, let's get it off our chests permanently by taking full self-responsibility in the creation of our own feelings. Ask yourself: "What have I *been doing* to get where I am right now?" "What life experiences have made me into who I am?" In the eMemory Inventory exercise tomorrow, you will answer these questions by graphically exploring the significant events along your road of life in a context of self-improvement.

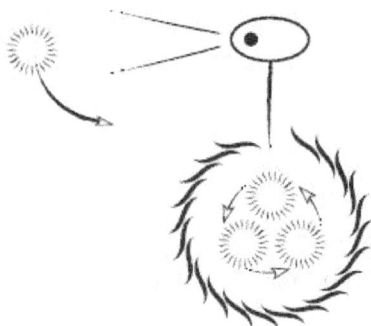

eMemory Inventory

Looking back on your road of life, there's some great news: Odds are that your most negative eMotions right now aren't yours! They were given to you by your parents, peers and teachers. They didn't mean to. They were just living the way *their* parents, peers and teachers taught them. Not knowing any different, they simply passed on their own emotional energy to you.

As a child, specifically from conception to around year seven, our brains are sponges—absorbing everything we see, taste, touch, hear and experience. Culture, education, religion and social environment all add flavor to our experience of life by instilling emotional programs that dictate how we behave in the world. If you had emotionally intelligent parents and teachers that taught you coping mechanisms for stress, you're probably not taking this program. But if you were like me—with authority figures who were perhaps well intentioned but had little clue they were passing on bad energy—your primal intelligence has learned some not-so-productive emotional habits. These bad behaviors more than likely express themselves under stress, when your rational brain is all but shut down and unable to think straight.

Back when you were a child, your brain was wide open to learning. It took in EVERY EXPERIENCE it was exposed to, and encoded those experiences into your primal intelligence. Your personality and behaviors today are a result of this vast inventory of collected life experience, laid on top of our genetic disposition for survival. Working together, this nature-nurture powerhouse of emotional energy strives to keep you alive—aware of and away from danger automatically. These survival-driven emotional programs tend to rear their ugly head when you're under stress. To know them is to discover a treasure of self-knowledge that will accelerate the self-improvement process.

As we explored a few days ago, eMemories are emotional memories. They are the subconscious programs that have fine-tuned our instincts and tell us how to move in the environment in which we've adapted. It's worth repeating that every eMotion you've ever experienced has been encoded energetically into your biology. Your environment may have changed since childhood, but the eMemories may remain programmed into your primal intelligence. Every painful embarrassment. Every exasperating failure. Time to take back conscious control and update the self-organizing living process!

To regain the health and happiness that is your birthright, you simply need to separate the trash from the treasure. Begin to discern high-energy states from low-energy states in the moment throughout the day. Tomorrow's exercise will help you do just that. But first, again, reflect on your day: TUNE IN and TURN ON your pings.

Day Twelve Exercise

Devote time today in the TURN ON portion of the methodology and concentrate on resolving your pings. This may require taking action and directly confronting the source of stress. This is what courage is all about. Again, complete the Quest Journal using the Odyssey Methodology.

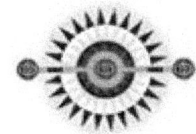

odyssey

The Odyssey Methodology

1. TUNE IN

Remember
your day

Close your eyes and mentally review your day.
Remember the pings—the people, places or events—that caused you stress, then determine the eMotion triggered by the ping.
- *A ping is a significant emotional experience that shifts your energy.*
- *You remember pings because of their emotional energy.*

Record
your pings

Pick the three most impactful pings of the day and record. [PING - box 1]
For each ping, choose the eState that best suits how you responded to the eMotion experienced and record. [TUNE IN - box 2]

Reflect
your energy

Focus on how the ping affected your energetic state.
Teach your brain what the ping feels like (i.e. grief, anxiety, apathy, etc.).
Mentally label the feelings with a rational understanding of the eMotion.

2. TURN ON

Raise
your eState

Choose an eState higher than the one experienced for each ping and record. [TURN ON - box 3]

Replay
your day

Close your eyes and with palm on forehead, visualize reliving each ping in the higher eState. Imagine the same people, place or event ping in the new eState.
- *Include all aspects of the more empowering eMotion. See yourself being confident, responding authentically with pleasant gestures, facial expressions, calm voice, etc.*

Resolve
your pings

Set action to neutralize the ping-energy. Ask yourself: What task or solution is necessary to fix a problem? Reconnect with a person? What steps are required to repair what is broken / disconnected? In courage, take action!
- *Set an intention to follow through on the commitment. With palm on forehead, mentally rehearse being courageous / optimistic / accepting of the situation. Visualize the new behavior. Train the brain for a high-energy response to stress.*

odyssey

The Quest Journal
- Day Twelve -

Date: ____ Day: S — M — T — W — Th — F — S

eState	eMotion	
Experience	*Feeling*	*Energy*
Enlightenment	Nirvana	1000
Peace	Bliss	600
Joy	Serenity	540
Love	Reverence	500
Reason	Understanding	400
Acceptance	Forgiveness	350
Optimism	Willingness	310
Trust	Neutrality	250
Courage	Affirmation	200
Pride	Scorn	175
Anger	Resentment	150
Desire	Craving	125
Fear	Anxiety	100
Grief	Regret	75
Apathy	Despair	50
Guilt	Blame	30
Shame	Humiliation	20

PING—a significant emotional experience

[box 1]

Duration: ___hr. ___min.

TUNE IN [box 2]

TURN ON [box 3]

PING—a significant emotional experience

Duration: ___hr. ___min.

TUNE IN

TURN ON

PING—a significant emotional experience

Duration: ___hr. ___min.

TUNE IN

TURN ON

GRATITUDE
1.
2.
3.

If the only prayer you say in your whole life is 'thank you' that should suffice.— Meister Eckhart

Emotion hierarchy adapted from Map of Consciousness: *Power vs. Force.* David R. Hawkins, M.D. Ph.D., 1995.

Day Thirteen—The eMemory Inventory

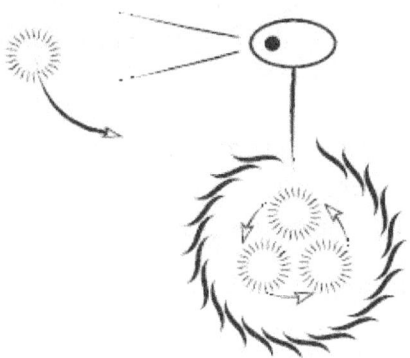

TUNE IN Your Road of Life

Along the road of life, we pick up both trash and treasure. In today's exercise, you will explore your past road of challenges and triumphs in a framework of self-knowledge. Plan to spend an hour somewhere quiet, where you can reflect on your life and examine the eMemories that are encoded into your physiology.

> **WARNING:** Remain in the Observer consciousness of your *road of life* during this exercise. Avoid reliving the physical experience of any emotionally charged event. You just want to observe what eMotions are associated with significant life experiences. The past may be painful, but it is the past. Use the knowledge encoded into your biology to enact a brighter future!

Taking an eMemory Inventory

What you remember about your significant past emotional experiences can serve as insightful information on the emotional programming that powers your ongoing state of mind. So, take time now to look back on your unique road of life and REMEMBER your past pings from an Observer consciousness. Then take a written inventory of what you consciously recall about your childhood. As these conscious memories are tagged with eMotion, reflect their subconscious energetic charges encoded into your brain.

The Observer rule of thumb is this: *Your memories of your past come with an emotional charge attached.* How you behave and experience the world today is a result of those emotional energies that are powering your perceptions. The quest is to become aware of these energies—be in tune to the spirit powering you right now—in order to ensure that you trust your instincts in the moment you need it most.

The Thought Inventory Exercise on Day Six was all about simple recognition of ongoing thoughts at the surface of your mind. Today's exercise requires more focused intention and depth of reflection. If necessary, complete this self-awareness exercise over a few days. It's an important one.

Each one of us has an individual road of life, our own set of growth experiences and eMemories that have formed the unique person reading these words right now. **The eMemory Inventory** will provide you with a simple way of capturing the most significant events of your life journey and correlating them with the energetic states you may be currently experiencing.

Before starting, find a comfortable spot where you will not be disturbed. Allow plenty of time to complete this exercise. Sit quietly and ask yourself, "What experiences have occurred in my life that I will never forget? What are the most significant memories I have of growing up?" "To now?"

Step One: Close your eyes and relax. Take a few deep breaths and begin to visualize your road of life. Remember the house and neighborhood you grew up in, your childhood room, your friends, family affairs and so on.

Step Two: Following the eMemory form on the next few pages, note your specific life experiences and events, ideally in sequence. Try to recall the key memories of your early life through adulthood. For example,

My kindergarten birthday party

The death of my dog Bobo

Step Three: Once you remember an experience, identify which eMotion best fits the experience in the right column. This is called the emotional tag. Sadness includes humiliation, blame, despair and regret. Happiness includes feeling trusted, accepted and understood.

My kindergarten birthday party   *Happiness*

The death of my dog Bobo   *Sadness*

Step Four: Once you have completed your list of memories and have correlated each with an eMotion, spend time in transcribing the significant emotional experiences onto the **My Road of Life** graph that appears on the page following the **My eMemory Inventory** forms. Record the event on top, then shade in the corresponding eMotion that appears below it on the graph.

WEEK TWO - THE QUEST
MY ROAD OF LIFE

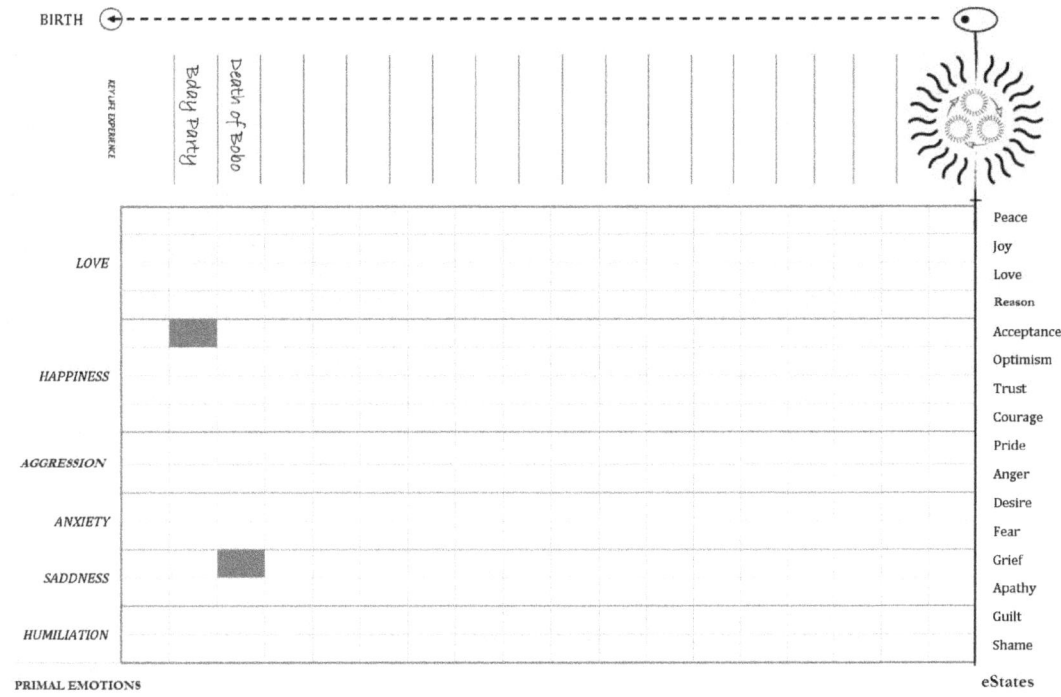

Step Five: By completing this exercise, you should be left with a graphical representation of which eMotions are encoded into your primal intelligence. You shouldn't be surprised if most of your pings TUNE IN to these experienced energies. These are your eMemories.

My eMemory Inventory

EARLIEST MEMORIES:

Associated eMotions:
humiliation, sadness, anxiety, resentment, happiness or love

CHILDHOOD MEMORIES:

Associated eMotions:
humiliation, sadness, anxiety, resentment, happiness or love

TEENAGE MEMORIES:	**Associated eMotions:** humiliation, sadness, anxiety, resentment, happiness or love

YOUNG ADULT MEMORIES:	**Associated eMotions:** humiliation, sadness, anxiety, resentment, happiness or love

RECENT MEMORIES:	Associated eMotions: humiliation, sadness, anxiety, resentment, happiness or love

WEEK TWO - THE QUEST
MY ROAD OF LIFE

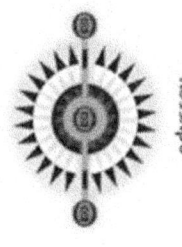
odyssey

BIRTH

KEY LIFE EXPERIENCE

Peace / Joy / Love / Understanding / Acceptance / Optimism / Trust / Courage / Pride / Anger / Desire / Fear / Grief / Apathy / Guilt / Shame

LOVE

HAPPINESS

RESENTMENT

ANXIETY

SADDNESS

HUMILIATION

YEARS OF AGE

Day Fourteen—Rest and Reflect on Your Week

Look back at the daily exercises and transcribe your pings in the boxes below. Note any commonalities and group accordingly. This exercise is not to assign blame, but to elevate your awareness of the people, places or events that are disturbing your energy. Observe any patterns. Also consider strategies that would help resolve the ping. Note any action necessary. Remember, courage is the gateway to high-energy states.

Day Eight Pings	Common Pings—People, Places and Events
1.	
2.	
3.	
Day Nine Pings	
1.	
2.	
3.	
Day Ten Pings	**Observations / Strategies for Improvement**
1.	
2.	
3.	
Day Eleven Pings	
1.	
2.	
3.	
Day Twelve Pings	**Action Items:**
1.	
2.	
3.	

odyssey

Our deepest fear is not that we are inadequate. Our deepest fear is that we are powerful beyond measure.

It is our light, not our darkness that most frightens us. We ask ourselves, who am I to be brilliant, gorgeous, talented and fabulous?

Actually, who are you not to be? You are a child of the Universe. Your playing small doesn't serve the world. There's nothing enlightened about shrinking so that other people feel secure around you.

We are born to make manifest the glory of God that is within us. It's not just some of us. It's everyone. And, as we let our own light shine, so we consciously give other people permission to do the same.

As we are liberated from our own fear, our presence automatically liberates others.

Marianne Williamson
A Return to Love

odyssey

WEEK THREE—THE LIVING MOMENT

Dynamics of Life Leadership

Right now, your spirit is alive within you. This mysterious life-force is in full command and control of your moment-to-moment experiences of feeling alive.

Travelling now with more self-awareness, you've become increasingly familiar with what pings you. You have increased self-knowledge of your spirit in action and have come to appreciate the eMotions your life-energy creates.

The quest continues as you learn to better recognize and neutralize pings in the moment as they occur. The continuous improvement process we call upon for this is the Odyssey Methodology.

Live in the present moment—that is the primary universal truth. For health and happiness, we must actively live its principle by managing our energy each and every living moment.

THE FIRST UNIVERSAL TRUTH
Live in the Present Moment

odyssey

The Quest Objectives

At the end of Week Three, you'll be able to...

1. Understand what is meant by the living moment and the energetic states of consciousness (eStates).

2. Understand the arousal response and how to TURN ON high-energy states.

3. Recognize when a loss of spirit occurs and know how to correct the imbalance of mind and body.

4. Begin your own hero's journey by applying the Odyssey Methodology.

The purpose of life is to be happy and useful.

The Dalai Lama

Day Fifteen—The Living Moment

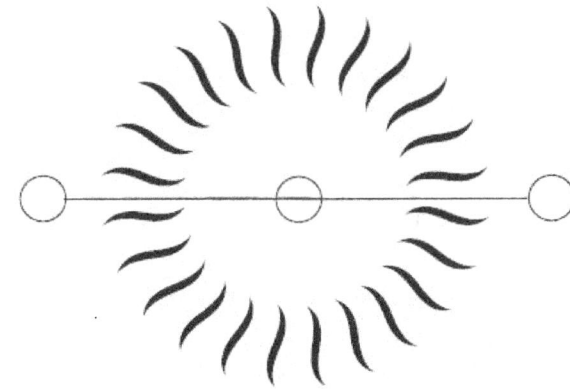

A few years back, a client—I'll call him Nick—professed to having a very busy mind. He rarely sat still and made other people nervous with his constant fidgeting and excessive talking. He would jump from one topic of conversation to another, which made it hard to get a word in edgewise. His own self-diagnosis was that he had Attention Deficit Hyperactivity Disorder (ADHD).

Nick was an intensely intelligent man, and worked as a strategic executive at a global I.T. firm. Without a doubt, one of their brightest and most gifted, he was responsible for procuring high profile customers to open up their bank accounts and sign multi-million dollar contracts. He was so bright, in fact, that he planned everything meticulously, both professionally and personally. After working together for a few weeks, I found out that Nick had meticulously strategized a dismal plan for his own suicide.

While his co-workers were praising Nick for heading to the Blue Mountains to hike on the weekends, Nick was secretly checking out something much more brooding—namely, which cliff was best to jump off from in order to kill himself. I was shocked at the confession. It seemed so out of character. With his jovial wit and charismatic charm, Nick was the last person I'd expect to have thoughts of suicide. After some investigation however, I understood that his rational brain was getting the best of him. Like a form of tinnitus, he was inundated by endless cognitive chatter and sought silence and solitude from his noisy thoughts, even if it meant ending his life.

It seemed that Nick's mind never stopped working. Paid for his intellect, he had trained his brain to think, and think it did, nonstop. With no off switch, late at night, on weekends and at times when he really wanted a rest from the world, his mind would remain active, analyzing every aspect of his life. He was literally going mad with the never-ending chatter—what to wear, who to see, where to go. Nick was also an avid smoker, and although he wanted to quit, he confessed it seemed to help his nervousness and calm the anxiety. With dismay, I remembered that many schizophrenics chain-smoked as a way to quiet the voices. I suggested an alternative. "How about we ground all that excessive chatter on your living spirit so you can get some rest?" As esoteric as that sounded, Nick was intrigued.

I had him imagine peaceful places, with little need to analyze, strategize, plan or think about what to do. Instead of pressuring his brain to make the right choice at the right time, I suggested he instead simply TUNE IN to his primal intelligence and trust his instincts to navigate the complexities he faced intuitively without thinking. He liked the idea. I then informed him that he would have to do brain-training. He needed to gain trust in his spirit to move him in the moment. He agreed to undertake *The Odyssey Quest* leadership program.

He was enthusiastic and soon became one of my best pupils. I told him that if he were to intentionally train his brain to neutralize pings as they occurred, then his anxiety would calm down, to the point where I believed he could give up cigarettes. That incentive gave him great motivation and he eagerly began the TUNE IN—TURN ON improvement process.

> TUNE IN: Are you choosing your thoughts? Or are your thoughts choosing you?

In the end, Nick didn't jump off a cliff. In fact, he gained so much from retraining his brain that he told the human resources director at his company that "Odyssey saved my life." Literally. Nick is still strategic in everything he does, but is now doing it in a much more grounded, happier way. He understands now that intelligence is much more than thinking alone. He understands how to use his in-tune-ition to navigate his world and not pressure his smarts to make the routine decisions.

Like Nick, once upon a time I too had wired my mind to be in constant analysis. Survival mode as I now call it. From the moment I woke to the moment I fell asleep, my brain would race with its own cognitive chatter. I too thought of suicide as the only way to quiet my overly active mind. My anxiety too, like Nick's, permeated everything I did. That was until I started learning from my life-energy and placing more trust in my spirit to guide my decisions and actions. Today, life is a lot easier. And happier.

In developing this program over the last two decades, it was my intention to clear my mind of thoughts and focus my attention. I simply wanted to find peace in everyday chaos and, like Nick, live a life untormented by an insecure and suicidal mindset. In hindsight, I am still amazed how zealous and unbridled thoughts, unfounded anxieties and needless depressions can get in the way of a life well lived. With mental illness escalating, the loss of spirit is epidemic. It's time to experience a new reality—a connective reality of feeling alive.

The Journey of Life

Years ago, I took a vacation and visited the magnificent mountains in Glacier National Park in Montana, USA. On one crisp summer morning with magnificent blue skies, I began a hike on a trail I had selected that would take me quite a long distance. It would be an arduous day. Steadily, I began walking up the long canyon. After a few hours, the footpath became steeper and steeper, and began zigzagging for the steep ascent. The mountains closed in around me as I made my way up through beautiful scenery and views until I found myself at the summit. That was only the beginning.

The trail then continued along a long, rocky, treeless plateau, where both sides of the trail dropped off into steep canyons below. The trail was wide, but I remember thinking that a misstep could send me plummeting down into the rocky ravine.

Earlier, I had noticed clouds building on the mountain to the west, but didn't think much of them until they covered the sun and an eerie darkness set in. I sensed that a major storm was brewing, and soon the mountain itself was hidden by a dark cloud cover. With nowhere else to go, I quickened my pace and stayed on the long, seemingly endless trail, high on top of the bald, rocky plateau. My heart started beating faster. I intuitively knew danger was approaching.

The storm quickly swept across the mountain, and what was once a clear blue sky was now a deep fog bank—I could barely see the trail before me. Suddenly, a hailstorm began. Golf ball-sized hailstones started to pelt down—a few at first, but then the clouds opened up to produce a deluge of frozen ice cubes. I covered my head with my backpack. With nowhere to take cover, I was starting to become genuinely concerned. The thought then occurred to me that people do die on mountains. Most—like me—probably didn't set out in the morning thinking their life was going to end.

The wind and rain increased, and soon hailstones covered the ground. The trail all but disappeared in the ice in front of me. Dressed only in shorts and a t-shirt, I began shivering in the cold, wet weather. Huddled under my backpack, I made my way forward, quickening my pace until I glimpsed a small rock outcrop. I slid into it, crouching under the tiny shelter it offered. Finally safe, I sat and waited for the storm to pass. I took a deep breath as I settled into my new tiny sanctuary.

After about 45 minutes, the harsh weather subsided. Soaking wet and shivering, I climbed out of my tiny cave and took in the scenery, covered in ice. Backpack on, I continued on top of the mountain along what I hoped was the trail. About five hours later, I arrived back at my car. A clear blue sky reigned above me again as if nothing had happened. I felt alive. Really alive.

When I'd left my car that morning, I'd never imagined that such an ordeal would await me. Back in the safety of the driver's seat, I reflected on my adventure and asked myself, "Would I have started the journey knowing what lay ahead?"

While I drove out of the park, I contemplated the question further and realized that I got up every morning to begin an adventure each day that was routinely filled with unexpected storms. I began to appreciate how many days I let my fears and anxieties get the best of me, anticipating work-related challenges and cowardly forcing myself 'up the mountain' instead of enjoying the journey. At that time, I would have admitted work was 'killing me' but I wasn't dying in a physical sense. I was dying inside, allowing my primal eMotions to take hold of my feelings. Looking back, I realized that I survived each storm, and that I should've enjoyed them more. So I began to contemplate how I could I face my daily weather challenges with a more courageous mindset.

I wonder how many other people are living in trepidation, worrying and over-analyzing potential storms that they routinely survive. It seems to me that as a soft society, we have lost what courage really means: to be scared to death but facing the fear anyway. After all, a storm of misunderstanding is far less hurtful than a hailstorm of golf-ball size ice. Emotionally speaking, we need to toughen up.

The Warrior Spirit

Every day when we wake and head out into the world, we have no idea what lies ahead. We could get into a traffic accident or a heated discussion with a co-worker. At times, I think about the hundreds of thousands drowned and lost in those terrible tsunamis, tornadoes and floods that have occurred in recent years, and I imagine that each of them began their day like every other, never expecting to die. I cannot help but have compassion for the refugees who flee their homes and leave everything behind. Civil wars, earthquakes, hurricanes, accidents, plane crashes, terrorist bombings—day in, day out, there is no guarantee of survival. Each day is a gift—a present—as we are truly blessed with being alive.

Regardless of how much we attempt to accurately plan our travel, the trip down the road of life forges ahead into an unknowable future that can be tarnished by negative eMotions—the survival responses to the pings of daily life. Taming emotional responses by strengthening your willingness to give the hard stuff a go is the recommended remedy for the roadblocks ahead. With each pelt, the pings of life provide an opportunity to TURN ON the courage to tackle the challenges we routinely face.

After the ordeal on the mountain, I was in a contemplative mood. The next day, I decided to head into the small town of Whitefish, Montana—taking the day off to hike seemed like a good idea. Walking down the promenade and past the shops along the quaint main street, I was drawn into a craft store where I discovered a wide variety of Native American artworks. One rather brilliant piece jumped out at me. Painted on a deerskin, I saw an ideal symbol of life leadership: The Lakota War Bonnet.

If you examine the war bonnet closely, you'll notice a couple of things. First, its most striking feature, the fiery center. The sunburst represents life-energy—the *wanka tanka*, or great mystery, that is alive within us right now. The black and white triangles represent life (white) and its polar opposite, death (black). The Lakota, like many native cultures, believe that the living spirit within us is locked in a continuous state of survival. Certainly, every morning we must face the day and all the challenges in courage—or die.

The next most striking feature of the war bonnet is the three circles, connected by a horizontal bar. This represents the road of life—the past, present and future. The left circle is the past; the right is the future. The middle circle is the core of the fiery center and represents the right here, right now.

The entire symbol is what I like to refer to now as *the living moment*.

After some research, I discovered that the Lakota Native American people were one of the most feared and powerful nations on the Great Plains of the central United States. Their leaders were also some of the most famous in Native American history. Today, the stories of Sitting Bull, Crazy Horse and Black Elk still inspire many people with their wisdom and bravery. Obviously, their war bonnet was good medicine. But how exactly did they utilize it to develop such an undaunted spirit?

As a spiritual symbol that immortalized their belief system, the Lakota War Bonnet helped focus the warriors' minds as they rode thunder into battle. Embracing the spirit of the moment, the Lakota neither thought about the past (failures and mistakes) nor the future (potential death). Instead, they set a clear intention and concentrated on taking action to resolve the challenge. They focused their attention, eMotions and willpower on what was necessary in the moment; namely, to protect their families and tribal members. Focused on their goal, they were undeniably courageous. Unified with a powerful singular intention, the Lakota gained a formidable reputation and were highly respected.

The concept of living in the present moment is common to all religious philosophies because of its grand merit. Indeed, when you go into any battle, be it a social conflict or a physical challenge, it's crucial to keep your wits about you and concentrate on what's needed in the moment. Any thought of past losses, regrets or mistakes, and you may miss the moment of opportunity that is essential in slaying the proverbial dragon. Likewise, allowing yourself to imagine a dire future and the potential for failure could fuel fear and anxiety and give the competition the unattended moment they need to slay you.

When faced with adversity, it is best to follow the leadership of the Lakota and focus on the most important moment—*the living moment* of right now. TUNE IN to your living spirit (rather than dwell on past mistakes or future defeats) and you will become more empowered in the moment to deal with the challenges lying right before you. This is the true realm of courage and life leadership—of being scared to death but facing the challenge anyway.

A Leadership Mindset

It is far more productive and energy-gaining to resolve a challenge than avoid it. Leaders initiate change, while all others worry and wait for change to run them over. We can find inspiration to help tame the fears that are exacerbated by the human condition by looking to rituals and beliefs that many native cultures have developed over thousands of years. Rather than being afraid and distracted, they trained their brains to focus on what needed doing, and then did it. Despite feeling fear, they turned on their brain by setting an intention and taking purposeful action. In contrast to our modern fragmented mindset (in which we analyze everything to death), we can learn from native psychology—a powerful immersion in the living moment, fully in tune with their spirit as the creator of their lives.

We can also find a similar mental paradigm in Australian Indigenous culture. Aboriginal people believed that there was little difference between the past and the future. For them, mind and body, time and space were one and the same. There was no road of life, just the here and now. With no words to describe time, the Aboriginal people considered themselves an intimate part of their surroundings. They were one with the world. Creators of their creation.

For us Western thinkers, such a heightened state of consciousness seems foreign and difficult to comprehend. We may have occasional glimpses of timeless bliss but we remain trapped in a self-absorbed consciousness where time is money and getting things done on time takes precedence in our everyday lives. With the concept of time being so pervasive in our modern minds, it's no wonder that people like Nick and I had such unstoppable chatter in our minds: We were unable to TUNE IN to our primal in-the-moment intelligence and gain control of the operating system. Instead, our attention got lost in analyzing or scheming what had happened or may happen in the future. Without a disciplined mind, it's nearly impossible to experience an enlightened one.

> TURN ON: You do not exist in yesterdays or tomorrows, but in your present thoughts, eMotions and behaviors. To your spirit, there is only right now.

The path to improvement involves training the brain to be in tune to the path itself—the good, the bad and the ugly. Living an enlightened, in-the-moment existence takes practice. And that means managing your life-energy at every living moment.

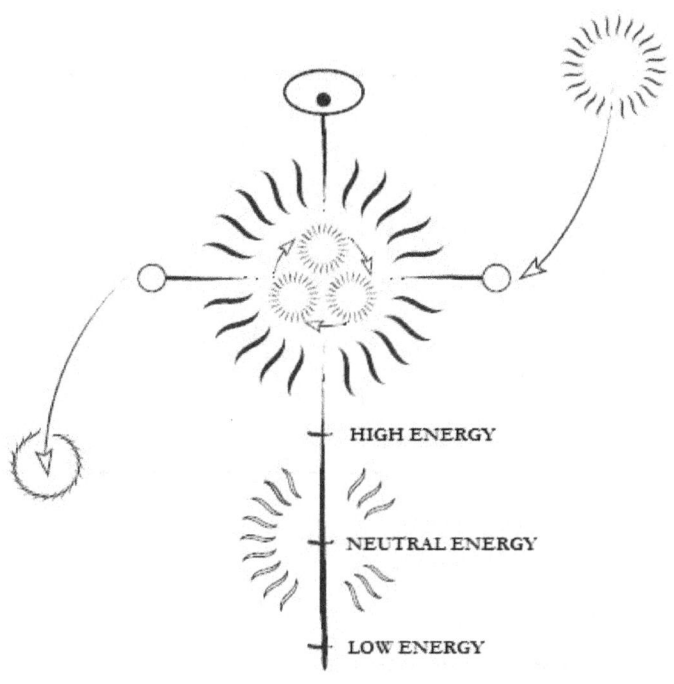

Energy Management 101

Consider that time is not a rigid, mechanical process, but rather a dynamic flow of energy. Our experience of time is always changing as our energy levels continually fluctuate in response to the people, places or events we encounter. Living in such a world of flux, our energy is undoubtedly subject to change. Without energy management, emotional energies can and do shift as our primal intelligence attempts to adapt to the ongoing changes in our environment.

Feelings are a self-awareness of your energy in motion. If you could shrink down to the size of atoms and roam around what is going on deep inside your body, you would find yourself immersed in a sea of energy. Glancing around, you would see yourself being built and maintained as if by magic. Molecule by molecule, energy bonds are being made, then broken, then made again. In this quantum world, nothing is ever just off or on. Instead, your energy levels fluctuate like the speed of a car. And like a speedometer, your feelings help gauge how fast (or slow) you are going. How do you then manage the speed in which you travel time? By taking more control of the biological engine and managing its high-energy performance.

Right now, all your subconscious activity is being conducted by the primal intelligence of your spirit. The energy of your spirit can be managed by simply using an improved self-awareness of what pings your energy. So now that you have collected information on what pings you and thus slows you down, it's time to learn how to speed things up.

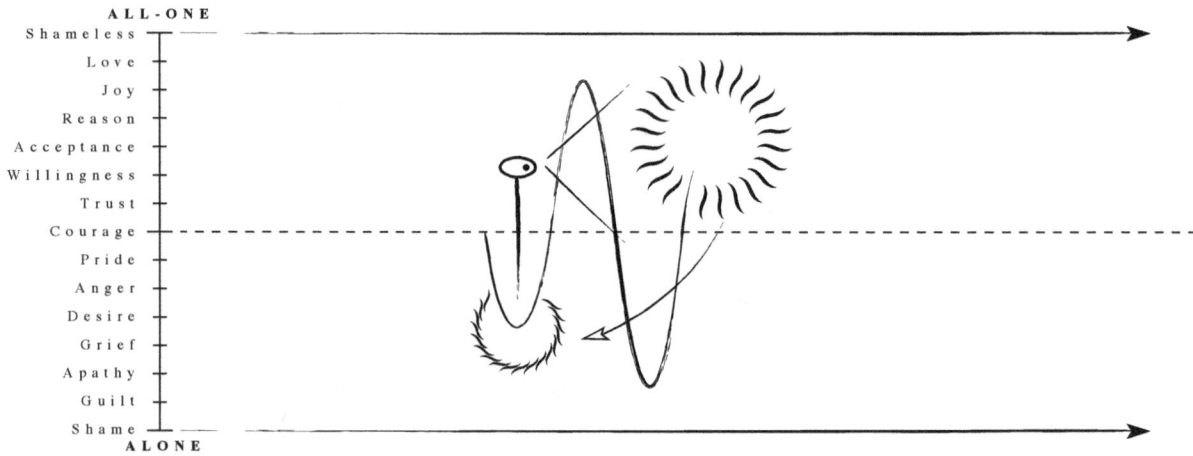

The Arousal Response

We have examined the stress response at length. But there is another, opposite energetic reaction known as the arousal response. Imagine living in a world of negativity but possessing a spirit powerful enough to protect your energy from the pings of life. How much more energized would you feel? How better motivated and enthusiastic would you be to take on the hard stuff? Now imagine being aroused by stressful challenges, while trusting yourself to survive and grow from them. This is possible when you teach your brain the TURN ON arousal response.

Remaining positive when real stress is on takes effort, but it is achievable. The key is to become fully aware of the thoughts, actions and behaviors that ping your energy. When you teach your rational brain what your emotional brain is doing, instead of reacting in primal eMotion, you respond in a positive way. This is a characteristic of a true leader: Maintaining high-energy when conflict occurs. It's called charisma. And it's a powerful spirit that people will follow into battle.

Everyone desires energy. When you have energy to give, people are attracted to you. You are better able to influence an argument and come out on top. We should remember that as animals with a core competency to copulate and reproduce, being turned on by another's energy is how life survives. Being sexy and charismatic is why celebrities and entertainers are paid huge sums of money. Their energy switches on other people's energy. This is the arousal response in all its energetic glory.

Being aroused is not always about intimacy with another person, however. Being aroused happens when you feel trustful, optimistic and accepting of situations. Sparking such high-energy feelings originates in the willpower to TURN ON your higher brain functions in the moment and to intentionally shift your energy to a higher eState. This is easily learned. In fact, you can arouse your state of mind anytime using your largest sex organ—your brain.

TURN ON: Arousing Energy on Command

When we become enthused over a new career opportunity, excited over an upcoming holiday or electrified by a romantic encounter, we feel aroused because of the positive energy those things spark. Our energy can also be shifted positively when we hear good news or learn of a successful result. In fact, just the act of thinking high-energy thoughts can initiate a biochemical change in our brain and we can experience real pleasure. Used intentionally, learning to think 'sexy' thoughts can serve as a valuable tool for energy management that can arouse our self-organizing living process at anytime.

Using our imagination, we can TURN ON our brain and visualize ourselves more positively within negative environments. We can imagine working at that perfect job, going on that dream vacation or conquering that mountain we've been meaning to climb. To our primal intelligence, intentionally thinking optimistically can and does initiate higher energy levels within the brain and body and we begin to feel optimistic. To spark this high-octane life-energy, all we have to do is imagine living in that higher eMotion. Einstein was right: Imagination is more powerful than knowledge.

As we have learned, a stress response is instinctual and automatic. When the heat is on, we can let our primal brain react emotionally or instead teach ourselves to think constructively. This requires the lifting of emotional weight. The TUNE IN—TURN ON strengthening process embeds a new empowering way of dealing with stressors in your subconscious. The goal is to train the brain to be aroused when we need it most—under stress!

You have already been doing this strengthening exercise. For the past fourteen days, you have become more familiar with what pings your energy. As you continue to collect data on your stress responses, you should now be more aware of the opportunities to TURN ON trust, optimism, acceptance and the higher eMotions that neutralize pings on contact. Remember that understanding is a high eState, so strive to maintain your ability to reason when stress does occur.

Again, continue to improve your self-awareness of your pings (the TUNE IN process), but also continue to TURN ON higher-level eMotions in the moment to neutralize the negative impact of a lower-level eMotion. For example, when I began using the TUNE IN—TURN ON methodology, I noticed that I got a ping of shame whenever I spoke out in a group. If I didn't get the response I wanted, I felt my energy sink and posture slouch. Left lingering in my pinged eMotion, the humiliation energy powered my thoughts and forced me into thinking self-doubt the rest of the afternoon. Learning to observe the ping's effect without falling into the eMotion, I intentionally aroused my energy by placing a palm on my forehead and imagined reliving that ping in a higher, more empowering state of mind.

Physically, I would augment this energy-shift by standing up straight, pulling my shoulders back and holding my head high. I intentionally turned on my self-organizing living process by trying on a courageous eState. I would stay in that TURN ON position until I felt the ping-energy dissipate and my mind more in-tune to the authentic me. In a few minutes, I felt the high-energy at work as the energy-positive biochemistry began powering my senses.

By applying the TUNE IN—TURN ON process regularly, I began to wire my brain to think in high-energy states automatically. I surprised myself by remaining calm and clear-minded when stress occurred. My senses switched on and I became more present in everything I did. For the first time, I began to enjoy feeling alive.

Again, intentionally imagine the higher eMotions at work within you. With eyes closed and palm on forehead, replay and reprogram your eMemories using visualization to next respond to the ping in high-energy. Feeling alive is a living improvement process—an intentional interplay of subconscious and conscious activity that helps empower the spirit. Continue to manage your energy and enlightenment will be yours.

More of the TURN ON process in the upcoming days.

Day Fifteen Exercise

Living in the moment is a continuous improvement quest that comes from an increased focus on what's going on right now within your mind, body and spirit. For today, continue to invest in the TURN ON visualization process to train your brain to deal positively with the pings of life. Imagine yourself being in tune in the moment should the ping occur again. Use the Odyssey Methodology to complete the Quest Journal.

173

odyssey

The Odyssey Methodology

1. TUNE IN

Remember *your day*	Close your eyes and mentally review your day. Remember the pings—the people, places or events—that caused you stress, then determine the eMotion triggered by the ping. - *A ping is a significant emotional experience that shifts your energy.* - *You remember pings because of their emotional energy.*
Record *your pings*	Pick the three most impactful pings of the day and record. [PING - box 1] For each ping, choose the eState that best suits how you responded to the eMotion experienced and record. [TUNE IN - box 2]
Reflect *your energy*	Focus on how the ping affected your energetic state. Teach your brain what the ping feels like (i.e. grief, anxiety, apathy, etc.). Mentally label the feelings with a rational understanding of the eMotion.

2. TURN ON

Raise *your eState*	Choose an eState higher than the one experienced for each ping and record. [TURN ON - box 3]
Replay *your day*	Close your eyes and with palm on forehead, visualize reliving each ping in the higher eState. Imagine the same people, place or event ping in the new eState. - *Include all aspects of the more empowering eMotion. See yourself being confident, responding authentically with pleasant gestures, facial expressions, calm voice, etc.*
Resolve *your pings*	Set action to neutralize the ping-energy. Ask yourself: What task or solution is necessary to fix a problem? Reconnect with a person? What steps are required to repair what is broken / disconnected? In courage, take action! - *Set an intention to follow through on the commitment. With palm on forehead, mentally rehearse being courageous / optimistic / accepting of the situation. Visualize the new behavior. Train the brain for a high-energy response to stress.*

odyssey

The Quest Journal
- Day Fifteen -

Date: _____   Day: S — M — T — W — Th — F — S

eState	eMotion	
Experience	*Feeling*	*Energy*
Enlightenment	Nirvana	1000
Peace	Bliss	600
Joy	Serenity	540
Love	Reverence	500
Reason	Understanding	400
Acceptance	Forgiveness	350
Optimism	Willingness	310
Trust	Neutrality	250
Courage	Affirmation	200
Pride	Scorn	175
Anger	Resentment	150
Desire	Craving	125
Fear	Anxiety	100
Grief	Regret	75
Apathy	Despair	50
Guilt	Blame	30
Shame	Humiliation	20

PING—a significant emotional experience

[box 1]

Duration: ___hr. ___min.

TUNE IN [box 2]

TURN ON [box 3]

PING—a significant emotional experience

Duration: ___hr. ___min.

TUNE IN

TURN ON

GRATITUDE

1.

2.

3.

If the only prayer you say in your whole life is 'thank you' that should suffice.— Meister Eckhart

PING—a significant emotional experience

Duration: ___hr. ___min.

TUNE IN

TURN ON

Emotion hierarchy adapted from Map of Consciousness: *Power vs. Force.* David R. Hawkins, M.D. Ph.D., 1995.

Know thyself.

The Oracle at Delphi

Day Sixteen—eStates: The Energetic States of Consciousness

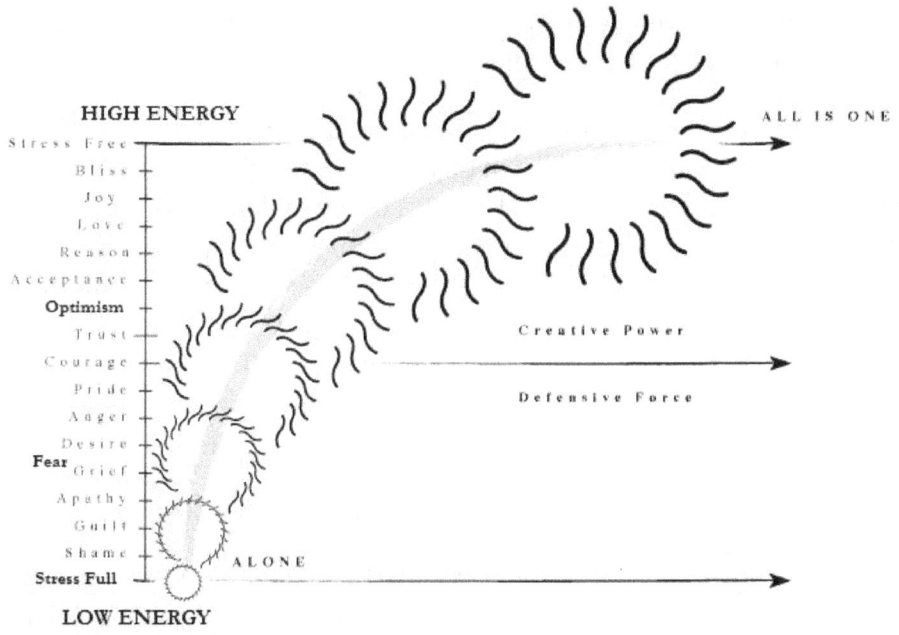

Right now, emotional energy is powering your state of consciousness. The current awareness you have of your own existence—the sensations, thoughts and perceptions of your surroundings—are all colored by the energy for motion being produced by your mind-body system. By feeling alive, in tune with the eMotions that move you, you achieve a more empowered awareness of the living moment. By recognizing ongoing energetic states of consciousness—eStates—you can determine where your life-energy is right now and where you want it to be in the future. This Odyssey of mind assists you in regaining full command and control of your thoughts and feelings by providing a strategy in which to neutralize negative energy states with a more positive, powerful life experience.

Under stress, life leaders strive to be in rational control of their emotional engine. With continuous improvement, they train their brains to be in command of the words and behaviors they use to navigate the challenging aspects of life. Rather than forcibly reacting to stress, life leaders know how to TUNE IN and TURN ON a courageous, optimistic mindset. They then use their positive energy to elevate the negative eStates of those around them. Aiming for high-energy consciousness, life leaders are on a mission to continuously improve their experience of feeling alive; striving to both survive and thrive in the challenges presented. Nirvana is the leadership quest—the evolution of the mind to an enlightened state of consciousness.

eStates affect everything you say, do and experience. For example, in an eState of anger, the aggressive energy drives your thoughts, words and actions. In anger, your energetic state of consciousness perceives life in a defensive, competitive manner. You become combative and process your daily encounters with similar survival programming. You may become intolerant of alternative points of views and entrench your mind with getting your way (the ugly side of pride). All the while, your spirit is driven by aggression and you feel increasingly resentful to sources of stress. Without self-knowledge of the eState, a rage-fueled explosion invariably occurs, releasing the built-up competitive tension. As being angry by defending your position consumes a lot of energy, angry people are soon exhausted. Not surprising then that depression, and feelings of apathy, are commonly experienced by those who are routinely angry.

Know yourself—this ancient advice is still pertinent on today's road of life. Often, our eStates change without notice. One minute we can be in bliss; the next, we're in guilt. Training the rational brain to recognize what the emotional brain is doing under stress, assists in moderating energy for motion. Maintaining a high eState means teaching yourself the physiological aspects of all your eStates, including the low-energy ones. For example, ask yourself, "When I am in a certain eState, how do I act? How do I think? How do I feel?" Take time to TUNE IN and rationally experience the visceral aspects of the different eStates. The better your rational intelligence is informed as to the motives of your primal intelligence, the better able you are to manage your ongoing eState.

Enlightenment is learnable. Really.

Today we will take time to explore the entire spectrum of eStates. Expect to gain a deeper understanding of the instinctual impetus behind what drives your behaviors in daily life. What stops most people from trusting their spirit is a lack of courage to actively learn from the lessons of life. Experiencing what it means to actively feel guilt, or shame or apathy in the moment requires a courageous mindset, the transformative gateway to the higher eStates.

Knowing yourself also means apprehending the life-energy powering your consciousness at any moment, and then doing something constructive with it. Let's start with the low-energy eStates, those usually termed negative states of mind.

DEFENSIVE FORCE: The Survive eStates

When energy is depleted, your self-organizing living process slows down to conserve energy. In the lowest eStates, the primary focus of your consciousness is on survival. Forced upon us by our primal intelligence, the survive eStates are what keep us alive instinctually. Although we may consider these energies unpleasant and even painful, survive eStates keep us safe by ensuring we escape the potential dangers around us.

There are eight survive eStates. They are deeply encoded into our human physiology and a foundation of who we are. When push comes to shove, our minds initiate a stress response, and it's these survival programs that dictate how we react instinctually and without thought. Genetically encoded via a 100+-million-year evolutionary journey, the survive eStates exist in us because we are survivors of the fittest. You have these eStates because they served every ancestor that survived before you.

The Survive eStates

Shame—"I feel alone"

When you have been rejected, punished or abused, feeling ashamed and humiliated becomes a natural stress response. The instinctual purpose of shame is to shut down all movement by collapsing your inner core of energy, which siphons strength and self-confidence. Like a blow to the belly, the visceral energy drain of shame causes your posture to slacken, and your head and shoulders to fall forward in a protective fetal position. In this submissive eState, you cut off eye contact with your abuser, separating yourself from the source of pain.

Guilt—"I feel bad"

When you have done something you know you shouldn't have done, you feel guilty. Guilt is pervasive in our society today, and (thanks to the Catholic Church and other guilt-inducing sources) has been deeply instilled in our cultural psyche for the past few hundred years. Feeling bad about something you've done keeps you in a state of low self-worth. As a regulatory, instinctual force however, guilt is essential for healthy social relations. Feeling guilty pings your consciousness to repair the connections you may have severed. To neutralize the energetic impact of guilt, courageous action is required to reconnect and right your wrong doings.

Apathy—"I feel depressed"

In terms of energy, apathy correlates strongly with despair and depression. When you experience a drain of energy over a longer period of time, your spirit deflates and you stop caring about your actions, flattening your motivation. Rudderless and without purpose, people in an eState of apathy often withdraw into isolation. In evolutionary terms, this depression of energy can be viewed as a sort of hibernation, where your spirit is allowed to rest and recharge. For our ancient ancestors, apathy kept them in their cave, protecting them from threats and allowing for healing and an increase in life-energy.

Grief—"I feel sad"

When you experience a loss, such as the death of a loved one or separation from a partner, you feel sad. Grieving helps remove the emotional energy associated with the dearly departed. In fact, tears produced when crying contain significantly increased quantities of prolactin and corticotrophin (stress hormones) and the elements of potassium and manganese[13] which may suggest that a good cry is helpful in healing an emotional wound. In energy terms, grief is seen as dark, yet it has more energy than apathy. When a depressed patient begins to cry, we know they are getting better.

Fear—"I feel anxious"

Acute fear is an essential eState for survival. The evolutionary advantage of fear is that it keeps your mind focused on what may harm you. Fear often inundates your consciousness as thoughts—mental reminders to watch out for threats in order to survive. However, while fear of danger is healthy, too much conscious attention to what can go wrong (chronic fear) can easily generate anxiety, and chronic anxiety often leads to apathy. Anxiety can be a self-destructive state of mind in that it drains copious amounts of energy by tensing your body in constant preparation for fight or flight.

Desire—"I feel hungry"

Before you can get something, you must first want it. As energy for motion, desire propels your spirit towards the object of want by instilling the motivation fuelled by the potential reward of pleasure. In instinctual terms, desire ultimately engages our most primal instincts; namely to eat, drink, breathe, be productive, socialize and have sex. If left unchecked, desire can also lead to the constant craving that characterizes addiction, which appears when our attention locks on the object of our desire. As desire motivates us, an inability to gain what we desire can easily lead to frustration and aggression, the more powerful energy of anger.

Anger—"I feel mad"

Anger has a negative connotation in our culture. However, anger as an evolutionary instinct is good in that it generates energy that gets us up and gets things done. Unbridled anger, however, is problematical as it causes us to lose grip on our rational intelligence. This quickly catapults us into rage with all its irrational thoughts and behaviors. However, if we can learn to harness the way we use anger, this eState has a range of positive attributes. In evolutionary terms, anger changes things. For those who've been victimized and oppressed, anger engages action, which can lead to the change of a person, society or culture.

Pride—"I feel important"

Individuals in pride feel attractive and revel in being the center of attention. When eyes are on you, you are validated and feel important. Indeed, in pride, you feel the first levels of positive energy at work. You look good and know it, strutting your stuff in life's parade. Prideful people

---

[13] Walter, Chip (December 2006). "Why do we cry?" *Scientific American Mind* 17 (6): 44.

generally speak in self-centered terms (i.e. "I've done that," "I've been there", "I have this", etc.) Pride becomes challenging when subjected to criticism which pings the ego (attachments of self-worth). This defensive positioning can easily ping an eState of anger if others challenge you. When you defend a mistake with excuses, it's the instinctual force of pride that is keeping you focused on gaining innocence (and self-worth) instead of having the courage to admit ignorance and grow from the experience.

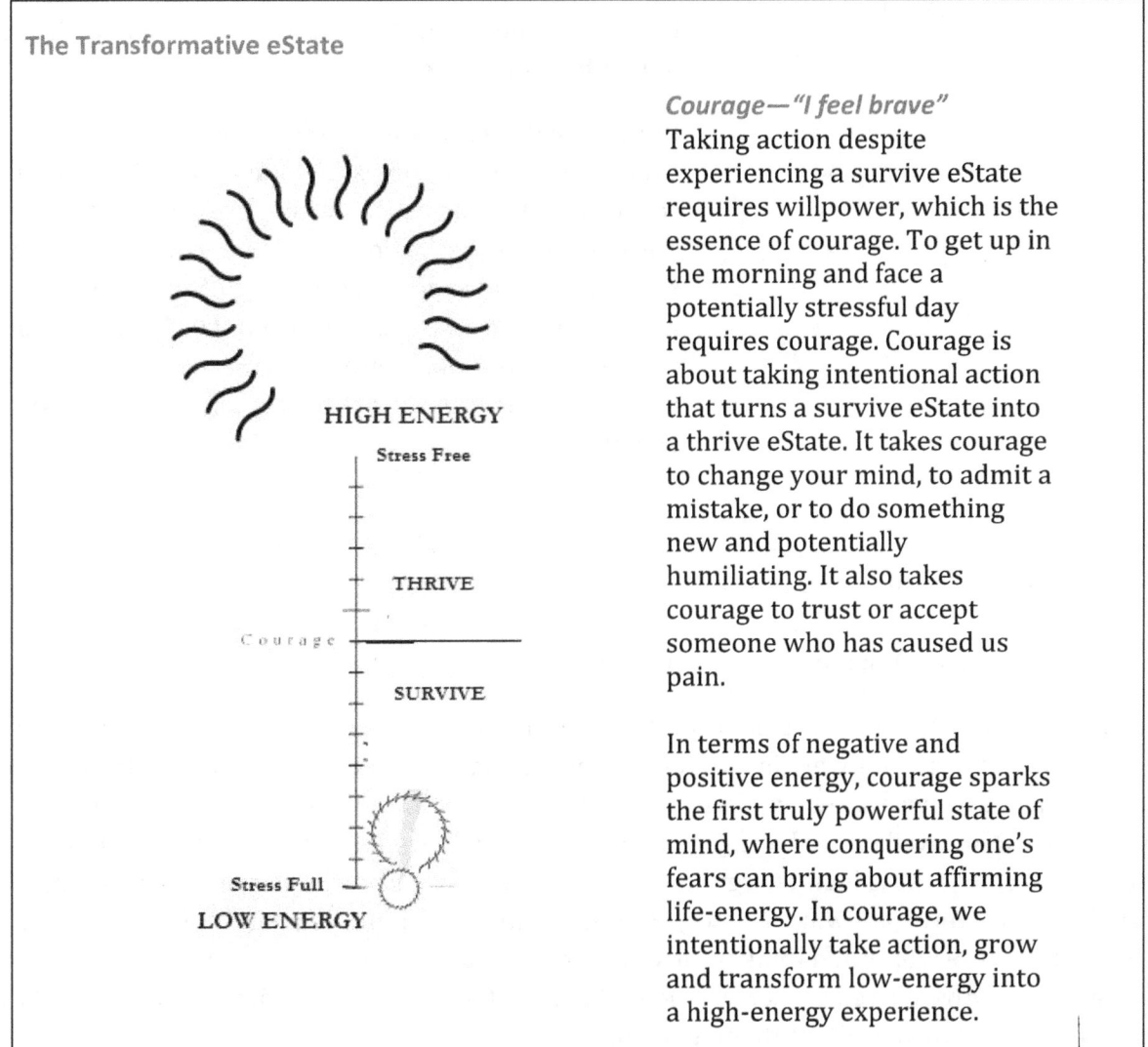

CREATIVE POWER: The Thrive eStates

While the survive eStates are negative (energy-draining), the thrive eStates are positive (energy-gaining). In energetic opposition to the stress response, the arousal response energizes our bodies by supplying them with feel-good biochemicals. Here at the more powerful eStates, the positive experience arouses our mind, body and senses, while bringing more enjoyment to everyday life. In these higher eStates, your spirit thrives.

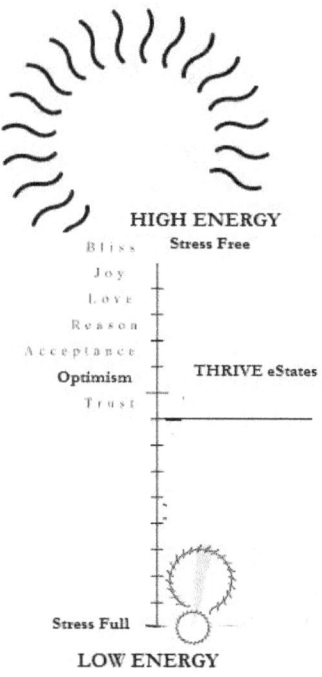

In the thrive eStates, physiological tension is released as we become less defensive to the people, places and events around us. Our bodies feel lighter and our minds sharper. As your energy increases, your spirit becomes exponentially electrified as you rise up the spectrum of eStates. As a result, your consciousness becomes increasingly powerful, looking beyond negative limitations and connecting more authentically with your higher human nature.

Within the thrive eStates, the survival-oriented, competitive "me" becomes the cooperative "we." As our consciousness becomes increasingly fuelled by more positive energy, we begin to see beyond differences and separations, and experience feelings of connectedness with everything and everyone around us.[14] As we gain more life-energy, our consciousness becomes more enlightened, energized with a brighter, more open and empowered way of perceiving ourselves and the world around us.

At the highest thrive eStates, your spirit soars in love, joy and peace. You feel connected to yourself and others. All-is-one as your mind-body-spirit operates in a holistic manner. As the survival instincts are satisfied, you experience feelings that are more carefree and enjoyable, experiencing the sensual moments of true happiness.

You may not readily experience many of these thrive eStates. If you were raised by parents or teachers who themselves were in survive eStates, you have some thrive training to do. If you do not experience thrive eStates regularly, you may simply not have the eMemories of optimism, acceptance or joy available to be engaged. Instead, you will need to teach yourself the TURN ON process to achieve these high-energy states of mind. Give yourself a lot of space to grow and transform the neural pathways. Mastery is about continuous improvement. It's not enough to simply read these words and think positive thoughts. You have to do the brain training to engage the positive energies when you need them most. Learn by doing, first by imagining these experiences, and then by living them in the moment.

Here are the thrive eStates that TURN ON a more powerful life experience.

The Thrive eStates

Trust—"I feel confident"

Trust is experienced as the first energy-gaining eMotion. In trust, we connect to the life-energy of others. The ability to feel trust at work represents a crucial shift from a singular "me" to a

---

[14] This enlightened "all-is-one" eState is the polar-opposite energy of feeling alone, the eState of shame.

plural "we." This me-to-we transition of consciousness comes about through courage. Indeed, it takes courage to trust, no matter whether you trust a stranger or your own skills and instincts. But once an eState of trust is programmed into your eMemory, you can access self-confidence at will. At the first thrive eState, you trust that all is okay and feel a neutral sense of energy buoyancy. You become less attached to expectations, as not always getting your way becomes self-actualization rather than self-defeat.

Optimism—"I feel willing"

When you are willing to learn and grow by experiencing new things, you empower your spirit with positive energy that lifts your capacity to take on new challenges. With a consciousness powered by optimism, you start experiencing the world as a positive place filled with a wide range of possibilities. In the energy-generating eState of optimism, a glass of water is naturally perceived as half-full rather than half-empty. Optimists generally feel that their lives and the lives of people around them are inherently good, and that most situations work out for the best.

Acceptance—"I feel cooperative"

When you accept others for how they are or what they've done, you acknowledge that their energy is no longer a threat to your survival. To be accepting means to feel more connected to the web of life of which we are all a part. In this evolved state of consciousness, you accept yourself and realize that happiness is an eState that is already inside you, not something found in the material world. When you embody acceptance, your self-awareness shifts as you observe the spirits of others, regardless of physical appearance, race, abilities, sexual preferences or political affiliations. By embracing diversity, you drop judgments and allow yourself to form a stronger energy-connection with others.

Reason—"I understand"

Rational intelligence rises to the forefront of your consciousness when the survival impetus of your primal intelligence is sated. In the eState of reason, you neutralize negative eMotions naturally as a result of your greater understanding of the people, places or events that ping your mind. Fuelled by this high-octane life-energy, you can discern, manipulate and analyze large amounts of information and make decisions rapidly and intuitively. Seeing both sides of an argument requires an eState of reason and understanding. The Dalai Lama has said that he sees himself as a scientist, remaining in this logical state of mind at all times, seeking greater understanding in every dilemma.

Love—"I feel connected"

In terms of energy and physiological response, love is the polar opposite of fear. Where fear is energy-draining, love is energy-gaining. In love, you give of yourself, your energy, your attention and time. Love perpetuates the health and happiness of a society and life itself. In an eState of love, you cooperate naturally with those around you. In terms of romantic love, you drop your defenses and become intimately connected to another person. Love should not be confused with desire; love is unconditional and exists without desire, because it is about connection rather than pursuing the need. Love focuses your consciousness on the goodness of life in all its expressions.

Joy—"I feel whole"

Love allows you to connect with Universal Energy more openly and freely. In the eState of joy, you live without shame and in a full and authentic expression of your personal values. Joy is the experience of a consistent feeling of happiness, contentment, and serenity that comes about from living in a high-energy perception of life. In joy, action is effortless because you truly enjoy what you do, whatever it is. With joy comes a sense of completeness. Nothing is missing. Everything is there. All is one.

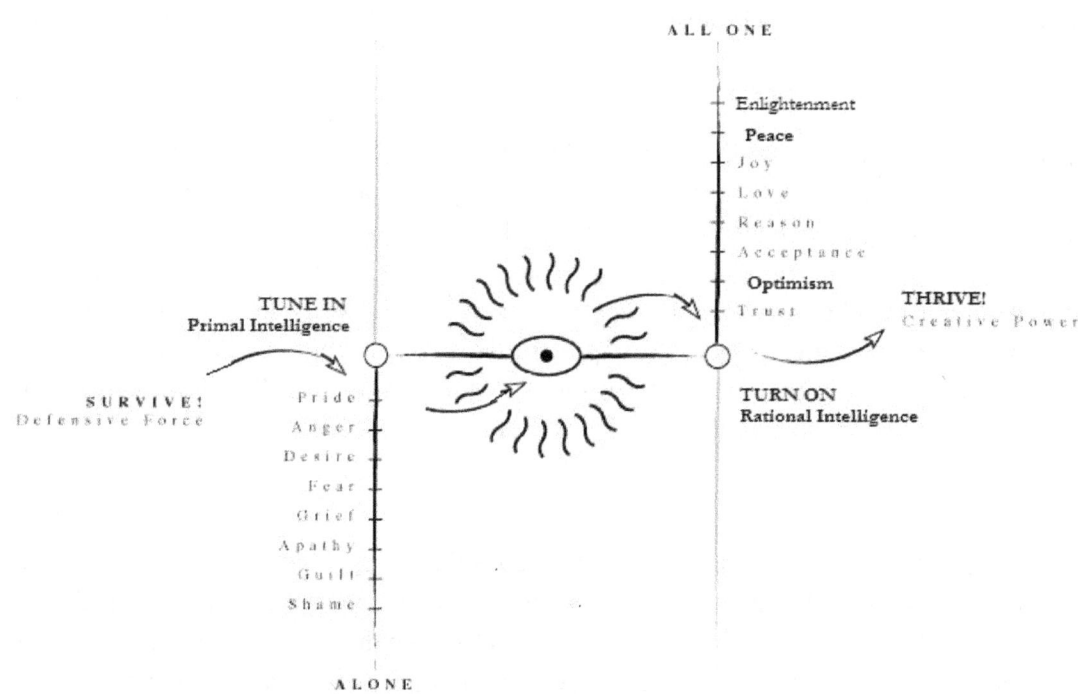

Above-the-Line Behavior

As we've read, there is an energetic threshold between the survive and thrive eStates—the eState of courage. Below this line of courage, energy is drained, and the mind and body become tense and defensive in the varying experiences of the stress response. Competition and survival is the name of the game. Many refer to these below-the-line eStates as negative energy.

In opposition, above the line of courage, energy is gained; defenses are dropped and physiological tension is relaxed. A competitive me-mindset becomes a cooperative we-consciousness. The higher eStates span the positive energies of trust, optimism, acceptance, understanding, love and joy. The journey up the ladder is one of continuous improvement— the path to enlightenment. Indeed, at the highest eState—above joy—is what Buddhists call Nirvana: a state characterized by freedom from or oblivion to pain, worry, and the external world.

> **FIRST UNIVERSAL TRUTH: Live in the present moment**

Whether we label eStates as negative or positive, or if our quest is to reach Nirvana, I want to emphasize that all eStates are good, not bad. (Those who do not experience guilt and shame are called psychopaths.) From an evolutionary perspective, every eMotion we experience plays a critical role in our survival and prosperity as a species. A life leader does not live solely in the thrive eStates. A true life leader is a captain and commander of every eMotion, embracing both the negative and positive. A life leader has learned to live in the present moment, no matter what life-energy he or she may be experiencing.

As we have learned in regards to the stress response, the survive eStates are emotionally encoded and energy-draining, and therefore their ongoing experience inhibits health and happiness. The arousal response, experienced as courage and the thrive eStates, is much more conducive to maintaining optimal mental health. As you are learning, courage—the transformative eState—is the warrior medicine necessary to go from destructive to constructive, negative to positive. Indeed, courage is the empowering eState that separates the two realms of emotional experience—from "me" to "we," from competitive to cooperative, from stress to arousal. In the days ahead, you will increasingly understand how to remain above-the-line; stronger, with greater appreciation for what courage is all about, and what it really means to be a hero in your own life story.

Tomorrow we will take the high road and begin to explore the above-the-line behaviors in more detail. Your quest now is turning the act of merely surviving the pings of daily challenges into calls to adventure.

Day Sixteen Exercise

All eMotions serve an evolutionary purpose in keeping you alive. Today, TURN ON and accept all the negative energy that you have been living with. Accept and forgive yourself profoundly for all the mistakes, misjudgments and misfortunes that may be plaguing your life. Love yourself intentionally and unconditionally—the good, the bad and the ugly. In today's exercise, devote time to more fully understanding that pings are there to help you improve your eState. Again, use the Odyssey Methodology to complete the Quest Journal.

odyssey

The Odyssey Methodology

1. TUNE IN

Remember your day	Close your eyes and mentally review your day. Remember the pings—the people, places or events—that caused you stress, then determine the eMotion triggered by the ping. - *A ping is a significant emotional experience that shifts your energy.* - *You remember pings because of their emotional energy.*
Record your pings	Pick the three most impactful pings of the day and record. [PING - box 1] For each ping, choose the eState that best suits how you responded to the eMotion experienced and record. [TUNE IN - box 2]
Reflect your energy	Focus on how the ping affected your energetic state. Teach your brain what the ping feels like (i.e. grief, anxiety, apathy, etc.). Mentally label the feelings with a rational understanding of the eMotion.

2. TURN ON

Raise your eState	Choose an eState higher than the one experienced for each ping and record. [TURN ON - box 3]
Replay your day	Close your eyes and with palm on forehead, visualize reliving each ping in the higher eState. Imagine the same people, place or event ping in the new eState. - *Include all aspects of the more empowering eMotion. See yourself being confident, responding authentically with pleasant gestures, facial expressions, calm voice, etc.*
Resolve your pings	Set action to neutralize the ping-energy. Ask yourself: What task or solution is necessary to fix a problem? Reconnect with a person? What steps are required to repair what is broken / disconnected? In courage, take action! - *Set an intention to follow through on the commitment. With palm on forehead, mentally rehearse being courageous / optimistic / accepting of the situation. Visualize the new behavior. Train the brain for a high-energy response to stress.*

odyssey

The Quest Journal
- Day Sixteen -

Date: ___ Day: S — M — T — W — Th — F — S

eState	eMotion	
Experience	*Feeling*	*Energy*
Enlightenment	Nirvana	1000
Peace	Bliss	600
Joy	Serenity	540
Love	Reverence	500
Reason	Understanding	400
Acceptance	Forgiveness	350
Optimism	Willingness	310
Trust	Neutrality	250
Courage	Affirmation	200
Pride	Scorn	175
Anger	Resentment	150
Desire	Craving	125
Fear	Anxiety	100
Grief	Regret	75
Apathy	Despair	50
Guilt	Blame	30
Shame	Humiliation	20

PING—a significant emotional experience

[box 1]

Duration: ___hr. ___min.

TUNE IN [box 2]

TURN ON [box 3]

PING—a significant emotional experience

Duration: ___hr. ___min.

TUNE IN

TURN ON

GRATITUDE
1.

2.

3.

If the only prayer you say in your whole life is 'thank you' that should suffice.— Meister Eckhart

PING—a significant emotional experience

Duration: ___hr. ___min.

TUNE IN

TURN ON

Emotion hierarchy adapted from Map of Consciousness: *Power vs. Force.* David R. Hawkins, M.D. Ph.D., 1995.

A human being is a part of the whole, called by us Universe, a part limited in time and space. He experiences himself, his thoughts and feelings as something separated from the rest, a kind of optical delusion of his consciousness. This delusion is a kind of prison, restricting us to our personal desires and to affection for a few persons nearest to us. Our task must be to free from this prison by widening our circle of compassion to embrace all living creatures and the whole of nature in its beauty.

Albert Einstein

Day Seventeen—#2 Road Rule: THRIVE!

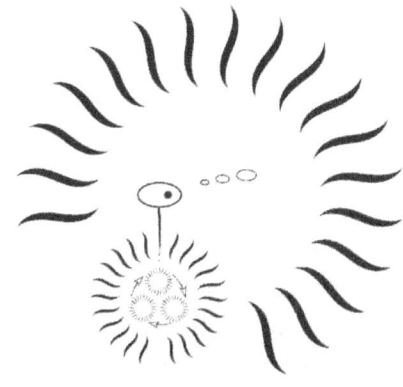

Life does not and cannot live alone. Life, by itself, soon withers and dies. As such, a powerful connection indicator that informs our consciousness as to the health of our relationships is encoded in our instincts. Your eMotions do more than just move you—they connect you energetically to others. By using the TUNE IN process (your in-tune-ition), you can gauge your connections to the people in your web of life and take intentional energy-gaining action when disconnection occurs. The act of feeling alive can now become a personal barometer as to the wellbeing of your emotional ecology. This living self-knowledge will help you thrive as you survive social challenges with an increasingly high-energy mindset.

For example, when you feel alone, you experience feelings of shame, guilt, grief, apathy and fear—the survive eStates. These uncomfortable feelings tell you that you are, even if only on a psychological level, disconnected from the web of life that is essential for survival. From an Observer consciousness, survive eStates are signals that prompt us to take action and connect with others. This requires courage—the gateway to experiencing the high-energy eMotions.

On the top end of the life-energy spectrum, the thrive eStates inform us of our level of association to the people around us. When relationships are healthy, we feel that all-is-one and experience the positive (connective) energies of trust, optimism, acceptance, understanding and love. Joy and true happiness develop when we are not only physically connected to others, but mentally and emotionally as well. This requires a TUNE IN to the defensive reactions we may have with other people, and a TURN ON of courage to trust, accept, understand and love them. It takes courage to reach out and love someone. To love means to give of our life-energy in the form of time, attention and affection. So why isn't there more love flowing from people? It's because most are hording their energy in an eState of fear—anxious and afraid of losing what little life-energy they have.

If you've ever been rejected or abused, or suffered an agonizing separation or divorce, the associated painful emotional energy of the disconnection experience (such as grief, guilt, or shame) was encoded into your eMemories. To your primal intelligence, people are now viscerally remembered as a source of pain and a threat to your survival. When you desire an intimate relationship, it is these eMemories of past painful connections that inform our state of mind and invoke feelings of fear and anxiety, which sabotage our connective efforts. As a result, social phobia and a generalized fear of people keep us away and at an emotionally safe distance. This leads to alienation and withdrawal in a primal effort to survive the challenges that come with people. Again, this is why courage is the transformative eState in the quest to thrive. Step One: TUNE IN competitive low-energy eStates. Step Two: TURN ON a cooperative high-energy mindset. Use acts of courage to overwrite fear-based eMemories and reconnect with people using more powerful, positive eMotion.

As an energy-gaining brain function, your primal intelligence can be taught to not be afraid of people. Again, this level of functionality requires you to TURN ON your higher brain functions and act courageously when pinged into a survive eState. It takes courage to confront a bully, admit a mistake, call an angry friend, or reach out to someone who has wronged you. Courage (i.e. taking action despite feeling anxious) is essential in rebuilding trust if we are hurt emotionally or if our pride is bruised. This energy-gaining exercise strengthens our ability to bounce back quickly from people's negative energy.

When we intentionally accept people the way they are, or understand and love them for their differences, we teach our brain that they are not enemies that can hurt us. To truly thrive is to feel alive and confident in your own ability to successfully survive around people. This is possible when you learn to trust your spirit to navigate challenging social situations.

Life is about survival of the fittest. In a society that promotes individual rights and freedom, we have been taught to survive by competing with our fellow man. As a result, when we are under stress, our primal intelligence powers up the primal survive eMotions automatically. In terms of life-energy, we become disconnected and end up feeling anxious, addicted or aggressive in a competitive effort to remain alive. This defensive low-energy mindset is an automatic survival response. We are pinged with anger when someone cuts us off in traffic or shuns our emotional needs—these are acts of disconnection. We are struck with sadness when someone close dies or moves away. And we feel bad when we do something that disconnects ourselves from others.

We often learn these emotional behaviors in childhood and may still use those 'how to behave' eMemories subconsciously, like riding a bike or driving a car without ever thinking about the skill. To thrive, pay close attention to your energy when people pings occur and TURN ON high-energy strategies in the moment to deal with social stress. The quest is to increasingly trust your spirit to successfully navigate people and their negative energy.

Surviving Among the Fittest

Survive eStates are instinctually forced upon us. Take desire for instance. Desire is fundamental to staying alive. We desire food, water, air, security and social connection without thinking about it. With a core sexual competency, our primal intelligence is driven by an insatiable yearning to unite with others and perpetuate the species. Powered by the energy of desire, our primal attention system searches incessantly for pleasurable energy-gaining sources, and once found, locks our rational mind onto those things automatically. To be certain, we must want something before we can have it. That's why life has instilled powerful primal eMotions that ping our consciousness and motivate us to take action to get what we desire.

As a primal life-energy, desire can easily lock down our state of mind by generating a constant craving for what we don't have. In time, the brain becomes wired to be persistently hungry for sources of positive energy. An addicted brain then forces attention on those things we think will make us feel better. Those whose brains have been wired with desire become easily unsatisfied with what's right in front of them, craving their next high-energy fix. Be it alcohol, illicit drugs, sex, binge shopping or porn, addicts become manically obsessed with getting the want of their desire, to the point of becoming anxious or aggressive. Likewise, addicts of all types can lock their thinking process in an eState of desire as their rational intelligence constantly schemes for the next fix of external, high-energy pleasure.

This makes rational sense. Nature has provided us with a core sexual competency that has already wired our brains to feel lonely, to desire companionship, and to have sex and make babies. Sex is at the heart of our social conscious. Our primal intelligence is always in tune with our emotional ecology and our prospects for the intimate connections that can make this happen. As being intimate and sexual are some of the most pleasurable experiences of humankind, it's no wonder then that the happiest people around are in loving, sexually fulfilling relationships. Their primal intelligence experiences the real, connected sensual aspects of another human being. This is where life not only survives as an individual, but thrives as a community.

The sexual connective competency of our spirit is why we compare ourselves to others, and why we worry about what people think about us. Being sexy and attractive is a desirable pleasure in that it draws attention to ourselves and connects us energetically to others. Feeling accepted, understood and loved, we experience the high-energy states of the emotional spectrum at work. The challenge with a rational pursuit for love is that prideful adoration provides only a temporary fix. The attention we receive may elevate us to feel good about ourselves for a while, but as competitive creatures, we easily fall back to a state of desire where we crave more attention. This is why people who seemingly have it all can remain unhappy and unsatisfied with their life—they become wired in the survive eState of desire.

In a society where looking good is a competitive sport, it requires more to thrive and feel alive than mere superficial remedies. When new clothes, a new car, a new body or a new partner fail to satisfy our fix, it's time for a new process of energy improvement—learning to TUNE IN to a survive eState and TURN ON a thrive one.

This means taking our energy-connections with others very seriously.

Spirit-to-Spirit Connections

Nature has hard-wired our brains to be energy-sensitive to others. Equipped with mirror neurons—specialized brain cells that reflect the emotional state in others—our brain remains in tune to the eMotions that power people. In this way, behaviors, physical gestures, facial expressions and tone of voice all inform our spirit as to the energetic state of another without thinking about it. A smile can ping us with a smile because our mirror neurons pick up the associated life-energy automatically. That's also why we can become angry when navigating around aggressive people. You do not have to think about the energy-connection. Your primal intelligence has already processed their state of mind. Through this subconscious messaging process, our spirit connects with the spirit of others.

Mirror neurons ensure we remain aware of the emotional intention of others automatically, if only subconsciously. In order to survive, we unknowingly feel what they feel. Their anxieties become our fears. Their negative emotional states soon affect our own state of mind. If we're not in tune to both their spirit and our own, their primal motivations can and do siphon our own energy stores. Primal intelligence will instinctually gear up our defensives to protect us from energy-draining—painful—sources. In order to thrive around negativity, we need a heightened in-tune-ition that keeps us high and feeling connected around energy-draining people.

The other day, an executive client confided to me about a work situation he was pinged with. No matter how hard he tried, he couldn't get the emotionally-charged experience out of his mind. Seems he heard from a coworker that his vice president had told a few people in his department that his work was of poor quality.

"Has he ever told you that directly?" I asked.

"Not at all. When I meet with him, he acts like everything is fine."

"Well, is your work *really* terrible?"

"No! I take pride in my work. We do have this new financial system I'm getting used to…"

I challenged his belief, "So he's lying about you?"

"Yes."

"What do you want to do?"

"I want him to stop thinking badly of me."

"Fair enough. Sounds like you need to resolve this challenge. What does your in-tune-ition say about his eState? What eMotions are driving his behavior?"

My client sat back and closed his eyes. After a few moments of TUNE IN contemplation, he answered, "Anger. He has a lot of anger. And fear. He's afraid of looking bad. And of course he's never satisfied with anything, so desire too." My client opened his eyes with an enlightened awareness, "He's gone primal! He's operating in survival mode! No wonder I can't get him off my mind. He's become a threat to *my* survival."

"Well done. To your primal intelligence, he is now an enemy to be dealt with. The PTSD of the experience and your associated thoughts are simply mental reminders to survive the threat."

"So how do I get him out of my head?"

"You already know the answer. Again, what does your in-tune-ition say? What eMotion did he ping in you?"

My client sat back, closed his eyes and again focused attention on his life-energy. After a quick TUNE IN, the answer was immediate, "Shame! He humiliated me! No wonder I've been feeling so lousy."

"Terrific. Let's neutralize the ping energy by connecting to your spirit. Step one: TUNE IN to the shame energy and experience it with a rational understanding of its instinctual purpose. Close your eyes, but this time, place a palm on your forehead[15]. Imagine your boss shaming

---

[15] A palm-on-forehead activates acupressure points, which allows blood to flow back into the frontal cortex, the executive center of the brain. This has a calming effect and facilitates learning.

you. Observe him from a distance, like a fly on the wall. See him being primal—angry, hungry and afraid. Visualize him operating in survival mode. Now, take a moment to really experience what shame feels like to you. Get familiar and comfortable with the low-energy state. Label the eState in your mind. Spend a minute and concentrate. Train your rational brain to recognize what your emotional one is doing right now with that ping." I allowed my client time to focus and encode the new awareness.

"Next, TURN ON your higher brain functions. Keep your eyes closed and place a palm on your forehead. Breathe deeply and relax. Continue to visualize your manager in the act of shaming you. Take a deep breath and intentionally relax your body. Teach your primal intelligence that he is not an enemy. "

"Begin to accept and forgive him because he's gone primal and is not thinking straight. TURN ON a new understanding of his low-energy motives. Keep focused until you feel the charged-energy dissipate and your mind relax. It's natural to feel anger as your energy returns, but remember, there is always an above-the-line leadership solution. Imagine being optimistic that there is a high-energy answer to the challenge." I let my client focus and train his brain for the optimal solution.

After a few minutes, I added, "Now, ask yourself, 'what action could you take to resolve the situation and rebuild trust in the relationship?'"

"I guess I could confront him directly, but that is scary. He has a strong personality and is intimidating. People avoid him if they can. He frightens everybody."

"Sounds like a scared bully to me. That's okay. As John Wayne said, courage is about being scared to death but saddling up anyway."

"Do I really have to face him?" I could tell fear was setting in.

"No, but your primal intelligence won't become wiser and braver. To your spirit, he'll still remain an enemy."

My client took this in and let out a breath. "Okay. What do I need to do?"

"Trust your spirit on this. Without thinking, if you were in an eState of optimism, what would you do?"

"I would just go up to him and ask, 'Is my work of poor quality'?"

"Great. Very courageous to walk up to the enemy and look them in the eye. Are you willing to do it?"

He looked perplexed. "I get that the Odyssey is necessary." He hesitated, and then looked me in the eye. "Sure. Why not? I can only get fired."

"Before you catastrophize it, what does your intuition say you need to do? Follow your gut instincts."

> He closed his eyes, focused inwardly for a moment. "Yep. I gotta do it."
>
> "Good. I'm proud of you. To help prepare you for the challenge, TURN ON and visualize meeting him with a calm and powerful personal authority. See yourself confident and courageous. Mentally rehearse what you'll say and do in your mind's eye so your primal intelligence gets comfortable with the idea. Practice asking 'Is my work of poor quality?' in a high eState. Say it in a cool and collected state of mind; body strong and the mind sharp. Look him straight in the eyes with your fortitude, and silently communicate you're a leader. A high-energy leader. Connect not in fear or anger, but in an optimistic acceptance that together you both will come to a new level of understanding. That's your Odyssey."
>
> A week later, I was curious to hear how it went. "How'd it go?"
>
> My client settled back on the sofa with a relaxed confidence I hadn't seen before. "I think he is my new best friend."
>
> "Really?" I pulled my chair closer, "Tell me about it."
>
> "A few days ago, he was outside his office and we caught eyes. I asked if he had a moment, and he said yes. When I walked up, my coworkers were close by and were taking notice. I wasn't feeling afraid or angry. I just did it. I felt my heart start beating hard but I simply walked up to him, looked him straight in the eyes and asked 'Is my work of poor quality'?' He froze. I think he was shocked. I couldn't help but grin. He got that I was serious. He looked around and shuffled me right into his office. We ended up having a very authentic discussion about my work with the new financials. It was a good chat. We both learned something about the other. He's really an okay bloke, just unaware of his energy."
>
> "Do you trust him now?" I asked.
>
> "It's better than before but he'll have to prove himself. I do feel less afraid of him. I'm not so worried about his opinion of me any more." My client reflected on his heroic feat. "It's good. It's all good. Every living moment. So, when's my next Odyssey?!"

Why do we care what other people think of us? After all, we can rationally understand that everyone is entitled to their opinion. But how often do we find ourselves with an energetic hook to someone else; our thoughts tied to theirs, overly concerned with what they may be thinking? Why does it bother us? It may be that our neurons are picking up their primal energy unbeknownst to our conscious mind and has deemed it a threat to our survival. That's because separation—even the thought of it—is painful. Words do hurt. A verbal assault or a nasty social media post can pack the same punch of negative energy as a physical blow when it enters our consciousness. Real pain can be experienced with virtual pings. Our spirit knows being disconnected means pain—feelings of shame, guilt, apathy and grief. For health and happiness, the social intelligence of our spirit must be respected yet strengthened. Anyone can go primal under stress—even the best of us! Continue to learn what specific behaviors people do to ping you and take action to resolve the connection positively, if only in your mind. TUNE IN—TURN ON three pings a day and stay energy-connected to those important to you.

Review your pings for the last two weeks and you'll likely discover that a majority of them originates from people. No doubt, people pings in survive eStates are at the root-cause of our biggest energy drains. Many people we meet are locked into primal eMotions that they cannot turn off. If we are not careful, they can act as black holes that suck the life-energy from our spirit. So, how do we remain in high-energy around dysfunctional friends and family? You must take active leadership of your spirit around the challenging spirits of others.

Spiritual Leadership

The first step in aspiring to be an inspirational leader is learning to manage your own energy under stress. Leadership by example is the preferred strategy, but before you can effectively lead others, your spirit should be high-energy and above-the-line most of the time. It is not surprising that we are attracted to leaders who remain calm, cool and collected under pressure. Like a magnet, we are attracted to their positive 'can-do' attitude. We will even follow confident leaders into battle by connecting to their power-fueled state of mind. We will also change our values and beliefs when we perceive others whose values have more powerful life-energy.

Since communication is more than 90% non-verbal, it's not *what* you say but *how* you say it that can influence others to take action and adopt your way of thinking. Management by fear and aggression will make people run away, whereas leaders in positive high-energy states attract the best and brightest to follow. All energy management (or spiritual leadership, as I like to call it) needs is that you TUNE IN your emotional states and TURN ON higher eStates on command.

Research routinely finds that the happiest people on the planet are those who are connected to a web of life that is bigger than they are. This is why religion (Latin, *ligare*, to tie), in its many forms, can play an important role in the health and happiness of individuals. Practicing one's religion can psychologically tie us to the energetic benefits of connecting to "all-is-one," be it God, Mother Earth, the Great Spirit or a Buddha mind—constructs that promote feelings of togetherness or community or "oneness." Despite our variable connections with other people, comfort and contentment comes when our mind, body and spirit experience the stable sanctity of connection to those energy sources that can provide us with the essential elements for our survival. Connecting consciously then to Universal Energy becomes a positive strategy that can elevate even atheists to higher energetic states of consciousness.

Our foundational beliefs are stored in our eMemories, and those emotional programs power our ongoing feelings of being alive. (Think of beliefs as eMemories formed by rational knowledge encoded with emotional energy.) And just like our feelings, eMemories, knowledge and experience can change with intentional re-engineering. We just need to train the brain to respond in high-energy when the stress is on.

In his book, *Man's Search for Meaning*, Viktor Frankl found that the power of belief meant the difference between people giving up and dying, or surviving in the midst of adversity. Imprisoned in the Auschwitz concentration camp, the Jewish psychologist began asking his fellow captives about their purpose in life. He discovered that those with a positive outlook of the future, who were able to immerse their imagination in that outcome, were better able to survive the horrid conditions. According to Frankl, the way a prisoner imagined the future affected his longevity.

> TURN ON: Feeling alone? TUNE IN the anxious feelings and TURN ON a connective reality of all-is-one.

Even without practicing an organized religion, agnostics and atheists are able to TURN ON an all-is-one mindset, tie fast to a higher social consciousness and feel better connected to the world around them. Amidst adversity, this means choosing high-energy beliefs that help you respond to stress in courage, trust and optimism. All of which leads to creating a better and brighter you.

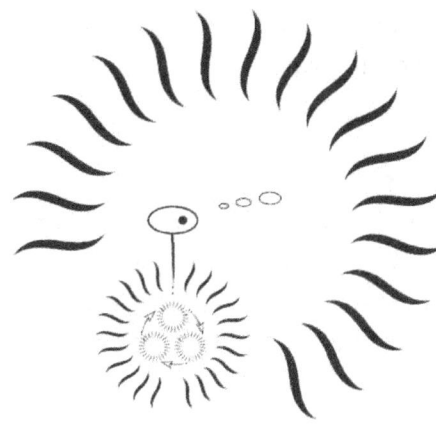

Thrive Intelligence

Having a belief system that promotes a cooperative connection (a thrive eState) to a community is essential for high-energy experiences. True leaders aim to instill thrive energy not only in themselves, but in others by bringing fragmented people and societies together. Leaders unite and connect people. They inspire others to change their competitive me-mindsets to a cooperative we-consciousness. Utilizing the willpower of their spirit, life leaders TURN ON beliefs that ping people positively with optimism, acceptance, understanding and love—each an important ingredient in a quest to thrive in a complex, energy-draining world.

Beliefs encoded with high-energy help spark feel-good biochemicals in the body, just as negative thoughts can drain energy and make you feel lousy. Remember, whatever you think or do, your primal intelligence is "in" on the conversation sparking your feelings.

In the everyday world, the rational modern brain and the emotional primal brain should ideally work together to get you to where you want to go. To use one by itself is to force yourself through life using an unbalanced mind-body system. Using both brains as if they were one is a more powerful alternative. The TUNE IN and TURN ON process enables you to manage the yin-yang duality of the cognitive-emotive system and to keep the living process in sync.

For example, let's say you desire to get to the other side of the road. Using rational intelligence, you start by making an intentional decision and setting a clear goal—to cross the street. You begin by focusing your mind on the objective. Listening to this call to action, primal intelligence powers up your body to get you there. If your attention is distracted, and the goal is not achieved, primal intelligence goes into stress (by not utilizing its generated eMotion) and a low-energy state is experienced.

If however, you steadfastly TUNE IN and follow through on the objective and make it safely across the road, you TURN ON pleasurable biochemicals in the body and you feel a rush of energy. Your primal intelligence rewards your brain for achieving the goal. Even if you TUNE IN and feel anxious or apathetic, take action anyway! TURN ON the courage necessary to walk across your next metaphorical street—and just do it! Your anxiety and fear will be left behind as high-energy is generated and you feel happier for making the journey. This is what thrive intelligence is all about—growing wiser and braver every step of the way.

The TUNE IN—TURN ON Process

Thrive intelligence is about both knowing where you are energetically (TUNE IN) and taking a more positive approach to dealing with the circumstance (TURN ON). With a living-in-the-moment awareness, you take action congruent with your primal intentions. The benefit here is that when you cross a metaphorical street often enough, the effort becomes habit. The once anxious challenge becomes an exercise in emotional strength-training. So, the next time you feel apathetic about going to a party, or feel anxious about having that terse conversation with a colleague, TURN ON your courage and just do it! The Odyssey will help encode more powerful eStates into your eMemory. Social efforts will become easier as your brain and body adapt to the challenge. Soon, you will begin to enjoy the journey of connecting with others.

All it takes to thrive is a living-in-the-moment awareness to step into social challenges with courage. Assuming you survive the effort, neurons will adapt and you'll begin to perform easier the next time. Again, practice makes perfect. Success builds on success as your brain becomes wired to be courageous. With thrive intelligence at the helm, you may still feel fear and apprehension, but know to take action anyway. This is the essence of the TUNE IN—TURN ON process of energy improvement.

This process re-engineering effort comes in handy when navigating everyday life. For example, when you send a text to a friend and do not hear back in a timely manner, your brain goes into stress because your desire—to get an immediate response—did not get fulfilled. We have no control over when another person will respond to a text. So, to thrive, TUNE IN to your negative reaction (the ping of anger, desire or fear in not receiving a reply) and TURN ON a high-energy response, such as being optimistic that they are not ignoring you, or simply accepting that they are not near their phone. Expectations that are not met have a draining effect on our spirit as disconnections set off a stress response.

> TURN ON: To remain high, it's important to manage your energy-connections with others.

Navigating the road of life with a clear, focused mind is paramount to high-energy experiences. It's also a birthright. When the mind is filled with negative pings and other distracting thoughts, it's hard to set clear intentions and follow through on them. Those diagnosed with ADHD may find it difficult at first to focus, but like a muscle, attention can be strengthened and fine-tuned. I often prescribe clients with ADHD to watch the burning flame of a candle, first only for a few minutes, working their way up to ever longer times. This helps strengthen the attention muscle. Counting your breaths is always a good TUNE IN exercise. So, too, is taking time to TURN ON your energy and neutralize ping-powered thoughts and stress responses. Yoga, meditation and other mindfulness exercises are ideal ways to wrangle in your desires and primal eMotions and replace them with high-energy.

Remember that our primal intelligence rewards us with pleasure when we take action congruent with our intentions. Creating integrity between our emotional and rational brain decreases stress within the two living systems and we naturally feel relaxed and more powerful. To thrive in stress-filled environments is an ongoing, continuously improving effort until it becomes habit.

> *Fear is a reaction. Courage is a decision.* Winston Churchill

A Spirited Adventure

It may be surprising to hear that Mike Tyson, a former undisputed heavyweight world champion, would be afraid of anything. The fact is, however, that Tyson struggled with fear throughout his career. He was very open about his own feelings of anxiety, and his trainers spent hours consoling him and helping him come to terms with his fear. Tyson even said himself, "I'm scared every time I go into the ring, but it's how you handle it. What you have to do is plant your feet, bite down on your mouthpiece and say, 'Let's go.'" Without question, Tyson learned how to TUNE IN his fear and ultimately TURN ON the courage to fight his foes successfully (even if controversially). In retrospect, fear became one of his most powerful weapons.

We may have evolved as human beings, but the same basic instincts that kept people alive before technology and sophistication took over, still dominate human physiology. Our core competencies are innate. No matter where we are—in combat, contemplation or copulation—survival remains at the heart of our existence. As we go forward on the road of life, primal eMotions will forever be a part of our lives. To not only survive but thrive, means to face our fears directly and welcome the journey along the path of challenges we encounter every day.

Again, there is a real impetus for taking the high road as science continues to provide us with insightful discoveries into what it means to fight our battles. As a social species, we are viscerally interconnected with other people because they are essential to our survival. Research from the University of Michigan[16] has found that how our spirit connects to other people plays a major role in the way we approach and deal with social stress.

The researchers placed volunteers in a variety of contests which pitted one against the other. After each challenge, both the winner and looser were tested for cortisol, the principal stress hormone. What they discovered was that social victory or defeat meant the difference between having low or high level of the biochemical but sometimes, not in the way you would think.

In the study, losing a contest against a stranger did not appear to be a uniformly stressful experience. In fact, it became clear that the volunteers who were power motivators (i.e. those who had a desire for dominance), were most cortisol-sensitive when it came to experiencing the stress response. Scientists found that it wasn't actually winning or losing that spiked cortisol levels, rather, it was the volunteer's belief in what winning or losing meant that triggered the response. For those volunteers who were not motivated to dominate another, winning might actually become more stressful than losing. Their conclusion was that "implicit power motivators as a personality trait played a role in determining physiological response to social stimuli."

Those who operate in a competitive spirit (a me-consciousness) apparently experience greater stress in social situations than those who operate in a more cooperative we-consciousness. When we loosen our grip on winning or losing and instead aim for win-win scenarios, we feel less stress at a biochemical level. Our health and happiness are elevated when we can adjust our win-lose beliefs and aim for a high-energy way of interacting with our fellow man.

The primary directive for our primal intelligence is to stay alive (#1 Road Rule: SURVIVE!). A positive attribute of the human condition is that we can intentionally adapt and grow stronger with every ping we encounter and learn to thrive when the road gets tough. We can identify patterns of survival thinking and feeling, and TURN ON a smarter thrive intelligence to understand the problem in a more empowering, solutions-focused way. This is an Odyssey of continuous self-improvement. The ongoing quest becomes a spirited adventure where we strive to remain high-energy amongst the people who ping us.

Day Seventeen Exercise

As people will forever play a connective role in our lives, take time to TUNE IN and TURN ON a healthier, happier way of interacting with them. Being a leader means inspiring and motivating others to operate as a team and get things done more effectively. Today, TUNE IN to a person who may ping you regularly. After identifying your own eState, ask yourself: What eState is the person who pinged me operating in? Did they hand me their own anger? Guilt? Apathy? Grief? Attempt to intuit what eMotion might be running their living process and record the eState in the new space provided.

---

[16] *Salivary cortisol changes in humans after winning or losing a dominance contest depend on implicit power motivation*, Wirth, Welch & Schultheiss, University of Michigan, November 7, 2005.

In today's RESOLVE process, enact courage and thrive eStates to more fully neutralize pings of social stress. TUNE IN to the adversaries' energy and, if required, set an intention to face your opponents directly in courage and other high-energy states. Positively resolve the issue by a TURN ON of trust, optimism, acceptance, reason and love. Remember, it takes courage to connect.

odyssey

The Odyssey Methodology

1. TUNE IN

Remember *your day*	Close your eyes and mentally review your day. Remember the pings—the people, places or events—that caused you stress, then determine the eMotion triggered by the ping. - *A ping is a significant emotional experience that shifts your energy.* - *You remember pings because of their emotional energy.*
Record *your pings*	Pick the three most impactful pings of the day and record. [PING - box 1] For each ping, choose the eState that best suits how you responded to the eMotion experienced and record. [TUNE IN - box 2]
Reflect *your energy*	Focus on how the ping affected your energetic state. Teach your brain what the ping feels like (i.e. grief, anxiety, apathy, etc.). Mentally label the feelings with a rational understanding of the eMotion.

2. TURN ON

Raise *your eState*	Choose an eState higher than the one experienced for each ping and record. [TURN ON - box 3]
Replay *your day*	Close your eyes and with palm on forehead, visualize reliving each ping in the higher eState. Imagine the same people, place or event ping in the new eState. - *Include all aspects of the more empowering eMotion. See yourself being confident, responding authentically with pleasant gestures, facial expressions, calm voice, etc.*
Resolve *your pings*	Set action to neutralize the ping-energy. Ask yourself: What task or solution is necessary to fix a problem? Reconnect with a person? What steps are required to repair what is broken / disconnected? In courage, take action! - *Set an intention to follow through on the commitment. With palm on forehead, mentally rehearse being courageous / optimistic / accepting of the situation. Visualize the new behavior. Train the brain for a high-energy response to stress.*

odyssey

The Quest Journal
- Day Seventeen -

Date: Day: S — M — T — W — Th — F — S

eState	eMotion	
Experience	*Feeling*	*Energy*
Enlightenment	Nirvana	1000
Peace	Bliss	600
Joy	Serenity	540
Love	Reverence	500
Reason	Understanding	400
Acceptance	Forgiveness	350
Optimism	Willingness	310
Trust	Neutrality	250
Courage	Affirmation	200
Pride	Scorn	175
Anger	Resentment	150
Desire	Craving	125
Fear	Anxiety	100
Grief	Regret	75
Apathy	Despair	50
Guilt	Blame	30
Shame	Humiliation	20

PING—a significant emotional experience
[box 1]

Duration: ___hr. ___min.

TUNE IN [box 2]

TURN ON [box 3]

PING—a significant emotional experience

Duration: ___hr. ___min.

TUNE IN

TURN ON

PING—a significant emotional experience

Duration: ___hr. ___min.

TUNE IN

TURN ON

GRATITUDE
1.
2.
3.

If the only prayer you say in your whole life is 'thank you' that should suffice.— Meister Eckhart

Emotion hierarchy adapted from Map of Consciousness: *Power vs. Force.* David R. Hawkins, M.D. Ph.D., 1995.

A belligerent samurai challenged a Zen master to explain the concept of heaven and hell.
The monk scorned, "You're nothing but a lout! I can't waste my time with the likes of you!"

His very honor attacked, the samurai flew into a rage and, pulling his sword
from its scabbard, roared, "I could kill you for your impertinence!"

"That," the monk calmly replied, "is hell."

Startled at seeing the truth that was in his grip, the samurai calmed down,
sheathed his sword, and bowed, thanking the monk for the lesson.

"And that," said the monk, "is heaven."

An old Japanese tale

Day Eighteen—The Human Condition: A Summary

We live permanently embedded in an energetic state of consciousness. We exist. We react. We respond. We do all of that depending on the eState we're in. If we're not self-aware, disapproval from a parent, partner or other can instantly ping our energy and trigger a snappy, even nasty reaction—a subtle resentment to an all out battle. Without an in-tune mindset, your eMotions can linger in energy-draining states for hours, remaining aggressive, addicted or anxious in an attempt to survive. All this self-destructive behavior is avoidable if we keep our wits about us and learn to TURN ON a higher course of action—under stress.

As children, we have limited abilities to reason. Until about the age of seven, a child's emotional brain is highly attuned to learning, and it adapts to everything the child sees, hears and experiences. At this age, our fundamental behaviors are formed. As our rational brain develops more slowly than our emotional brain, behaviors, gestures and vocal tones provide much more meaning and learning to a child than do spoken words.

If you were lucky enough to be raised by encouraging, high-energy role models, they would have instilled in you a good dose of wisdom and courage by showing you by example how to overcome your fears; that is, how to proverbially get back on the horse when life throws you off. Your eMemories would be well-armed with positive behaviors, wired to respond constructively to stress. If, however, you were raised by parents who were absorbed with survival, your ongoing emotional states may reflect those same low-energy eMotions. When stress strikes, and without emotive wisdom to guide a positive response, your primal intelligence will reference your eMemories and use the encoded emotional programs found to move you automatically. That's why even the best and brightest can react in aggressive, addicted or anxious—primal—ways. Without positive eMemories, you can get stuck in the negative.

Without strengthened self-awareness, the human condition can leave people feeling trapped in their own anger, desires and fears. Many lack suitable life strategies for dealing with stress directly. In survival mode, they find it difficult to construct positive meaning or behave in a reasonable manner when faced with a challenge.

Like a fish that doesn't know it's in water, we often do not recognize that everything we perceive and experience is a direct reflection of our own eStates and eMemories. Emotive life-energy powers not only our state of mind and behaviors, but colors the way we see, feel and interpret the world. The world inside our heads is governed by billions of neurons that use our energetic state to filter and make sense of reality. That's a heap of complexity. For many, there is a real difference between the outside world—out there—and their own self-organizing living process—in here.

The Loss of Spirit

If we regard self-awareness as the highest order of human mental function, we must acknowledge that the underlying eMotion generated by our primal intelligence is the creator of our moment-to-moment life experience. Without improved self-awareness of what's going on beneath the surface of our lives, we may unknowingly create a virtual hell for ourselves and for those around us. With a disconnection to spirit, we fail to feel alive.

As an explorer of human behavior, the psychologist Carl Jung set out a century ago to study primitive cultures and discover how they managed the conscious-subconscious relationship. His quest led him to remote parts of the world where he studied a multitude of rituals and patterns of behavior as they related to psychological and emotional health.

Jung found that many native cultures were already well aware of the human condition. When a tribal member became imbalanced, they were regarded as having lost their spirit. Without a balancing agent, how a person reasons or experiences the world can be dramatically thrown out of kilter, one becoming dominate over the other. Jung noticed there were two ways in which this happened: The first was where eMotions overwhelmed the individual (known as body without mind); the other, where their conscious mind was over-ran with cognitive chatter (known as mind without body).

Let's explore both of these instances in detail.

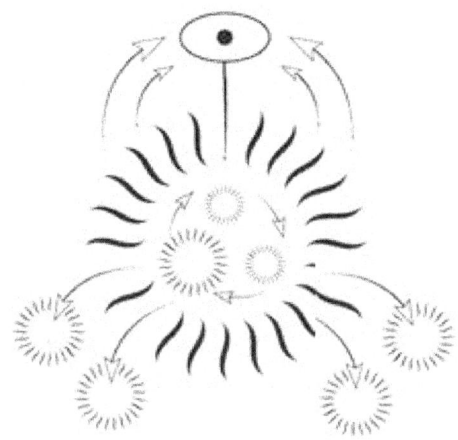

Body without Mind

The human condition allows us to be aware of our own feelings and eMotions. Under stress, primal intelligence commandeers rational intelligence, and we end up losing this higher order, self-regulating brain function. Without rational control, primal eMotions can be automatically generated that may overwhelm our conscious experience of life. When the emotional brain dominates our behavior, our energy for motion enslaves our brains and bodies and we fall into that eMotion hook, line and sinker. In an instance of body without mind, we are unable to think straight and we become emotionally imbalanced. This rational-to-primal reaction takes only 1/500th of a second—faster than you can think a thought.

Such an imbalance occurs naturally to animals in spring, when mating season occurs. As a core competency, sexual instincts instigate the desire to mate. These emotional drivers shut down the animals' rational behavior and a deep instinctual force to procreate spurs them to forego food and security in favor of satisfying the primal hunger.

Likewise, as humans we can suffer from overriding emotional forces that make us feel depressed, anxious or aggressive. Experiencing body without mind, our eMotions get the best of us and our spirit becomes lost in the self-organizing chaos.

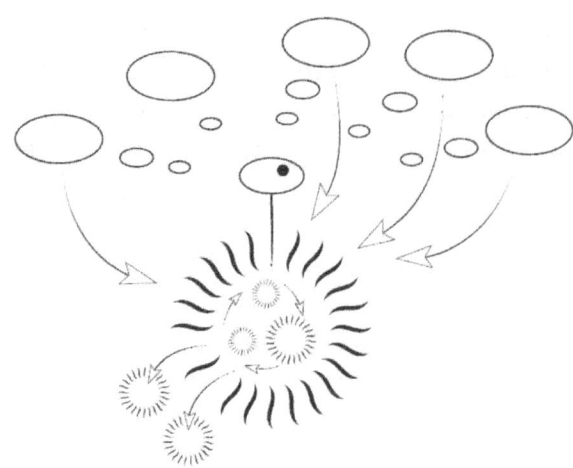

Mind without Body

A loss of spirit also occurs when active thoughts and mental chatter dominate the mind. In the cognitive dysfunction, the conscious mind disconnects from its subconscious operating system, your primal intelligence. This can become a real problem when you become locked in your own fear-driven thinking process, unable to quiet the anxious voices.

Although an educated intellect brings advantages in today's competitive world, getting lost in your own thoughts can open a Pandora's Box of evils. In pride, we can become defensive and aggressive when other's challenge our thinking. Noisy cognitive chatter can also fog our perception of reality and we can fail to experience the joys that are right in front of us. In prideful arrogance, we become myopic, only seeing what we want to see. When we lose ourselves in survival-driven imagination, our mind goes wild with analysis, judgment and paranoid perspectives of life. This is mind without body.

Evidence of this mind-body imbalance is noticeable when you find yourself continually analyzing stressful people, places or events. In the resultant nervous energy, you can talk excessively about your problems, jumping from one self-absorbed ping to another, powered by an anxious or aggressive mindset. With such unconstrained burning of energy, it's no wonder that smart people find themselves depressed. Constant cognitive chatter burns a lot of energy.

Experiencing mind without body, without limits that contain the thinking process, the conscious mind runs amok, embedding mental habits that lock people into analysis-paralysis—where making even a simple decision becomes difficult. Too much thought, not enough feeling.

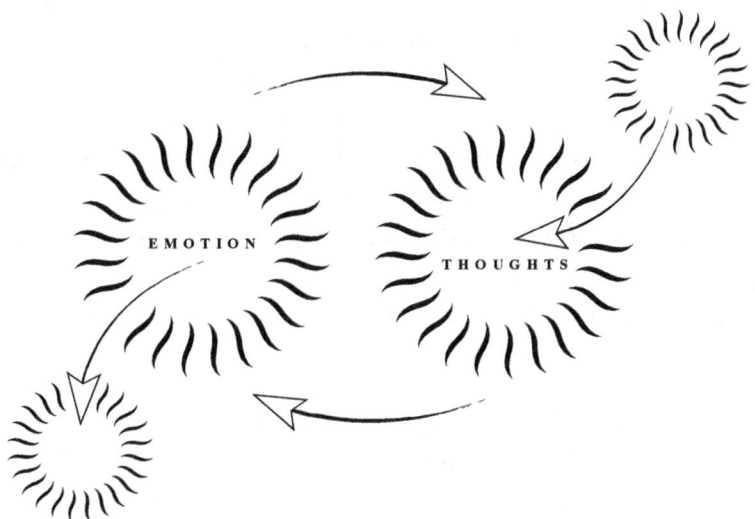

Balancing the Mind-Body System

Today, attention deficit disorders affect nearly everyone to some degree or another. Stimulated by the constant flow of news and information, emails and instant messages, gossip and deadlines, our attention gets tossed about like a cork on a turbulent sea. Indeed, it's a testament to the power of the human spirit that we're as sane as we are.

As we've learned many times by now, our primal intelligence remains active in our subconscious, and the emotional energy that is generated can stir up our brains to think about negative things. In the adaption-to-stress process, our eStates become anxious, addicted or aggressive automatically. Depression eventually follows. Still, we force our rational intelligence forward, dealing with the onslaught of pings with an unacknowledged spirit that is helping us survive the stressors. Soon, a cognitive-emotive feedback loop begins. Our conscious thoughts ping our subconscious body into primal states of anger, desire or fear, which in turn powers negative thoughts such as worry, craving and resentment. That's why left unattended, such cycles of psychological distress can turn our lives into a living hell.

Whether the imbalance is experienced as emotionally overwhelming or rational over-analysis, our mind and body need to be intentionally balanced so that our spirit is not lost in the dualistic disposition.

The Yin-Yang of Human Nature

While our spirit keeps us alive, it can easily become lost in the imbalance of thoughts and eMotions. As an animal species that has evolved rational intelligence, we pressure our modern mindset to move us away from trouble, forgetting all the while that our primal intelligence is in charge of our energy for motion.

In considering our mind and body as two aspects of the same living process, it's important that we come to understand that the dual cognitive-emotive process utilizes both our conscious and subconscious minds. In our quest for increased self-knowledge, we should remember that our state of mind is ever-changing. Feelings come and go, as do the ups and downs. If you're feeling sad today, you may well feel happy tomorrow. As much as we want to feel balance in our lives, it's the job of our spirit to balance the human condition. Connect with spirit, and you'll balance both thoughts and eMotions. This may sound esoteric, but through experiential self-discovery—a TUNE IN to subconscious energy, then a TURN ON of higher brain function—you'll find yourself better balanced and stable to authentically navigate stressful challenges in the moment.

Many of my clients are bright professionals who depend on their intellect to get things done.

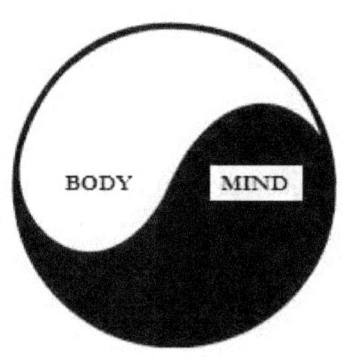

The tool they use for this work is their rational intelligence. Some are literally paid for their smarts. They spend the majority of their days moving information around in their heads, or initiating the movement of thoughts in other people. As much as our modern intelligence helps us survive, and no matter how smart you may pride yourself in being, your thoughts are still governed by the primal intelligence our ancestors used hundreds of thousands of years ago. The ill-effects of sitting at a desk for hours on end have now been compared with the ailing health of a chain smoker. This means we need to move more than thoughts if we are to be healthy and happy.

Thomas Jefferson, the third U.S. president, was a big believer in walking. He suggested walking two hours a day if you were a hard thinker. As a noted intellectual (and principal author of the Declaration of Independence), he intuitively recognized that we need to provide our rational minds a break. So, next time your thoughts get the best of you, take a walk or do yoga or engage in some other physical exercise. Make time to balance your mind, body and spirit.

Since thoughts are energy in motion (eMotion), then the process of observing our thoughts can reveal a lot about our state of mind. It's from the Observer consciousness that our spirit can gently remind us that we are neither our thoughts nor our eMotions, but a self-organizing living process of both. Like time and space, our minds and bodies are interdependent aspects of the same *living moment*, continually transforming energy into matter and back again. It is best if we understand the continually transforming process, and befriend its intelligence with courage and acceptance, for in the end, it's our spirit that is keeping us alive.

Day Eighteen Exercise

How is your spirit right now? What eState are you operating in? Is your mind-body system balanced? Are you able to relax the body with a TUNE IN of feeling alive? And, are you able to quiet the mind with a TURN ON of energy? Increasingly TUNE IN and TURN ON when necessary out in the real world, not only when completing the daily exercise. Your brain should be better in tune to your self-organizing living process with each passing moment. For today, again use the Odyssey Methodology to complete the Quest Journal.

odyssey

The Odyssey Methodology

1. TUNE IN

Remember
your day

Close your eyes and mentally review your day.
Remember the pings—the people, places or events—that caused you stress, then determine the eMotion triggered by the ping.
- *A ping is a significant emotional experience that shifts your energy.*
- *You remember pings because of their emotional energy.*

Record
your pings

Pick the three most impactful pings of the day and record. [PING - box 1]
For each ping, choose the eState that best suits how you responded to the eMotion experienced and record. [TUNE IN - box 2]

Reflect
your energy

Focus on how the ping affected your energetic state.
Teach your brain what the ping feels like (i.e. grief, anxiety, apathy, etc.).
Mentally label the feelings with a rational understanding of the eMotion.

2. TURN ON

Raise
your eState

Choose an eState higher than the one experienced for each ping and record. [TURN ON - box 3]

Replay
your day

Close your eyes and with palm on forehead, visualize reliving each ping in the higher eState. Imagine the same people, place or event ping in the new eState.
- *Include all aspects of the more empowering eMotion. See yourself being confident, responding authentically with pleasant gestures, facial expressions, calm voice, etc.*

Resolve
your pings

Set action to neutralize the ping-energy. Ask yourself: What task or solution is necessary to fix a problem? Reconnect with a person? What steps are required to repair what is broken / disconnected? In courage, take action!
- *Set an intention to follow through on the commitment. With palm on forehead, mentally rehearse being courageous / optimistic / accepting of the situation. Visualize the new behavior. Train the brain for a high-energy response to stress.*

odyssey

The Quest Journal
- Day Eighteen -

Date: _____ Day: S — M — T — W — Th — F — S

eState	eMotion	
Experience	*Feeling*	*Energy*
Enlightenment	Nirvana	1000
Peace	Bliss	600
Joy	Serenity	540
Love	Reverence	500
Reason	Understanding	400
Acceptance	Forgiveness	350
Optimism	Willingness	310
Trust	Neutrality	250
Courage	Affirmation	200
Pride	Scorn	175
Anger	Resentment	150
Desire	Craving	125
Fear	Anxiety	100
Grief	Regret	75
Apathy	Despair	50
Guilt	Blame	30
Shame	Humiliation	20

PING—a significant emotional experience

[box 1]

Duration: ___hr. ___min.

TUNE IN [box 2]

TURN ON [box 3]

PING—a significant emotional experience

Duration: ___hr. ___min.

TUNE IN

TURN ON

GRATITUDE
1.

2.

3.

If the only prayer you say in your whole life is 'thank you' that should suffice.— Meister Eckhart

PING—a significant emotional experience

Duration: ___hr. ___min.

TUNE IN

TURN ON

Emotion hierarchy adapted from Map of Consciousness: *Power vs. Force.* David R. Hawkins, M.D. Ph.D., 1995.

Make me wise and brave.
Clear the way, in a sacred manner I come.

Lakota Native American Prayer

Day Nineteen—The Human Spirit

Many are traveling the road of life with a lost spirit. Some you can spot straight away—they're usually aggressive or anxious and rarely satisfied with their life. They often talk excessively about their problems or continually complain about what's not right with the world. Those with lost spirits find it hard to take in other's viewpoints or admit they're wrong. Many smoke cigarettes, drink alcohol and do drugs to drown out how lost they feel. However, there are people whose behavior does not point to their troubles and you would never guess they were feeling off-track. For the most part, they act normally. On the inside, however, they may experience feelings of poor self-worth or guilt and remain chronically unsatisfied with their life. Many appear to have it all together, but as Henry David Thoreau said, "The mass of men live lives of quiet desperation."

For years, I operated with a lost spirit—tossed between being angry, anxious and depressed. In public, I acted as if everything was fine, complete with a bogus smile on my face. From my own experience, I have learned never to judge a person by their appearance. Remember Doug from Day One? He was a good-looking professional who came to experience panic attacks and chronic insecurity. With a lost spirit, he became afraid of his own shadow. Greg, who we met on Day Eight, was lost in his anger and addictions. And this week we learned about Nick, the strategic executive who was so lost in his own smarts that he began strategically contemplating suicide. When your spirit is lost, the road of life becomes a tough trail to navigate. Without a trusted inner guidance system, there is no compass that can tell you which direction to take. Decision-making becomes difficult as actions are weighed down by apathy. Without a connection to spirit, no wonder so many are lost in today's fast-paced competitive world.

> TUNE IN: How connected are you to spirit? Do you trust your life-energy to move you?

No matter how lost you may be, an intelligent spirit is keeping you alive right now. Your spirit operates continuously with every heartbeat and at each *living moment*. Like many, you may have lost touch with your intuition, which lingers in the realms of a busy mind, but your spirit remains a highly effective navigator. Even now, your spirit influences your every decision, thought and eMotion. Learning to listen to your spirit is paramount to successfully navigating the challenges that come your way. Use in-tune-ition to find yourself back on track and at the helm of your psyche, where you will feel alive, confident and courageous—in tune with your inner power source. Decisions and actions come easily when your mind is connected to a high-energy spirit.

Much has been written about the human spirit, perhaps because of its amazing ability to intentionally change and improve our lives. It's the human spirit that can imagine new ways of doing things, create solutions to problems, invent work-saving devices, and develop ways to overcome difficulty. With the human spirit, the impossible becomes possible. As human beings, we can grow wiser and braver by putting our minds to it. Even if you feel lost, with intentional effort you can put the wind back into your sails and find your way once again.

Today we'll summarize what we've learned in the past three weeks, reflect on where we've been and where we're going. Remember, connecting to spirit is an ongoing process. We must actively train the brain to balance thoughts and eMotions until it becomes an unconscious habit. To successfully gain this skill, I'll formally introduce **The Odyssey Methodology**—the process re-engineering technique that will help you TUNE IN and TURN ON eStates. The higher your eState, the more connected you are to your spirit, and the quieter your mind.

Courage and constructive cognitive skills are necessary to effectively manage your energy and to remain healthy and happy, strong and confident no matter what life throws at you. This means taking greater control of your thoughts and eMotions. It means balancing the human condition with an empowered attitude toward your self-organizing living process.

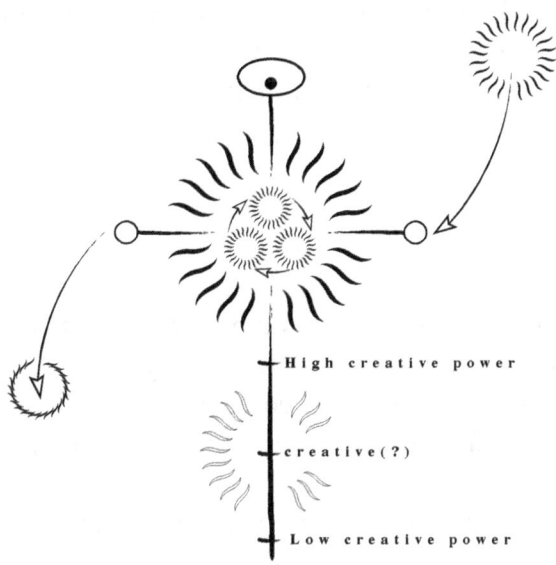

Developing an Alpha Consciousness

Ask yourself: Do you choose your thoughts or do your thoughts choose you? Who's in charge?

From a spirit perspective, we are neither our thoughts nor our eMotions. We are an interdependent living process of both mind and body. In simple terms, if your thoughts choose you, you've created habits of active thinking that lack self-management—there is no governor to moderate the habitual cognitive activity. Better energy management is required. This means drawing your attention from the thought itself to its power source—your eState. Managing the energy that moves the thought in the first place is incredibly efficient in clearing the mind—it allows you to influence the thought's origins. Think of it like tuning the engine of your car. With a smoother running spirit comes a clearer, more focused state of mind.

> TUNE IN: What eState is powering your thoughts right now?

As you continue to learn about your own eStates, you'll naturally begin to understand the subtle mechanisms that balance your thoughts and eMotions. Being more in charge of your eState, your spirit connection will automatically strengthen. I like to call this enlightened self-awareness alpha consciousness—control over the living processes operating within. An Alpha consciousness is both self-aware and energetically resilient. It has the heightened self-awareness of knowing where one is psychologically and emotionally, along with the prowess to do something positive with it. Instead of being distracted, an Alpha consciousness is clear and focused; it is both director and producer, and in full conscious control. It's this leadership mindset that gets you to where you want to go.

Begin to think of your own body and mind as a vast social community filled with living processes—thoughts and eMotions—all of which require conscious alpha leadership. Your Alpha consciousness is your willpower to tame the animal within. It's your courage to face and conquer the emotional demons. It's the trust built in your core self to get you through the tough times. And it's your willingness to forgive, understand and love others despite what they may do to you. In this way, your Alpha consciousness can increase your spirit's energy and enthusiasm.

Strengthening the Spirit

If you're not in tune with your body, your mind will get the best of you. If you cannot TURN ON higher eStates, negative thoughts will continue to interrupt your consciousness. Thoughts are energy, and negative thoughts disturb your emotional energy. So the more effective you are at managing your energy, the healthier and happier you will be. This means using your Alpha consciousness to set your mind to learning from everything you do. By intentionally adapting from each ping you experience, you eliminate their emotional stings. You grow "wise and brave" because you are strengthening rational intelligence and emotional resilience. Ultimately, it's the willpower of your Alpha consciousness to change eStates that affects this outcome. Develop your Alpha consciousness intentionally to instigate neuron change in your brain and you'll be able to influence thoughts and eMotions from a higher consciousness.

In quantum physics, scientists have documented fascinating yet still unexplained cause-and-effect relationships between consciousness and energy. In experiments that require observations of certain minute realms of the physical world, they have found that the way in which they observe these experiments has a direct effect on the results.

For example, if scientists observe an experiment in progress from a certain perspective, they get a certain result. If they leave the room and turn off the recording equipment, they get a different result. Quantum scientists now advocate that the power of consciousness itself—attention and awareness—plays a pivotal role in how the world is experienced. In other words, how we look at things affects our thoughts and feelings toward them. Change your point of view and you may well change your eState.

If you pay attention to a particular aspect of a situation, you experience a particular result. But if you change your eState and observe the situation from a different angle, you can obtain a different outlook—a different feeling—from the same situation.

Neuroscientists have also noted that the way in which we observe and perceive the world has a direct effect on the living processes within our brains. Studies have shown that refocusing our attention actually changes the physical structures of the brain. Like learning to play tennis or to speak a new language affects neural pathways, the intentional directing of your attention can change your state of mind and thus the way you perceive a challenging situation. Let's use this insight as we continue to TUNE IN to our pings, and TURN ON a different, more empowering way of looking at them.

> TURN ON: What is really valuable about the pings you experience? How does each ping serve you?

There is value in pings. For example, in learning from my pings, I find that a common anger trigger for me is someone saying one thing but doing another. They break a promise or cancel at the last minute. In mining my pings for what was valuable, I discovered that INTEGRITY is an important value to me. I still experience a subtle ping when integrity is jeopardized but I am able to remain in a high eState and respond in a reasonable way.

This conscious mastery plays a vital role in influencing our ability to focus attention. Without the leadership of an alpha consciousness, our concentration can wane and become scattered. We must treat our attention like a muscle—with a use-it-or-lose-it mentality. Indeed, your ability to focus your mind is directly proportional to the strength of your alpha consciousness—the ability to control your state of mind. The first step in energy management is to stop energy drains, and that means being self-aware of what pings your eState. Continue to embrace and experience what it means to feel alive. I challenge you to live above-the-line in the spectrum of eStates for the next 10 pings. Begin by aiming to be courageous in everything you do from this moment forward.

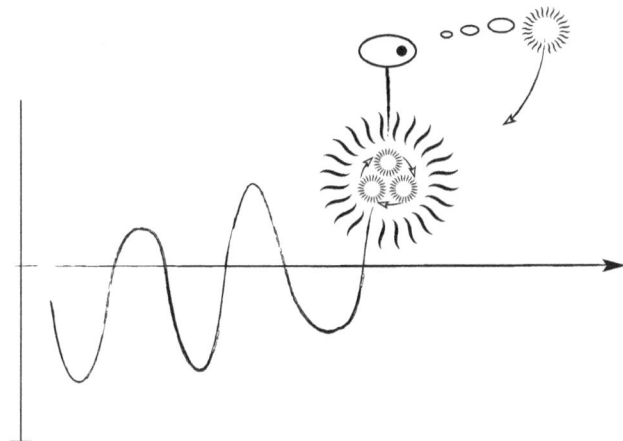

The Hero's Journey

Have you ever wanted to be a hero? Someone who steps in and gets things done amidst adversity? A hero is someone who is both producer and director of his own life. He is someone who has experienced the negative eMotions but intentionally chooses to live above-the-line by knowing what courage really means. A hero knows how to survive and thrive on the road of life. He has had his share of bumps and bruises, and has gained strength and wisdom from the experience. In terms of spirit, the hero's journey is the path to enlightenment. The experiential journey transforms him for the better, and it starts by being courageous in all he does.

Imagine being on top of a high mountain. To get there, you would have to dedicate yourself to a steep and treacherous climb that would call upon your strength and stamina. Not everyone makes it. It is a hero's journey. Once you reach the top, you would have conquered your perceived limitations. You would be rewarded with a beautiful vista; seeing the world as very few do, from a higher perspective.

Metaphorically speaking, the same exertion is required to reach a higher consciousness. We cannot take a helicopter to such a place; quick fixes and weekend seminars never get or keep us there. A methodical path is necessary, where continuous improvement raises your eState—permanently. It's a hero's journey where you become smarter and stronger with each ping you encounter. Along the way, success builds on success and your spirit's operating energy increases, strengthened by the intentional Odyssey. The hero's journey is a trail to the top, where only few have seen the grand view.

Joseph Campbell was a famous mythologist who first identified a common pattern found in "every story ever told" and named it the hero's journey. From blockbuster movies to bestsellers, the hero's journey is the singular thread that weaves its way through every storyline. Campbell discovered that path-to-enlightenment stories were common in every culture, and that they always called upon an individual to face their fears directly. In the heroic experience, the individual would be transformed, made "wise and brave" by the adventure. Campbell noted that this way of living can be applied to our everyday life. Indeed, the hero's journey can be one of continuous improvement, where we face each demon directly and grow from the experience.

The path of the hero's journey is a direct reflection of the way in which the natural world operates. First, there is the comfort of the known. The would-be hero lives unaware and ignorant of the world outside his domain. Then, a stressful challenge pings the individual's consciousness, and he becomes aware of something that isn't right. Taking the hero's journey, he faces the challenge head on and does something positive about it. As a hero, he regains comfort, made sharper and stronger from the experience. Inevitably, another stress is encountered, and the hero is again faced with another adventure. And again, he grows smarter and stronger from the effort. The continuous improvement path continues repeatedly. With every ping, the hero becomes "wise and brave".

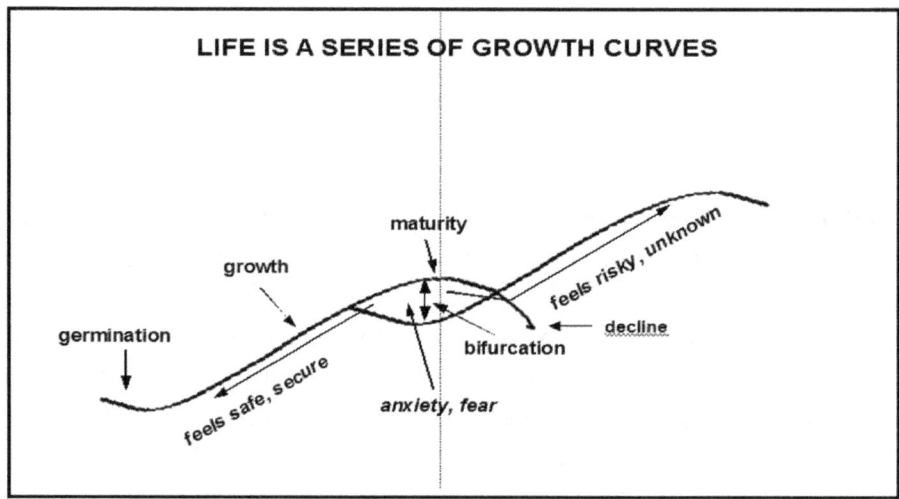

This improvement pattern has also been noted in scientific circles. In 1977, this methodology was termed the stress-growth process and was officially recognized by Nobel Laureate Ilya Prigogine, who surmised that stress is the essential element that moves living systems to adapt and evolve. Without stress, most self-organizing living systems fall apart. Indeed, without stress to keep us on our toes, we lose strength. We become couch potatoes, growing weaker by not exercising our aptitudes of life. We either use it or lose it. Adaption, after all, is a core competency. Best to use the adaption process for the highest benefit.

> TURN ON: As stress will always be a part of our lives, face challenges as a hero in a spirit of courage.

The Spirit of Courage

The ancient tale of Odysseus and his endless struggles on his journey back home after winning the Trojan War is one of the oldest stories ever told. Homer's Odyssey is a testament to the enduring will of the human spirit to overcome challenge after challenge. For sure, it may seem that the gods continually torment us. However, the hero's quest is not about eliminating stress (we have little control over the outer world), but about growing wiser and braver with each stressful challenge we encounter. That's why we're so attracted to heroes. We enjoy reading about them, even daydream of being one in our own life story. So what's stopping you? Do you know what being a hero really means?

The word courage comes from the Latin word *cordis*, which means heart. While we are alive, the spirit of life ticks endlessly within us, tirelessly, forever active in the rhythmic beating of our heart. It's little wonder that our distant ancestors considered the heart to be the center of courage. The heart is really the beating drum of every living moment. In their primitive mindsets, our ancestors intuitively knew that being courageous meant listening to their hearts.

From a scientific perspective, our ancestors were spot on. We now know that the heart has its own complex network of neurons, just like the brain does. Indeed, your heart beats of its own free will and generates its own electrical impulses that pump blood (energy) throughout the body. When our heart stops, we stop. With each heartbeat, our spirit manifests a spark of courage, spurring the energy and movement that keeps us alive.

A hero understands that courage means following his heart's calling. Living with a warrior spirit may require you to embrace the entire spectrum of eMotion and to take action (courage) toward resolving a particular life challenge. If so, best to ground such daunting endeavors with solid intuitive knowledge of what is real and important. Being a hero means that you will be feeling fear—your heart will be beating hard—yet using your willpower, you "saddle up" and overcome the anxiety by taking action anyway. This is when you begin to thrive. Movement is the excitable aspect of feeling alive.

Think of the survive eStates. They can keep you still. The feelings of sadness, fear and depression all but shut down a spirit. Even if you are burdened with a heavy heart, your spirit still drives your life despite the circumstance you may be experiencing. A hero allows himself to cry or be depressed, because a hero has heightened self-awareness to the meaning of those eStates. Sometimes, being sad, anxious or depressed is appropriate. But knowing there's an exit—relying on an Alpha consciousness and knowing your state will change—is very empowering. This is the essence of courage—to intentionally change your state of mind.

The hero mindfully chooses his battles and the dragons he will fight. Whether it's confronting the neighborhood bully or the corrupt corporation, a true hero tackles the challenges undaunted by self-doubt (fear), knowing that in his action (courage) he will experience more peace and wisdom (optimism, understanding, joy).

A hero lives in alpha consciousness, in the forefront of his mind. He is captain on the bridge. The hero chooses the road less travelled creating his own life story as he goes. Despite feeling fear and anxiety, apathy and weakness, a hero dives in to save others—a hero doesn't just think, a hero does. With an enlightened consciousness, he intuitively takes in the big picture (we) rather than capitalizing on personal gain (me). This is true leadership. Despite the very real consequences of painful rejection or death, a hero is not held back by emotional sabotage. He is unafraid of his own shadow for he knows what lies beneath. In contrast, the trust in his instincts—following his heart—leads him into new adventures. At the helm of his psyche, his passionate behavior can't help but be noticed by others. Living with a heroic spirit, he inspires others with a can-do energy.

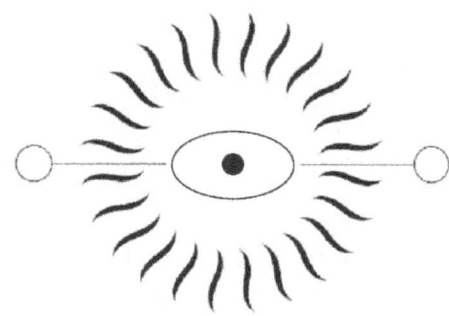

Quest for Feeling Alive

If indeed we are spirits having a physical experience, then we must embrace all the experiences life has to offer. As a hero in your life story, be willing to step into every eMotion and undertake a quest to continually improve your experience of feeling alive.

Your lifetime Odyssey is to increase life-energy and to move from a state of surviving to an enlightened state of thriving. Strengthen your Alpha consciousness throughout the journey and feel the spirit of courage working within. Step by step, climb the arduous mountain before you. Conquer your inner demons and continue to grow stronger and evolve consciously. With continual improvement, your new heroic nature will help transform the stings of pings into the joys of living and learning. Armed with an enlightened self-awareness, TURN ON a new way of seeing the world and become aroused by what you find. Transformation is the promise of the hero's journey.

As energy beings, we are powered by the energy for motion flowing within us. By empowering our self-awareness with our knowledge of our eState, we feel more stable and optimistic and take on more with less effort. With positive energy flowing through our brains, we thrive in everyday complexity. Living with high-energy consciousness, we smile at the face of adversity. We find the little things don't bother us when we understand how to live above-the-line and continually aim for higher eStates. Challenges and their pings become calls to adventure.

Only through the hero's journey—the path of continuous improvement—does enlightenment occur. Whatever religion or spiritual belief you may hold, continue the quest for feeling alive. The Odyssey is an ongoing, never-ending story. As spirits having a physical experience, we do well to enjoy each and every *living moment*.

Tomorrow we'll summarize how to do this by applying **The Odyssey Methodology**.

Day Nineteen Exercise

What energy powered your spirit today? What dominant eState did you operate in? Were you able to TUNE IN and TURN ON when pinged? Heroes utilize and develop an Alpha consciousness to remain on top of their thoughts and eMotions. As hero in your own life story, you become wiser and braver with each ping, and courageously step in to resolve the challenge. Continue to TUNE IN and TURN ON, neutralizing pings as they occur. To master this skill, once again use the Odyssey Methodology to complete the Quest Journal.

odyssey

The Odyssey Methodology

1. TUNE IN

Remember your day	Close your eyes and mentally review your day. Remember the pings—the people, places or events—that caused you stress, then determine the eMotion triggered by the ping. - *A ping is a significant emotional experience that shifts your energy.* - *You remember pings because of their emotional energy.*
Record your pings	Pick the three most impactful pings of the day and record. [PING - box 1] For each ping, choose the eState that best suits how you responded to the eMotion experienced and record. [TUNE IN - box 2]
Reflect your energy	Focus on how the ping affected your energetic state. Teach your brain what the ping feels like (i.e. grief, anxiety, apathy, etc.). Mentally label the feelings with a rational understanding of the eMotion.

2. TURN ON

Raise your eState	Choose an eState higher than the one experienced for each ping and record. [TURN ON - box 3]
Replay your day	Close your eyes and with palm on forehead, visualize reliving each ping in the higher eState. Imagine the same people, place or event ping in the new eState. - *Include all aspects of the more empowering eMotion. See yourself being confident, responding authentically with pleasant gestures, facial expressions, calm voice, etc.*
Resolve your pings	Set action to neutralize the ping-energy. Ask yourself: What task or solution is necessary to fix a problem? Reconnect with a person? What steps are required to repair what is broken / disconnected? In courage, take action! - *Set an intention to follow through on the commitment. With palm on forehead, mentally rehearse being courageous / optimistic / accepting of the situation. Visualize the new behavior. Train the brain for a high-energy response to stress.*

odyssey

The Quest Journal
- Day Nineteen -

Date: Day: S — M — T — W — Th — F — S

eState	eMotion	
Experience	*Feeling*	*Energy*
Enlightenment	Nirvana	1000
Peace	Bliss	600
Joy	Serenity	540
Love	Reverence	500
Reason	Understanding	400
Acceptance	Forgiveness	350
Optimism	Willingness	310
Trust	Neutrality	250
Courage	Affirmation	200
Pride	Scorn	175
Anger	Resentment	150
Desire	Craving	125
Fear	Anxiety	100
Grief	Regret	75
Apathy	Despair	50
Guilt	Blame	30
Shame	Humiliation	20

PING—a significant emotional experience

[box 1]

Duration: ___hr. ___min.

TUNE IN [box 2]

TURN ON [box 3]

PING—a significant emotional experience

Duration: ___hr. ___min.

TUNE IN

TURN ON

GRATITUDE
1.
2.
3.

If the only prayer you say in your whole life is 'thank you' that should suffice.—Meister Eckhart

PING—a significant emotional experience

Duration: ___hr. ___min.

TUNE IN

TURN ON

Emotion hierarchy adapted from Map of Consciousness: *Power vs. Force*. David R. Hawkins, M.D. Ph.D., 1995.

The future is not a forecast.
It is created right here, right now, with what you do today.

Unknown

Day Twenty—The Odyssey Methodology

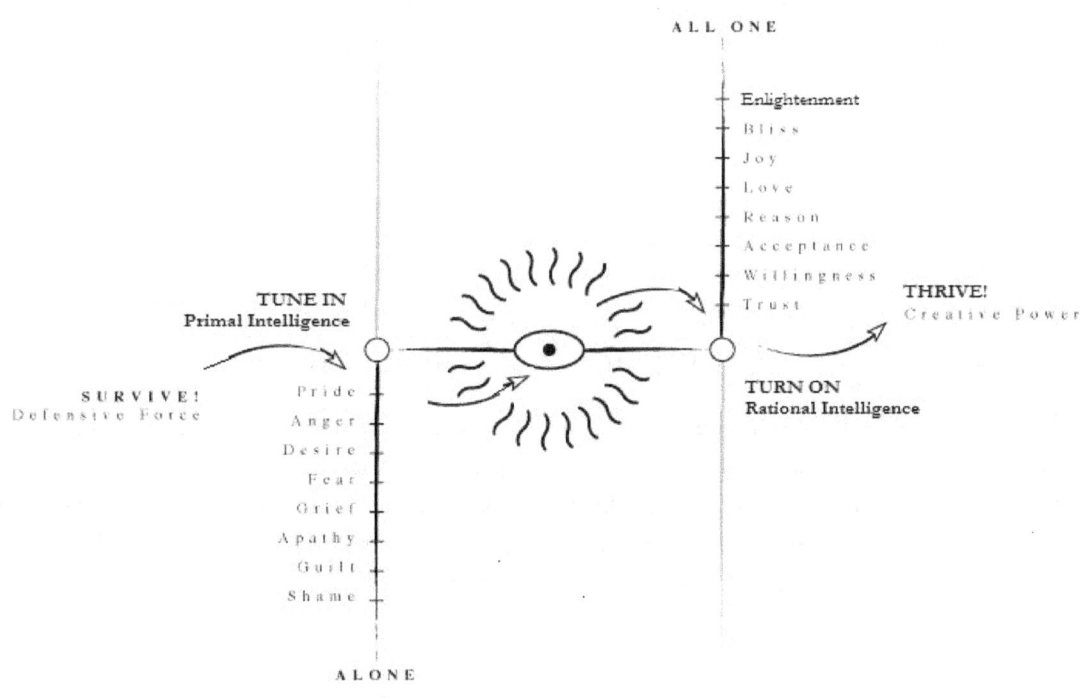

Beneath your conscious awareness lies a domain that is inaccessible by thought or spoken language. Yet, running beneath the surface of your conscious mind, a highly intelligent living process occurs. It's driven by a spirit that strives to keep you alive—aware of and away from danger automatically.

As humans, we are gifted with a condition that separates our conscious from our subconscious mind. Possessing both rational and primal intelligence, human beings can have a dualistic experience of eMotions. To the Observer consciousness, eMotions are interpreted as feelings.

The energy states we experience can be improved upon with intentional continuous improvement.

For the last 20 days, you have become more in tune to your ongoing energetic states. Through increased self-awareness, you have taught your rational brain what your primal brain is doing under stress. You should have more insight into how to improve your feelings and manage your energy with each ping. Today, I will summarize what you have learned so that the new neural habit of self-improvement forms and embeds properly.

Pings of Continuous Improvement

Any effort meant to improve a process is called continuous improvement. These efforts can be incremental over time or an all-at-once breakthrough experience. Improvement of a living process requires consistency—a methodology that collects and evaluates data, and that uses the findings to improve the efficiency, effectiveness and flexibility of the process itself.

You have been improving your energetic state using **The Odyssey Methodology**. In the incremental effort, you have intentionally improved your rational-emotional process by enabling a heightened self-awareness and energy management of pings when they occur. Beyond this program, pings will continue to be key growth catalysts in your quest for thriving in stressful challenges.

The Stress-Growth Process

Science has discovered that, when met with stress, living processes spontaneously reorganize their internal functions and update themselves automatically. Spurred by perturbation, living things have been found to have a competence for turning chaos into order. In other words, living organisms spontaneously self-organize and grow stronger when subjected to stress.

As previously mentioned, Ilya Prigogine won the 1977 Nobel Peace Prize in Chemistry by identifying this stress-growth process found in living systems. He surmised that stress is the essential element for how living systems adapt and evolve. Without stress, living systems fall apart. Without stress, muscles become weak, emotional prowess looses integrity. Like all living things, we grow stronger, wiser and braver when we meet with stress.

> TURN ON: Feeling stressed and overwhelmed? Congratulations. You're improving!

The Universal Pattern

Since growth from stress is natural, it is not surprising that there is a common pattern within every story ever told, including the world's great religious philosophies and current scientific methods. This universal pattern described by Joseph Campbell—the hero's journey—is an archetypal road map that can help us to intentionally step into a stressful challenge and come out transformed, wiser and braver by the stress-growth experience.

Christianity
Birth → Baptism → Transfiguration → Crucifixion → Resurrection → Ascension (Heaven)

Hinduism
Doubt (question) → Sravana (hearing with being) → Manara (thinking) → Hdhidyásan (mediation) → Buddhi (wake-up)

Zen Buddhism
Profound Dissatisfaction → Scripture & Study → Kon (paradoxes) → Zazen (meditation) → Surat (awakening) → Satori (Nirvana)

Science
Anomaly → Study & Research → Frustration → Insight → Resolution → New Anomaly

Continuous improvement is the remarkable common thread that weaves its way through every global philosophy. When met with something new—stress, dissatisfaction, doubt or anomaly—it's time to begin the hero's journey. Follow the path and be transformed.

Let's now summarize the Odyssey and what that path to enlightenment entails.

TUNE IN and SURVIVE!

Our eMotions keep us alive by prompting us to act. The energy for motion produced by our brain and body are auto-responses to stress, responses that are fine-tuned with life experience. Without warning, primal eMotions can easily lock our consciousness in survival mode. We become aggressive, addicted or anxious without choice. On the hero's journey, first TUNE IN to the primal response and learn from the emotional experience.

STEP ONE: TUNE IN to your energy for motion by becoming more self-aware of the eMotion in action. Use rational intelligence to become in tune with the primal energies operating within.

Remember your day.
– What you remember has an eMotion attached to it.

Record your pings.
– Collect data on your stress triggers and their energy.

Reflect your energy.
– Rationally learn what is happening at an emotional level.

TURN ON and THRIVE!

Stress and survival will be forever part of our lives. Use pings to TURN ON the ability to thrive in chaotic situations. In this manner, mental disturbances and anxieties can provide a positive influence on growth and evolution. Learn from your negative experiences by improving your cognitive-emotive process, helping your brain to reorganize and become stronger in the stress-growth process.

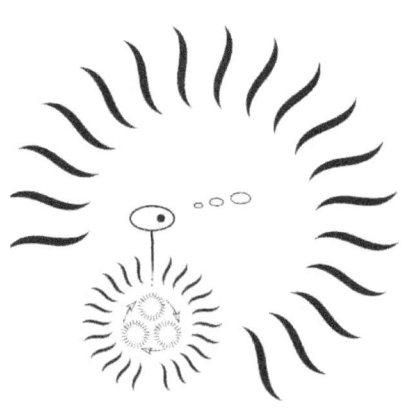

STEP TWO: TURN ON your eState using your willpower to imagine high-energy necessary to resolve the ping in your consciousness. With palm-on-forehead, close your eyes and visualize the energy-draining experience from a higher, more empowering state of mind. Train your brain how to best respond should the ping occur again.

Raise your eState.
– Intuitively choose an eState higher than pinged.

Replay your day.
– Close eyes and visualize living the ping in the higher eMotion.

Resolve your pings.
– Set an intention or take action to neutralize the ping.

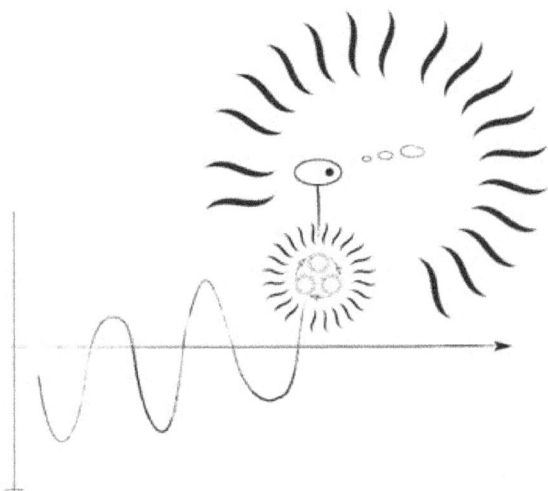

The Path to Enlightenment

When we accept and understand the pings that are necessary for our growth and evolution, we are better informed and increase our capacity to step into stressful situations and intentionally transform to become a better person. The hero's journey is a path to enlightenment, a process of continuous improvement where you grow "wise and brave" from every ping.

On the hero's journey, we are both aware of our eStates and the energetic lens through which we see the world. Being in tune to our spirit, we can better turn on positive intentions that assist in resolving the challenges set before us.

Day Twenty Exercise

Rest and Reflect on your Week.

Look back at the daily exercises and transcribe your pings in the boxes below. Note any commonalities and group accordingly. This exercise is not to assign blame, but to elevate your awareness of the people, places or events that are disturbing your energy. Observe any patterns. Also consider strategies that would help neutralize the ping. Note any action necessary.

Day Fifteen Pings	Common Pings—People, Places and Things
1.	
2.	
3.	
Day Sixteen Pings	
1.	
2.	
3.	
Day Seventeen Pings	
1.	**Observations / Strategies for Improvement**
2.	
3.	
Day Eighteen Pings	
1.	
2.	
3.	
Day Nineteen Pings	**Action Items:**
1.	
2.	
3.	

Follow your bliss.

Joseph Campbell

Day Twenty-One—The Never Ending Story

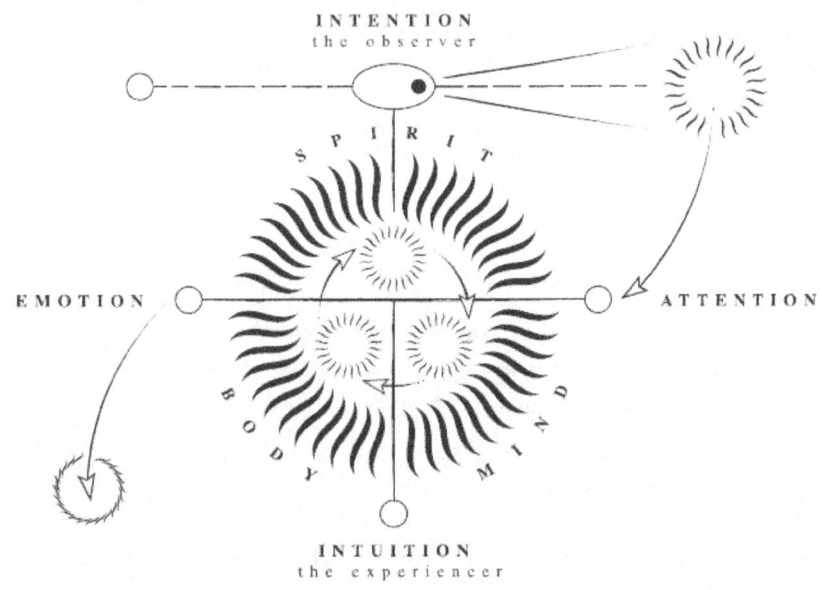

No one can promise you a stress-free life. I routinely tell clients that the methodology taught here won't make their stressors go away; instead, the intention is to strengthen the fortitude necessary to tackle the hard stuff that may come their way. Life is stressful by nature. Our aim on the road of life should be to continually improve the experience of feeling alive in the never-ending stress-growth process.

However, there are a few fundamental barriers to avoid if you want the best out of life.

Roughly 3,000 years ago, King Solomon wrote in the Book of Proverbs 6:16-19 that there are "six things the Lord hateth, and seven that are an abomination unto him." According to Catholic moral thought, the seven deadly sins are not discrete from other sins, but instead are the origin of the others. The prescribed punishment for living a life of vice was severe. In the Epistle to the Galatians (Galatians 5:19-21), Saint Paul says that people who practice these sins "shall not inherit the Kingdom of God."

What is so deadly that Heaven would be denied?

The Seven Deadly Sins

Latin	Vice	eState
Superbia	Pride	Pride
Ira	Wrath	Anger
Avaritia	Greed	Desire
Invidia	Envy	Desire
Luxuria	Lust	Desire
Gula	Gluttony	Desire
Acedia	Sloth	Apathy

(Ira through Acedia: PRIMAL EMOTIONS)

The seven deadly sins may not be lethal in clinical terms, but living them certainly has its drawbacks. Namely, life-energy is drained from our spirit every time we live in negativity. Going primal places a lot of stress on the mind-body system. An increase in the stress hormone cortisol is known to put pressure on the circulatory system, cause heart and digestive problems, break down tissue and cause many diseases. To be healthy and happy, the act of living a virtuous life may have medical merits.

Perhaps not coincidently, these ancient sins directly reflect the experiences of the survive eStates. It seems that from the dawn of humankind, people have struggled with the negative consequences of their animalistic nature. Acting in a primal manner in a corporate environment is not regarded as an affirmative leadership trait. But why pride? Isn't being proud supposed to be a positive trait?

In many religions, pride is considered the original and most serious of the seven deadly sins, and the source of the others. Take Adam and Eve for instance. It took individualist pride to go against God and choose what was forbidden. Eating fruit from the tree of knowledge surely provided them a new self-awareness, most notably the shame of being naked. Pride was the original sin and for that, humankind was cast out of paradise.

Pride is identified as believing that one is essentially better than others, a self-centered me-consciousness. It shows when you fail to acknowledge the accomplishments of others, or when you admire yourself excessively. As pride goeth before a fall, those in pride can easily loose self-confidence and fall into resentment. Not surprisingly then that anger is the next deadly sin.

As we've explored the primal eStates at length, it is noteworthy that we find so many desires in the list. That's not surprising if we acknowledge that our sexual competency is a powerful force in our lives. We cannot help but go primal to reproduce. Sex is perhaps the most naturally pleasurable act and we cannot help but crave the high-energy sexual intimacy provides. The key to health and happiness is to enter into primal situations with a higher, rational understanding of the desire.

The other vice of note is apathy. Going back to the Latin *acedia*, which means neglecting to take care of something we should do, being apathetic is equivalent to being depressed, living a life without joy. Melancholy, gloom, dejection, heavyheartedness, dispiritedness and misery all describe the feelings of apathy. The real vice however is knowingly living a life that drains energy away from yourself—and others.

Courage to Lead—Energy to Inspire

People can tell if you're feeling weak and insecure by your body language. With 90% of communication being non-verbal, no one can truly hide anxiety or depression. Subconscious behaviors—bouncing a knee up and down, jittering, tapping, fidgeting or failing to make eye contact—are a sure sign someone is nervous and not in control. Your slack posture, hunched back, crossed arms and head bowed to the ground, signals the weight you are carrying. Science has recently discovered that doing those things may actually be the root cause of the problem.

Amy Cuddy, a social psychologist at Harvard Business School, found that when volunteers were put in "high power" and "low power" body language, their saliva chemistry reflected the same highs or lows. Remarkably the results showed that only a mere 2 minutes of holding a "power-pose" was enough to increase testosterone levels by 20%, and reduce cortisol levels by 25%. Conversely, the "low-power" group saw a 10% reduction of testosterone levels in their salivary and experienced a 15% increase in the stress hormone.

What is a power-pose? It is intentionally taking the stances associated with confidence, power and achievement—chest lifted, head held high, arms either up or propped on the hips. Over time, we become wired to act and behave in a certain way, and often do things without noticing ourselves. But change your body to reflect a high energetic state and the biochemicals will follow. This means when you TUNE IN to your body you can TURN ON your state of mind. The more you stand straight with your head held high, the more powerful and confident you become.

There's an altruistic fortune in physically taking a thrive stance: People take notice. The saying goes that people can smell fear; similarly, they can be influenced positively by the way you carry yourself. Imagine the famous leaders of the world: Mahatma Gandhi, Nelson Mandela, Abraham Lincoln, Thomas Jefferson, Winston Churchill, Dalai Lama and Jesus Christ, among others. They all radiate high energetic states that continue to influence others to achieve a higher way of thinking and living. Even after death, their we-consciousness continues to be infectious.

You too can be an inspiring leader, a hero in your own life story. Without question, it takes courage to live life. Visualize and model your heroes: Believe in Jesus' miraculous energy and "ye will be saved." Or try emulating Buddha and his approach to non-attachment to the expectations of others. Ask how your spiritual leader or role model would handle the pings you experience and you may find yourself with an answer that may surprise you. Whatever religious belief or methodology inspires you, it's all about maintaining high-energy when challenges occur. TURN ON your potential so you can effectively TURN ON others. Fake it until your brain rewires to operate in the new higher eMotions and eStates naturally under stress.

Pay it Forward

Instead of being primal in your management or parenting style, proceed with courage—standing straight, shoulders back, chin up and eyes wide—and take positive action in resolving your pings. Train your brain to deal with the vicissitudes of life in a high-energy, leadership mindset. Decide to influence others to higher ways of thinking. You'll get more done with less effort. Your children will better respect you. Your staff or boss will thank you. And your health will show remarkable improvement.

On the road of life, you can make your own rules. As we are fortunate to live in a free world that nurtures free will, the personal values you have are yours and yours alone. Aim to remain wise and brave in stressful situations and you'll be appreciated for taking the high road when it's needed most.

TUNE IN to your cognitive chatter and eStates. Then TURN ON loving yourself unconditionally. Immediately accept and forgive mistakes. Give yourself a lot of room to grow and evolve. The road of life should be one of never ending self-improvement. Joy and bliss will inevitably follow your higher aspiration.

odyssey

THE FIRST UNIVERSAL TRUTH

Live in the Present Moment

The human condition hinders us from living in the present moment. Our higher intelligence of thought and imagination fuels emotional fires of past mistakes or future worries. As a result, we fail to attend to right now—*the living moment*.

Because of our dual nature, a two-step methodology is required to realign mind and body. Our spirit is the Alpha consciousness we use to balance thoughts and eMotions.

With every moment of every day, and with each ping we experience, we are presented an opportunity to grow and evolve, and become wiser and braver in everything we do.

The only reason for time is so that everything doesn't happen at once.

Albert Einstein

Day Twenty-One Exercise

What's Valuable to Me?

On the road of life, what do you most value? What is so viscerally important to you that you will go to battle to protect it? When you're under pressure, what is real and meaningful?

You are about to find out.

In this closing exercise, I will lead you through a meta-thinking exercise that will enlighten your awareness as to what your primal intelligence holds dear. Thus far, you have become aware of what pings you. Now we will explore the recorded ping-data for reason and understanding. When push comes to shove, what you most value is locked away in what you have learned so far. It's been with you all the time and it's time to bring it to the surface.

As you look back at the last twenty days, take this opportunity to ascertain the spirit-driven values within you right now. These are rational labels for the most powerful eMemories you have, driven by the intelligence of your spirit. These emotionally-charged personal values are the important arousal triggers that get you up and going.

Knowing your values is of the utmost importance for maintaining effective healthy relationships. We often run into people with different values and ping ourselves in the process. To remain high, you need to live your values. As part of an organization, you bring your personal values with you, where they are challenged and influenced by others, contributing to the overall culture of the community. Answering the question, "Who am I?" means knowing what you value most while navigating social challenges with style and charisma. Making decisions is also made easier when you know what is important to you.

Life leaders live their personal values. They bring fractions together by inspiring others with their authenticity. People will even change their values when they notice others that are more powerful. This is the inspirational aspect of the warrior spirit in all its energetic glory.

Living your personal values means living authentically in the moment—in tune and turned on by the natural expression of your spirit. In the quest for feeling alive, you will now identify what is real and valuable to your spirit by examining the pings of your past 20 days. To begin, first turn to the Personal Values List and browse the values. Explore the values and intuitively circle the ones that most resonate with you. Do this rather quickly and without thought. Select the ones you feel best describe who you think you are. Circle as many as you feel are reasons for living. After you have circled the values you resonate with, follow the steps to complete the Value Assessment.

Personal Values List

STEP ONE: Circle the Values that most resonate with you.

ambition	competency	individuality	equality
integrity	service	responsibility	accuracy
respect	dedication	diversity	improvement
enjoyment/fun	loyalty	credibility	honesty
innovativeness	teamwork	excellence	accountability
empowerment	quality	efficiency	dignity
collaboration	stewardship	empathy	accomplishment
courage	wisdom	independence	security
challenge	influence	learning	compassion
friendliness	discipline/order	generosity	persistency
optimism	dependability	flexibility	accuracy
adventure	trust	fairness	harmony
accomplishment	connectedness	acknowledgement	growth
aesthetics	beauty	authenticity	collaboration
community	adventure	culture (art, etc.)	movies
purpose	spirituality	empowerment	contribution
excellence	free spirit	focus	orderliness
hustle	family	freedom	personal power
freedom	leadership	fun loving	health
helping others	service	humor	creativity
carefree	good income	independence	self-expression
integrity	nurturing	joy	comradeship
lightness	love	nature	directness
partnership	risk taking	peace	participation
performance	prestige	elegance	romance
recognition	religion	security	productivity
lack of pretence	honesty	success	team player
tradition	to be known	vitality	zest
	productive (hard worker)	variety (doing different things)	

odyssey

Taking a Personal Values Inventory

Step One: Review the Personal Values List and intuitively circle all the values you feel are important to you. This will give you a targeted list to which you can refer.

Step Two: Look back to Days Seven, Fourteen and Twenty, and transcribe the pings (or stress triggers) onto the Personal Values Assessment Form [1. My Pings]
Include a tick mark to note the eState experienced. [4. My eStates]

Step Three: Referencing your circled Personal Values, start at your first ping and ask, "What did I most value in this ping? How did the experience ping what was valuable to me? Why did I have the reaction in the first place?"

For example, if you find you were pinged because your felt controlled, you may choose FREEDOM as a personal value. If you felt criticized, you may find AMBITION or CONTRIBUTION valuable. This is an intuitive match-up exercise.

Write in the value [2. What I Valued] and tick the occurrence. You will find that the values you record repeat. Note the consequent reoccurrences.

Step Four: When you have completed matching values to pings, use the My Personal Values Summary to compile the number of value occurrences. Identify the most to least frequent incidents.

Step Five: Complete the "I value…" dialog using your personal values. Speak this aloud.

Step Six: Memorize your Personal Values Statement.

Step Six: With each future ping, TURN ON a smile—you are living your values!

Below is a sample of what your Personal Value Assessment form should look like after completion.

WEEK ONE

Personal Value Assessment

	DAY OF WEEK	Monday			Tuesday			Wednesday			Thursday			Friday					
4. My eState	Peace																		
	Joy																		
	Love																		
	Reason																		
	Acceptance																		
	Optimism																		
	Trust																		
	Courage																		
	Pride											√							
	Anger	√			√						√			√					
	Desire												√						
	Fear		√				√								√	√			
	Grief					√													
	Apathy							√	√										
	Guilt									√									
	Shame																		
3.	POSITIVE																		
	NEGATIVE																		
2. What I valued	efficiency	√		√	√	√		√	√		√			√					8
	teamwork		√		√			√			√		√		√				6
	integrity			√		√	√			√	√				√				6
	productivity					√			√	√				√	√				5
	responsibility				√	√			√	√		√		√	√				7
1. My Pings		Arrived late—traffic	Email from Joe	Computer locked up	Argument with Sally	Left wallet at home	Boss wanted to see me	Quality dept delays	Too many emails!	Not prepared 4 meeting	Supplier missed deadline	Drama with Kyle	Son wants new iPhone	Run-in w/Prod Mgr	Sales low for quarter	Expenses over budget			

odyssey

WEEK ONE

Personal Value Assessment

DAY OF WEEK							
4. My eState							
Peace							
Joy							
Love							
Reason							
Acceptance							
Optimism							
Trust							
Courage							
Pride							
Anger							
Desire							
Fear							
Grief							
Apathy							
Guilt							
Shame							
3. POSTITIVE							
NEGATIVE							
2. What I valued							
1. My Pings							

odyssey

WEEK TWO

Personal Value Assessment

	DAY OF WEEK														
4. My eState	Peace														
	Joy														
	Love														
	Reason														
	Acceptance														
	Optimism														
	Trust														
	Courage														
	Pride														
	Anger														
	Desire														
	Fear														
	Grief														
	Apathy														
	Guilt														
	Shame														
3.	POSTITIVE														
	NEGATIVE														
2. What I valued															
1. My Pings															

250

odyssey

WEEK THREE

Personal Value Assessment

	DAY OF WEEK							
4. My eState	Peace							
	Joy							
	Love							
	Reason							
	Acceptance							
	Optimism							
	Trust							
	Courage							
	Pride							
	Anger							
	Desire							
	Fear							
	Grief							
	Apathy							
	Guilt							
	Shame							
3.	POSITITIVE							
	NEGATIVE							
2. What I valued								
1. My Pings								

odyssey

My Personal Values

Value (from PVA form)	Quantity
efficiency	*8 times*

Personal Value Statement

"My name is _____ and I value _____, _____, _____, _____, _____, _____, and _____."

odyssey

Postscript

I hope you enjoyed the Odyssey. If you felt a bit emotional reading your own Personal Values Statement, you know you're on the right track. Continue to live your values unashamedly. Remain on the path of continuous improvement and learn from everything you do. Master the ability to navigate the ups and downs of life feeling connected to your personal values and authenticity. Do not be afraid to shine brightly. As practice makes perfect, continue your quest with an enlightened, empowered spirit knowing that every ping is making you wise and brave.

You can also look forward to my next book, *Odyssey—The Universal Truths*. In it, we'll explore the world's great philosophies to find the ancient wisdom that has served humankind for centuries. We'll examine the six remaining Universal Truths in a scientific light, and learn how to TURN ON their psychological insights—wisdom that will elevate your energy and supercharge your hero's journey.

I invite you to continue using the methodology in the weeks to come.

Nirvana is a never-ending quest, so I wish your journey high-energy in everything you do.

Enjoy the living moment!

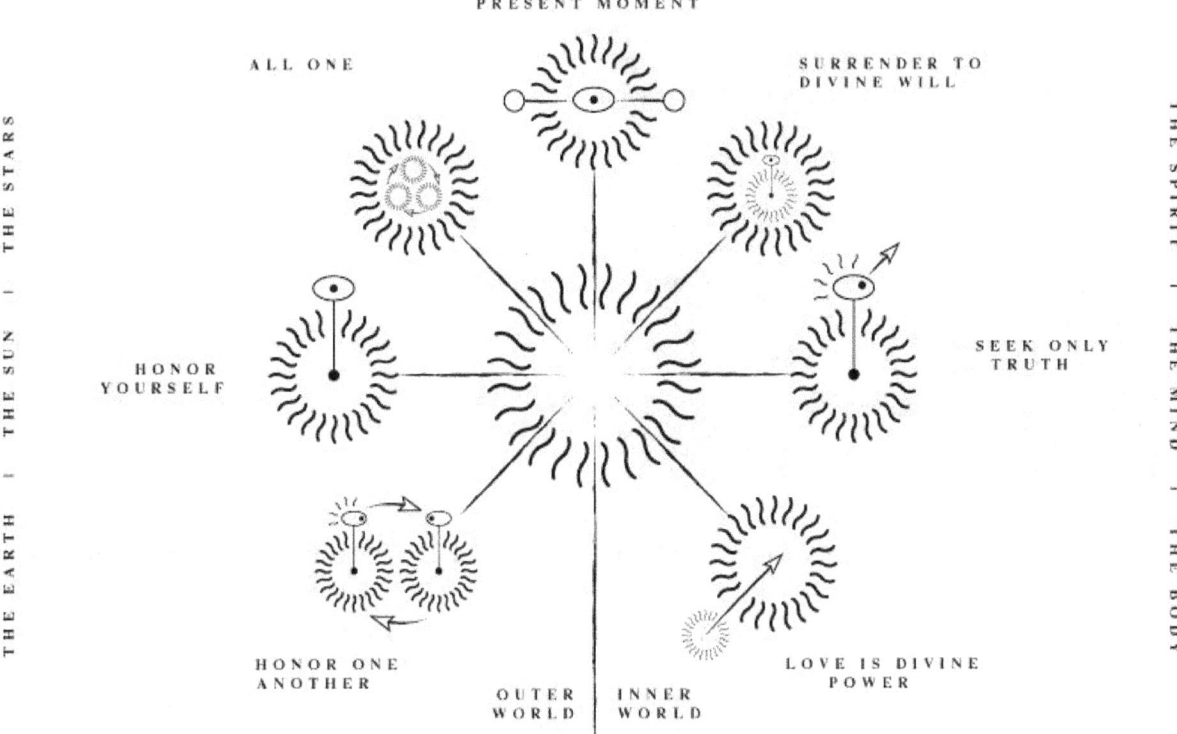

The Seven Universal Truths

The Seven Universal Truths

Russell R. Hassler
Odyssey Leadership

Odyssey: The Living Moment represents the first three weeks of the twelve-week program, *The Odyssey Methodology*, that was RUSSELL R. HASSLER's life's work. It is the result of decades of research, years of practice, and a boundless passion for helping others.

Russell was born and raised in Texas, and went out into the world with a firm belief that the anxieties and insecurities that he felt within himself were a product of environmental and social programming. He believed that, with the right tools, anyone can learn to overcome the driving factors behind reflexive negative emotions that harm our relationships, happiness and productivity. Russell spent two decades working in corporate positions, focused on process engineering, marketing and client relations. His experience identifying and resolving structural weaknesses within manufacturing systems, software, and management, complemented the research he had begun into the influences that we all face in our daily lives; influences that cause each of us to respond to certain triggers with automatic and unconscious negative emotions.

A decision to leave the corporate world and focus on his passion was followed by a move to Australia, where Russell honed his research and started his practice as *Odyssey Leadership*. Russell worked with clients from all walks of life, and assisted them in furthering their goals, whether those goals ranged from running a large corporation, navigating the challenges of a marriage, or finding peace in a complicated world. Clients of his program reported significant improvements in interpersonal relationships, balanced emotions, and even an ability to escape a history of self-medication.

In 2014, Russell returned to the United States to care for his aging mother, and to focus on finishing *Odyssey: The Living Moment*, intended as the first of three books describing *The Odyssey Methodology*. But a rare and aggressive form of cancer took him far too young, in late 2016, when he had so much more to give others through his work. He approached the disease with a positive spirit, and with the same wonder and curiosity that guided him throughout his own fifty-three year *Odyssey*. It was his wish that this book be allowed to reach others who might benefit from his work.

odyssey

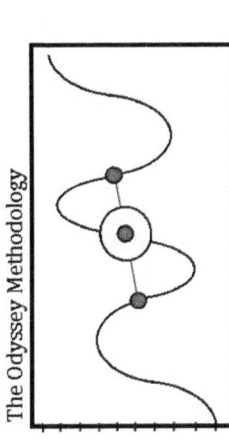

The Odyssey Methodology

The Odyssey Quest

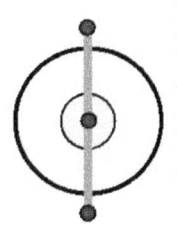

THE LIVING MOMENT
WEEKS ONE TO THREE

The Great Mystery
Life & creative power

The Road of Life
Stress & defensive force

The Living Moment
Dynamics of life leadership

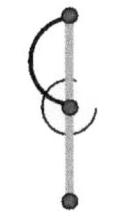

THE OUTER WORLD
WEEKS FOUR TO SIX

The Stars
Mystery, Myth & Transformation

The Sun
Energy, Ritual & Intuition

The Earth
Instincts, Connectivity & Co-evolution

THE INNER WORLD
WEEKS SEVEN TO NINE

The Body
Sex, Arousal & Integration

The Mind
Consciousness, Willpower & Intention

The Spirit
Transcendence, Courage & Compassion

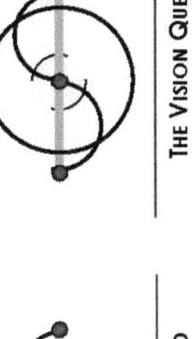

THE VISION QUEST
WEEKS TEN TO TWELVE

Relation - who am I
Yin: Connection to Value

Profession - what am I
Yang: Expression of Value

Vision - where am I going
Living "In sync" with Value

Copyright © Russell R. Hassler 2004-2014 All Rights Reserved
www.odysseyleadership.com

NOTES

NOTES